Studies in Emotion and Social Interaction

Paul Ekman
University of California, San Francisco

Klaus R. Scherer
Université de Genève

General Editors

Nonverbal vocal communication

What is the meaning of the wordless vocal expressions of animals and human infants? Are they merely expressions of affect or are they related to human speech? Specialists from several disciplines discuss this question and review the present knowledge on neural substrates of vocal communication, on primate vocal communication, on precursors and prerequisites of human speech, on the way human infants learn their mother tongue, and on some aspects of speech disorders. There is evidence that parents are well fitted to support infant communicative development. Their capacities represent a primary, biological model of didactic educational support.

Studies in Emotion and Social Interaction

This series is jointly published by the Cambridge University Press and the Editions de la Maison des Sciences de l'Homme, as part of the joint publishing agreement established in 1977 between the Fondation de la Maison des Sciences de l'Homme and the Syndics of the Cambridge University Press.

Cette collection est publiée co-édition par Cambridge University Press et les Editions de la Maison des Sciences de l'Homme. Elle s'intègre dans le programme de co-édition établi en 1977 par la Fondation de la Maison des Sciences de l'Homme et les Syndics de Cambridge University Press.

Nonverbal vocal communication

Comparative and developmental approaches

Edited by

Hanuš Papoušek
Max Planck Institute for Psychiatry, Munich

Uwe Jürgens
German Primate Center, Göttingen

Mechthild Papoušek
Munich University

CAMBRIDGE
UNIVERSITY PRESS

and

Editions de la Maison des Sciences de l'Homme
Paris

Published by the Press Syndicate of the University of Cambridge
The Pitt Building, Trumpington Street, Cambridge CB2 1RP
40 West 20th Street, New York, NY 10011-4211, USA
10 Stamford Road, Oakleigh, Victoria 3166, Australia
and
Editions de la Maison des Sciences de l'Homme
54 Boulevard Raspail, 75270 Paris, Cedex 06

First published 1992

Printed in the United States of America

Library of Congress Cataloging-in-Publication Data
Nonverbal vocal communication : comparative and developmental
approaches / edited by Hanuš Papoušek, Uwe Jürgens, Mechthild
Papoušek.
p.   cm. – (Studies in emotion and social interaction)
Includes indexes.
ISBN 0-521-41265-X
1. Nonverbal communication in children.   2. Interpersonal
communication in children.   3. Parent and child.   4. Psychology,
Comparative.   I. Papoušek, Hanuš.   II. Jürgens, Uwe.
III. Papoušek. Mechthild.   IV. Series.
BF723.C57N66   1992
153.6'9 – dc20   91-43005
                                                                        CIP

A catalog record for this book is available from the British Library.

ISBN 0-521-41265-X hardback
ISBN 2-7351-0447-8 hardback (France only)

To
Detlev Ploog, in appreciation
and
David Symmes, in commemoration

Contents

Preface

Books on communication may elicit ambivalent feelings. Postmodern society suffers from social satiation, and excessive communication is believed to be one of the causes. Conversely, communication has occupied a remarkable area of scientific research, beside technology and mass media, and continues to nourish a growing interest within the biological, psychological, and medical disciplines. It has gradually become obvious that misuse of communication should not lead to underestimation of something that belongs to innate needs, functions as a means of evolutionary adaptation, and is vital to social coexistence.

Interest in human communication used to be narrowly focused on verbal communication, and the presence of speech was viewed as a categorical attribute of human beings. There was no room for consideration of phylogenetic or ontogenetic continuities or for precursors of verbal communication and, consequently, no space for a proper interpretation of speech acquisition. That situation has changed, and as in many other areas of research, static, two-dimensional concepts have made way for dynamic, interactionistic thinking, even concerning human languages. The old question of whether languages are products of culture or, like culture, are codetermined by nature has been reapproached, owing to improved communication, on a higher level of the critical interdisciplinary forum, where data mean more than mere speculation.

Thus, the need for the mutual exchange of information, especially about methodological procedures, has become obvious to students of communication in both animal and human research. Primatologists are using psycholinguistic methods; psychologists and researchers in human development are considering biological aspects of communication. Interdisciplinary cooperation has proved useful and has motivated the contributors to the present volume to discuss developmental and comparative aspects of nonverbal or preverbal vocal communication, where some interesting discoveries have been reported recently.

The original impetus for this discussion came from a group of Central European scientists, especially an interdisciplinary team at the Max Planck Institute for Research in Psychiatry in Munich. The director, Detlev W. Ploog, an advocate of biologically oriented psychiatry and an eminent neurologist, realized very early the decisive role of communication in both human mental development and mental health. He brought together neurophysiologists, psycholinguists, developmentalists, and psychiatrists engaged in either experimental or clinical research on communication in humans and other primates. Some of the American contributors to the present volume participated in this research as guest researchers in Munich and now work at the National Institutes of Health in Bethesda, Maryland. The engagement of both institutes clearly indicates the significance attributed to comparative and developmental research on communication by clinicians in medical fields.

The Max Planck Society generously enabled the entire group of contributors to meet at an editorial symposium in the society's magnificent conference center, Ringberg Castle in the Bavarian Alps. There our chosen conceptual frame of reference found a most pleasant physical setting. It would be much easier, of course, to describe the beauty of the landscape than to capture the scholarly atmosphere of the meeting.

Comparative and psychobiological approaches made us aware of the general position of communication in the animate world as an important means of evolutionary adaptation. In many species, living in social groups increased the survival rate. At the same time, some kind of communication had to develop to allow sharing of tasks, space, and food and to establish most adaptive forms of social integration. Taking into account the rich variety of communication, including the use of abstract symbols in honeybees and categorical vocal signals in some primates, we necessarily have to admit both phylogenetic and ontogenetic continuities with the presence of precursors of speech in preverbal forms of communication.

Human speech not only had biological roots in animal communication; it also led to biological adaptive consequences affecting survival and resistance to biological dangers. Biologically relevant means of adaptation are generally characterized by a number of mechanisms securing their effectiveness: They are based upon innate, relatively stable and universal programs; they develop rather early during ontogeny; and they find adequate behavioral counterparts that coevolved in social partners, often in surplus. Similar assumptions can be legitimately applied to human speech, if we view it as a crucial means of biological adaptation. However, the application points out gaps in evidence, rather than sets of solid data.

Psychological and clinical interest in preverbal communication mirrors several complexes of problems: (1) Since Sigmund Freud's time, the effects of early experience on later development have gained increasing attention, but communicative development has been neglected in conceptual domains and underresearched in science. (2) The study of the early ontogeny of speech acquisition allows an insight into the process of speech evolution that escapes paleontological investigation. Comparative approaches play a particularly useful role in this connection. (3) Biogenetic factors of behavioral regulation are usually more visible during early development. Their evidence may serve as indirect proof of innate predispositions for human speech which escape direct experimental verification in human subjects. (4) Early dependence of human infants on caregiving draws attention to social interactions between infants and caregivers and reveals gaps in knowledge on a potential support to speech acquisition which may be included in caregiving behaviors. Cross-cultural adoptions make it evident that social environment guides speech acquisition in infants; however, the mechanisms of this guidance have long remained unknown.

Obviously, the present state of research on nonverbal communication confronts us with findings that contradict some former concepts and raise questions requiring investigation. Yet this circumstance does not contradict the need to review periodically the state of the art and consider new directions and methods. At such opportunities, participants also learn by using the same, or at least a commonly understandable, working vocabulary in an area with a surprising redundancy.

Jürgens's review of present knowledge of the neurophysiological structures involved in the perception and production of vocal signals offers a much-needed basis for discussions of the comparative and developmental aspects of vocal communication. Particularly interesting are evolutionary changes in the brain, since a phylogenetic comparison compensates to some degree for the missing fossil records of soft intracranial tissues. Careful analyses presented by Ploog allow detection of branch-points in cerebral evolution and throw a new light on the old question of the sequential primacy between phonatory and bodily gestures.

Nonverbal vocal signals have often been viewed as mere expressions of affects. However, elaborating on Bühler's concept, Scherer stresses the threefold significance of vocal signals: a symptomatic expression of the sender's internal state; a symbolic representation of contextual aspects; and an appeal signaled to the receiver to answer the signal. Microanalyses of early social interactions illustrate convincingly that the process of preverbal communication cannot be interpreted satisfactorily if any of these three aspects is neglected.

The search for discrete categorical entities in vocal signals seems to be outweighed by attributional approaches, stressed in Newman and Goedeking's essay. The authors view vocal signals as multivariate complexes in which variability of individual subunits decreases with increasing signaling value. Similarily, as Marler, Evans, and Hauser argue, motivational and referential characteristics, which were formerly viewed as functioning independently in vocal signals, have been demonstrated to function in essential relation. Marler and coauthors recommend new methodological approaches for the analysis of meaning in animal signals.

Symmes and Biben reveal another new aspect of adult–infant communication in squirrel monkeys which immediately captured the attention of researchers in the field of communicative development and led to improved methodology. The authors show that the earliest face-to-face communication between an infant squirrel monkey and adults, which cannot occur between a mother and an infant sitting on her back, takes place between the infant and other female conspecifics. This finding indicates the importance of universal predispositions for caregiving stressed by Papoušek and Bornstein in relation to human infancy research. The participants in the symposium could not anticipate, however, that they were seeing David Symmes for the last time. To their deep regret, David Symmes died on April 8, 1990.

So far, the progress in research on nonverbal and preverbal vocal communication has been greatly influenced by methodological innovations. Methodological problems are still much in evidence, but awareness of these difficulties may spur further progress, as exemplified in the present volume: Scherer has profited from the work of Marler, Marler from that of psycholinguists, infancy researchers from Marler, and so on. New techniques are reported in the analysis of vocal signals; microanalyses are introduced in studies of early social interactions; and longitudinal observations are used in evaluating the role of social scaffolding in speech acquisition. Rather provocative findings reported by Owren, Seyfarth, and Hopp point out the role of acoustic processing in differences among primate species and suggest that psychoacoustic analyses should be included in the methodology of research on vocal communication in general. In human infancy research, naturalistic strategies have been utilized to explore innate propensities, since direct experimentation is ethically inconceivable. Almost every chapter includes useful methodological recommendations or caveats.

The first form of human vocalization is typically crying. Lester and Boukydis outline the present methodological status of the field, as well as examining what clinical studies of crying have to offer. Detailed analyses of non-cry vocalizations and studies of the first vocal interchanges between infants and caregivers provide evidence of the developmental shift from crying to deliberate forms of non-cry vocalization, including an unpretended, specific preverbal vocabulary in prosodic elements, as reported by Mechthild Papoušek and Anne Fernald.

Two clinical syndromes – developmental retardation and early autism – were studied by Amorosa in order to illustrate the participation of separate functional systems in the development of vocal communication, as well as to point out gaps in our understanding of the nonlinguistic aspects of vocal development.

A new area of research, devoted to early vocal communication in human infants, requires microanalytic approaches employing audiovisual documentation, spectrographic analysis of vocal signals, adequate descriptive systems, and open conceptual systems. Oller and Eilers recommend replacing the former alphabetic description of sounds with an infraphonological system, which may be of particular interest to comparative researchers analyzing animal sounds.

Present theory attributes to the preverbal phase of human vocal communication quite new dimensions, for instance, the presence of a "primary, intuitive didactic support" for speech acquisition, revealed by Papoušek and Papoušek, or the use of prosodic contours as primary categorical messages prior to the first verbal categorical messages.

Didactic support concerns not only the production and use of vocal signals but also, and perhaps more importantly, the training of integrative processes involved in the structuring or decoding of vocal signals. In fundamental aspect, those processes have been shown to function at birth or very soon thereafter. However, they function rather slowly at the beginning and have to function much faster to cope with the rapid strings of messages in speech at the end of infancy.

On the whole, preverbal vocal interchanges in humans appear in the concluding essays in a new light, revealing their dual and crucial significance: On the one hand, communication per se serves the need of co-existence within a social group; on the other hand, it provides the infant with numerous teaching experiences, which facilitate learning and enhance the cognitive processes of mental integration. Experimental verification of the effects of social support on early integrative growth and speech acquisition is difficult, and yet Bornstein reports encouraging data from a "natural experiment" involving the mothering of twins.

Last but not least, the smooth course of the symposium and subsequent interchanges were facilitated by the quiet and effective cooperation of three colleagues: Kim Bard, Charles Rahn, and Roberta Turner. Their help is gratefully acknowledged.

The new conceptual and methodological framework offered at the symposium opens important avenues for further research, both animal and human, and both experimental and clinical. It was this belief that motivated the participants to share the results of the interdisciplinary discussions with a broader community of readers.

Hanuš Papoušek

Contributors

Hedwig Amorosa
Hecksche Klinik – Solln
Munich, Germany

Kim A. Bard
Yerkes Regional Primate Center
Emory University
Atlanta, Georgia

Maxeen Biben
National Institute of Child Health
    and Human Development
Bethesda, Maryland

Marc H. Bornstein
National Institute of Child Health
    and Human Development
Bethesda, Maryland

C. F. Zachariah Boukydis
Brown University Program in
    Medicine
Bradley Hospital
East Providence, Rhode Island

Rebecca E. Eilers
Mailman Center for Child
    Development
University of Miami
Coral Gables, Florida

Christopher S. Evans
Department of Zoology
University of California
Davis, California

Anne Fernald
Department of Psychology
Stanford University
Stanford, California

Philipp Goedeking
National Institute of Child Health
    and Human Development
Bethesda, Maryland

Marc D. Hauser
Department of Zoology
University of California
Davis, California

Steven L. Hopp
Department of Psychology
Emory and Henry College
Emory, Virginia

Uwe Jürgens
German Primate Center
Göttingen, Germany

Barry M. Lester
Brown University Program in
    Medicine
Bradley Hospital
East Providence, Rhode Island

Peter Marler
Department of Zoology
University of California
Davis, California

John D. Newman
National Institute of Child Health
   and Human Development
Bethesda, Maryland

D. Kimbrough Oller
Mailman Center for Child
   Development
University of Miami Medical School
Miami, Florida

Michael J. Owren
Department of Psychology
University of Colorado
Denver, Colorado

Hanuš Papoušek
Free University
Amsterdam, The Netherlands

Mechthild Papoušek
Institute for Social Pediatrics
University of Munich
Munich, Germany

Detlev W. Ploog
Max Planck Institute for Research in
   Psychiatry
Munich, Germany

Klaus R. Scherer
Department of Psychology
University of Geneva
Geneva, Switzerland

Robert M. Seyfarth
Department of Psychology
University of Pennsylvania
Philadelphia, Pennsylvania

David Symmes (deceased)

PART I

Systems of communication

Introduction and review

UWE JÜRGENS

Part I provides the reader with some general information about the biological foundations of nonverbal vocal communication. It starts with an anatomical description of the phonatory apparatus. In accordance with the aims of this book, the description follows a phylogenetic line, delineating the changes and specializations that have taken place in the development of the larynx and supralaryngeal tract from lungfish to humans. It thus recapitulates the morphological transformation of the larynx from a pure respiratory organ (lungfish) to a respiratory organ with some vocal capability (amphibian, reptiles, lower mammals) and finally to that highly sophisticated instrument that we use when singing or producing variegated emotional intonations. This description makes clear the degree to which the rich vocal repertoire typical of humans and of nonhuman primates (squirrel monkeys, for instance, with their extraordinary vocal range of more than eight octaves) depends upon specific morphological prerequisites.

As chapter 1 further points out, the phonatory apparatus, as it evolved toward its form in humans is paralleled not only by an increase in vocal repertoire but also by an increase in voluntary control over vocalization. At the lowest level at which vocal communication can take place, a subject reacts innately to a specific stimulus, with a specific call. In ethological terms, this is called a vocal "fixed action pattern," activated by an "innate releasing mechanism." In such a case, neither the vocalization, which represents a genetically preprogrammed motor pattern, nor the eliciting stimulus, which elicits vocalization without any prior experience, has to be learned. At this lowest level of vocal communication, voluntary control is absent. Instead, the vocal repertoire corresponds to a reflex reaction, comparable to coughing as a response to an irritating stimulus in the pharynx. Nevertheless, such completely genetically determined vocal reactions occur not only in submammalian vertebrates but, as chapters 1 and 2 show, also in primates, including humans.

The next-highest level of communication is represented by a situation in which a subject reacts with a genetically preprogrammed vocal motor pattern, but the eliciting stimulus is learned. In other words, the subject has to learn in what adequate context to use a particular vocal utterance which until then has been called for more or less indiscriminately. Most of the monkey calls and a number of the nonverbal emotional vocal utterances of humans seem to belong to this category. The alarm calls of the vervet monkey and the squirrel monkey are the most intensively studied examples of this kind; consequently, they will be discussed in the following chapters in greater detail. In some mammalian species, such as the cat, the dog, the sea lion, the dolphin, and several monkey species, it has been shown that these animals can be trained to master a vocal conditioning task, that is, to emit a species-specific vocalization for a food reward when a conditioned stimulus is presented (and to refrain from vocalizing during presentation of a different stimulus). Such animals clearly have some voluntary control over vocalization. This control, however, is limited to the initiation and suppression of vocalization; it does not extend to the acoustic structure – which still is genetically determined.

The highest level of vocal communication is represented by learned vocal motor patterns uttered in response to learned stimuli. In this case, there is not only voluntary control over initiation and suppression of an utterance, but also voluntary control over the acoustic structure of the utterance. This type of communication is the common communicatory mode in humans. In nonhuman primates and other mammals, it seems to be the rare exception.

As chapter 2 shows, depending on the level at which vocal communication takes place, the brain structures involved differ. For the production of learned vocal motor patterns, a number of brain structures are necessary that are not needed for the production of innate vocal utterances. Furthermore, the capability of initiating or suppressing vocalization volitionally depends upon brain structures not needed for the production of unconditioned vocal reactions. The message of the second chapter thus is that, parallel to the behavioral hierarchy of complexity in vocal communication, there is a hierarchy of brain structures underlying the different forms of vocal communication.

The last chapter of part I deals with the functional properties of nonverbal vocal utterances. It is asked, what type of information is transferred by such utterances and how do they influence the partner. With respect to the first question, it is shown that the information transmitted carries a subjective and an objective component. The subjective component consists of the vocal expression of the momentary emotional state. This component signals the preparedness of the vocalizer to react in a specific way. As acoustic analyses reveal, different emotional states are represented by different acoustic patterns. This holds especially for non-human primates and humans: Both possess a rich vocal repertoire of nonverbal emotional utterances enabling them to express a wealth of emotional shades. In man, this is not limited to nonverbal utterances: By way of emotional intonation superimposed on the linguistic component of speech, it extends to verbal utterances as well. As chapter 3 points out, there are first indications that the acoustic features characterizing specific emotional states are similar across species. In other words, there seem to exist universals of emotional vocal expression. This again argues for a genetic – more specifically, phylogenetic – basis of emotional vocal utterances.

The second, objective component in the information transmitted by nonverbal vocal utterances relates to states outside of the vocalizer. Vocalizations often are reactions to specific situations. In these cases, vocalizations reflect specific external events in their acoustic structure – provided that the partner is able to decode the signal. According to Scherer, this may be regarded as a symbolic component inherent in nonverbal vocal utterances. In this sense, not only learned but also innate vocal patterns may have a symbolic function.

With respect to the question of how nonverbal vocal utterances can influence a partner, again two principal modes can be distinguished. The better-known mode is that of the vocalizer trying to provoke a reaction in the partner(s) that is different from the vocalizer's own; for instance, when the partner is forced to retreat by the emission of a threatening call or, conversely, when the aggression of a dominant partner is dampened in response to a flattering utterance. The other mode is characterized by a process that might be called "emotional infection," or emotion transfer by identification. In this case, the vocalizer attempts to evoke a response in the partner(s) that is identical to the vocalizer's own. A well-known example from the animal kingdom is the mobbing response found in many species against potential predators. Here, one animal starts to emit alarm calls against the predator. This serves to draw attention of other group members to the source of excitation. They join the first animal in uttering alarm calls, thus forming a louder and louder chorus. Corresponding examples from the human sphere are presented in chapter 3.

1. The evolution of vocal communication

DETLEV W. PLOOG

It is our interest in the evolution of human language and speech that inspires our interest in the evolution of vocal communication. Around the middle of the nineteenth century, this topic met with so much abuse that in 1866 the Paris Société de Linguistique enacted its famous ban against papers dealing with the topic. The subject of dispute then was – and it still is – the question of whether early humans used gestures for communicating before they learned to use the voice, or whether vocal sounds formed the primordial language (Harnad, Steklis, & Lancaster, 1976). I would like to show that comparative biology of the mammalian voice clearly points to a process of natural selection leading to an optimization of audiovocal communication.

The voice is, and most probably always was, an outstanding means of social signaling in nonhuman primates and in humans. Hence, it is promising to study the physical structures and functions of the organism which produces and controls vocal behavior. Phylogenetic comparison will, to a substantial degree, compensate for the missing fossil records of the nonbony tissue involved in vocalization; that is, not only parts of the larynx, tongue, and the like, but also of the brain. Moreover, it is the whole system which is involved in audiovocal communication that must be considered in an evolutionary context.

From a neuroethological point of view, a signaling system must consist of at least four parts: (1) the peripheral apparatus, which generates the species-specific signal; (2) the cerebral motor system, which produces the patterning of the signal; (3) a sense organ, which receives the species-specific signal; (4) the cerebral decoding apparatus, which transforms the signal into a message that may or may not produce a modification of behavior on the receiver's side – for example, a vocal response to a vocal signal. The way in which the cerebral motor patterning and the decoding systems are linked seems to be the key to understanding

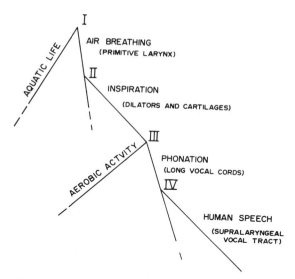

Figure 1.1. A functional branch-point diagram for the evolution of the upper respiratory system (Lieberman, 1984, p. 266).

communication processes in general. The four subsystems function as an interdependent system in communication processes. Therefore they should be studied together in order to appreciate the evolutionary progress in regard to the behavior achieved, that is, the audiovocal mode of communication.

The peripheral signal generator

Let us first consider the peripheral apparatus which generates the species-specific signal. During evolution a gradual transformation of the larynx and the supralaryngeal tract took place (Fig. 1.1). The first appearance of the larynx can be traced back to the ancient lungfish. Here, it is essentially a valve that is positioned in the floor of the pharynx. In the water, the simple sphincter closes. Out of the water, the sphincter opens and allows air to be forced into the fish's swim bladder, which is homologous with the lungs. A first functional branch-point was the new condition of life out of the water. A *branch-point* is that point at which the course of evolution can potentially be changed by virtue of selection for a new mode of behavior that is of value to a group of animals (Lieberman, 1984; Mayr, 1942). The next stage in the evolution of the larynx was the development of fibers to pull the larynx open to allow more air into the lungs during breathing. Later stages of evolution yielded lateral cartilages that facilitated the opening movements of the larynx. The elaboration of the larynx enabled it to act as a sound-generating device and marked a second functional branch-point.

Negus's (1949) comparative studies demonstrate that the larynges of many animals are specialized for phonation at the expense of respiration, whereas other animals like horses maximize the flow of air to and from the lungs. The human larynx is designed to enhance phonation for the process of vocal communication. Canids – vocalizers and hunters – represent an intermediate solution to the competing selective forces deriving from respiratory efficiency and phonation (Lieberman, 1984).

The evolutionary condition of the sound-producing apparatus corresponds with the organism's vocal behavior. For instance, frogs have an early tripartite primary larynx skeleton, consisting of arytenoid cartilages and tracheal cartilages. Male frogs are provided with a vocal repertoire of only up to five calls, chiefly the mating call that is to attract a female and the release call that serves to repel other males. Other calls signal territorial defense, warning, and distress (Capranica, 1968). The calls are innate; the mating call, especially, is strictly species-specific and has a selective effect on the female.

In contrast to the primitive condition of the sound-producing apparatus in amphibians with only a few calls, the highly evolved larynx of nonhuman primates corresponds with a rich vocal repertoire used not only for the purpose of procreation but for differentiated vocal communication in complex social interactions. The vocal repertoire of the squirrel monkey will serve as an example (Fig. 1.2). Five classes of calls, first described in 1966 (Winter, Ploog, & Latta), are shown as graded signals from the center toward the periphery. The individual sounds are depicted in frequency by time sonagrams, with shrieking close to white noise in the center of the circle. Each class – and probably innumerable graded signals – are associated with a certain function.

From this example it is obvious that the evolution of the sound-producing apparatus from the amphibians to the nonhuman primates has led to an enormous range and diversity of communal vocal communication. How did this materialize? In the scaffolding of the mammalian larynx, the fourth cartilage, the thyroid emerges and hinges on the cricoid cartilage, which facilitates the opening and shutting of the laryngeal aperture. The definite secondary laryngeal skeleton, then, consists of four parts: the thyroid, the cricoid with superadded aryte-

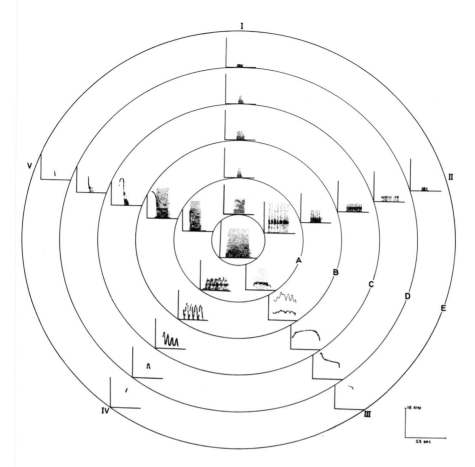

Figure 1.2. Vocal repertoire of the squirrel monkey. Calls represented as frequency–time diagrams. *Class I* (groaning-cawing-shrieking): Calls of this group act as protest calls. With increasing spectral energy (toward the center), their function changes from an expression of slight uneasiness to one of intense defensive threat. *Class II* (purring-growling-spitting): Calls of this group express a challenging or self-asserting attitude. With increasing spectral energy, there is an increasing probability that a directed aggressive action will ensue. *Class III* (chirping–isolation peep-squealing): These calls serve a number of cohesive functions to express the desire for social contact. *Call IIIc* is the isolation peep, sometimes also called "separation peep." *Class IV* (twittering-chattering-cackling): The function of these calls is to confirm social bonds and to create companionship; with low energy, pleasurable events are announced; with high energy, intraspecific mobbing against one or several outsiders is set about. *Class V* (clucking-yapping-alarm peep): Its function is warning, ranging from disagreement with a conspecific to alarm calls against aerial VC or terrestrial predators VB. (Jürgens & Ploog, 1976.)

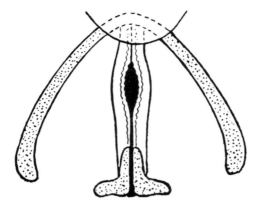

Figure 1.3. Function of the vocalis muscle in humans only. Falsetto mechanism. The central part of the glottis is blown open *(black)*, and only a short length of vocal fold is in vibration. The thyroid cartilage and the arytenoid cartilage are stippled (Negus, 1949).

noid cartilages hinged on the cricoid, and the tracheal ring. The epiglottis is also a new formation (Negus, 1949; Paulsen, 1967).

Further evolutionary differentiation in higher mammals developed in the shapes of the cartilages, in humans especially the arytenoids, and in the laryngeal musculature. The arytenoid transversus muscle is singularly observed in all primates. In apes, an oblique interarytenoid muscle detaches itself as a separate unit, becoming increasingly conspicuous along the line orangutan – chimpanzee – gorilla – human (Kelemen, 1963). The thyroarytenoid muscle is located in all nonhuman primates at the base of the vocal cords (vocalis muscle). Only in humans does it reach into the medial part of the vocal cords, thus making a finer vocal adjustment possible. The glottis became a perfect vocal organ with the insertion of muscle fibers at the vocal cord (Fig. 1.3). It grows a considerable length during ontogeny, from 3.0 mm at 3 days of age, to 5.5 mm at 1 year, and to 9.5 mm at 15 years. The adult male has a vocal fold of 17–23 mm and the adult female, of 12.5–17 mm (Negus, 1949).

For humans, the most important change concerns the supralaryngeal tract (branch-point IV in Fig. 1.1). The functional divergence at this point involves the competing demands of selection for vegetative functions like breathing, swallowing, and chewing as opposed to nonvegetative functions like phonetic efficiency. Lieberman (1984) demonstrated that the supralaryngeal airways of anatomically modern *Homo sapiens* evolved to enhance vocal communication at the expense of these vegetative func-

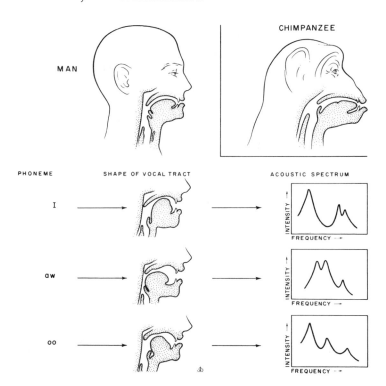

MAN

CHIMPANZEE

PHONEME   SHAPE OF VOCAL TRACT   ACOUSTIC SPECTRUM

I

ɑw

oo

Figure 1.4. The phonatory apparatus of humans and chimpanzees. The configuration of the mature human vocal tract enables him or her to produce sounds that the chimpanzee (and the human infant) cannot produce, e.g., the three vowels presented in their articulatory positions and their intensity–frequency spectrum (Wilson, 1975).

tions. Interestingly enough, Darwin already noted "the strange fact that any particle of food and drink which we swallow has to pass over the orifice of the trachea, with some risk of falling into the lungs" (1859/ 1964, p. 191). Thousands of deaths occur every year when people, especially children, asphyxiate because a piece of food lodges in the larynx. Swallowing the wrong way, however, does not occur in newborn infants. They can simultaneously swallow fluid and breathe. They are obligate nose breathers. The high position of the larynx relative to the nasopharynx allows them to do this. The epiglottis and soft palate overlap and form a double seal. The larynx, in effect, functions as a tube that extends upward from the trachea into the nasopharynx.

This situation changes drastically within 3 months, at which age the descensus of the larynx is almost completed, an age at which the vocal activity of the infant is already remarkable. The angulation between the mouth and the upper respiratory tract is increased, the pharyngeal space is lengthened, and the back half of the tongue has come to form the front wall of the long tract above the vocal cords. This ontogenic transformation recapitulates Branch-point IV in evolution.

Humans deviate from the standard-plan supralaryngeal airway, whereas the rest of the primates, the pongidae included, do not. The angulation between the mouth and the glottis creates a two-tube supralaryngeal airway, as opposed to the single-tube system of the standard-plan vocal tract. Lieberman and coworkers have in various ways demonstrated that only the two-tube system can produce the vowels / i /, / a /, and / u /. These three configurations are the limiting articulations of a vowel triangle that is language-universal (Lieberman, 1973). Just like Neanderthal man, neither the newborn human nor the adult chimpanzee can produce the vowel space that is necessary for any language of *Homo sapiens*. This is illustrated in Figure 1.4. In this connection, a human genetic finding is of interest: Children suffering from a severe case of Down syndrome have a supralaryngeal tract similar to that of a newborn baby. These children are unable to speak intelligibly (Benda, 1969).

There is still another major change in the evolution of the peripheral sound-producing system which needs to be mentioned. These are the articulators within the oral cavity: the pharyngeal constrictor muscles, the velum (which seals the nasal cavity), the tongue, the cheek muscles, and the facial musculature, especially the lips, to mention only some. In addition, the extrinsic laryngeal muscles are also involved in the process of phonation and articulation, and all these muscles (and bones), originally designed for the ingestion of food, were gradually adapted to a second function: vocal communication by speech.

The central vocal system

The structural and functional evolution of the vertebrates' phonation system suggests that those species physically qualified to vocalize selectively benefited from audiovocal communication. Furthermore, the great variety of vocal expressions made possible by the ever-increasing structural changes probably helped speciation. The final product of evolution, namely speech, is the human being's most complex motor skill.

The execution of a movement, its speed, and its segmentation are important factors in all motoric precision performances. This is so also in the case of speech. Two hundred twenty syllables per minute is the normal speed of speaking; up to 500 syllables per minute can be produced (Lenneberg, 1967). Articulation runs at a speed of about 15 phonemes per second (Levelt, 1989). Speech requires the coordinated use of some 100 muscles. The adult speaker executes the movement automatically and involuntarily. How these synergistic motor configurations are produced by the central nervous system is as yet virtually unknown.

The cerebral motor system governing the peripheral apparatus which generates vocal behavior and selects the appropriate vocal signal for a given situation are discussed by Jürgens (chapter 2 of the present volume). My task at this point is to outline the evolutionary context of this system.

It is quite clear that the brain underwent numerous changes in the course of mammalian evolution, although these changes affected the various portions and subsystems differently. When human evolution and the unprecedented increase of neocortex are discussed, however, concomitant changes in subcortical structures are usually neglected. The limbic system is one of these structures. Since this system is heavily involved in vocal behavior, it is important to know that morphometric analyses of limbic structures revealed more neurons in the human anterior thalamic limbic nuclei (anteroventralis and anteromedialis) than expected in an anthropoid of our brain size (Armstrong, 1986). The increased number of neurons in the human anterior thalamus produces an increased limbic input into the human neocortex, especially into the supplementary motor area, premotor and orbitofrontal cortex (Fig. 1.5). The larger source of thalamic limbic information for the cingulate and parietal association cortex in the human brain, compared with that of other anthropoids, suggests a change in the human motivational system. The enlargement of the thalamic limbic pool of neurons may represent an increased differentiation of the limbic message being sent to the cortex. Vice versa, the enlarged thalamic limbic pool through reciprocal connections may represent an increased ability to activate and control limbic structures via neocortical input (Armstrong, 1986).

By far the most developed part of the nonhuman brain and – much more so – the human brain is the frontal lobe, especially the prefrontal cortex, which appears in primates relatively late. It receives projections from the secondary sensory areas and from the limbic anterior and dorsomedial thalamus. It is therefore in a position to integrate limbically and perceptive-cognitively processed data. This transition in evolution is of great significance for communication processes, particularly for vo-

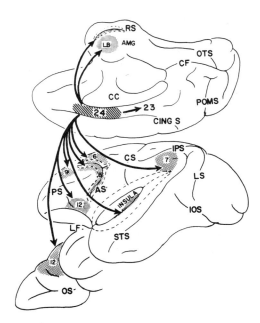

Figure 1.5. Diagram of projection patterns from area 24 of cingulate gyrus in rhesus monkey on medial, lateral, and basal surfaces of cerebral hemispheres: Premotor areas 6 and 8; prefrontal area 9; fronto-orbital area 12; rostral part of inferior parietal lobule of area 7; anterior insular cortex; perirhinal area (RS); laterobasal nucleus of amygdala (LB). (Pandya, Van Hoesen, & Mesulam, 1981.)

cal communication, since the anterior cingulate gyrus, the supplementary motor cortex, and some prefrontal structures are in one way or another involved in vocal behavior and its control (Müller-Preuss & Jürgens, 1976; Ploog, 1979; Pandya, Van Hoesen, & Mesulam, 1981).

The concept of branch-points in evolution was introduced earlier, in the discussion of the evolution of the larynx. An example of such a branch-point in cerebral evolution may be the following: Electrical stimulation of the rostro-inferior part of the cortical face area, the larynx area, yields movements of the vocal folds in nonhuman primates but no vocalization (Jürgens, 1974, 1982). Some authors (e.g., Hines, 1940) reported inconsistent results on electrically elicitable vocalizations in the chimpanzee. There are well-established projections from the cortical larynx area of the monkey to the cortex around the anterior cingulate sulcus and to those brain stem structures which are relevant for vocalization. Cortical stimulation, however, can play only upon the vocal folds. The complete phonatory pattern consisting of vocal-fold adduction, expiration, and adequate movements of the oropharyngeal muscles is not integrated with cortical stimulation of the monkey and ape. In humans, however, vocalzations can be elicited readily from the cortical face area. The difference between humans and nonhuman primates – with the chimpanzee possibly taking a position in between – can be considered another example of progressive corticalization of functions in the ascending phylogenetic scale.

More direct evidence for the active participation of the supplementary motor area (SMA) can be demonstrated by regional blood flow measurements in human subjects (Larsen, Skinhöj, & Lassen, 1978). The diagram in Figure 1.6 depicts the results of a left-sided intensive activation of the premotor region which corresponds to the SMA, as well as a second activation of the larynx / tongue area. To a limited degree, the right hemisphere participates in this activation. Measurements were taken while the subjects, in so-called automatic speech tests, repeatedly counted from 1 to 20 (Ingvar, 1983).

An activation of the classical speech center of Broca, just in front of the face area, also may be assumed, based on data collected at an aphasia clinic. What role this area plays in speech is still not sufficiently clear. It is conceivable that there is a stage in ontogeny where the "raw material" of innate vocalization – a child's cooing and babbling – is formed into templates for phonemes. These templates would be released via the face / larynx area as articulatory gestures learned by matching and screened against motorically active neighboring cortical areas (Ploog, 1988). Deficits in fine motor coordination in children with unintelligible speech, the timing of speech and hand–motor coordination in language-delayed children, as well as the conspicuous associative movements of the hands which accompany the articulatory movements of a child learning to speak (Amorosa, 1982; Amorosa, von Benda, Dames, & Schäfersküpper, 1986) may be indicative of a functional differentiation process taking place within and between the respective areas of the premotor and motor cortex.

Ontogenetic aspects of phonological development

Phonological development in humans is treated in depth in part III of the present volume. Therefore only a few remarks regarding evolutionary aspects may be in order here. Three points should be made: (1) Phonological development in humans is different from that in nonhuman primates, from the very beginning. In my opinion, the latter are born with a repertoire of sounds which undergoes hardly any subsequent changes in structure (Winter, Handley, Ploog, & Schott, 1973). This is-

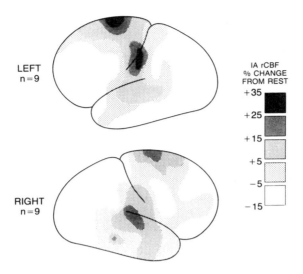

Figure 1.6. Automatic speech. Superimposed diagrams of nine right-sided and nine left-sided regional cerebral blood flow (rCBF) studies in patients without neurological disturbance and with normal speech. The rCBF changes have been calculated in percentages, relative to the resting state. Scale to the right denotes magnitude of flow change. During automatic speech the subjects were asked to count repeatedly from 1 to 20. The subjects had their eyes closed. Note z-like flow change on the left side, with a clear-cut flow peak in the premotor/prefrontal regions, another peak in the mouth/tongue/larynx area, and also an activation of the middle temporal region. On the right side a similar pattern was recorded, but the peaks were not as high and were less well defined, especially in the temporal region. (Replotted after color television display; Ingvar, 1983.)

sue is controversial, however; it is discussed in detail in chapter 7 of this volume by Symmes and Biben. Nonhuman primates are not endowed with the ability to imitate sounds and can hardly learn any new kinds of sound pattern. In the human species, however, the range of vocalizations expands and changes in a process that begins in the first few weeks of life and proceeds through a course of predetermined stages before the development of actual speech. (2) Although the development of vocalization in humans is unique, during the first 6 months of life there are similarities with phonation in nonhuman primates, such as (a) the great variety of vocalizations and the innumerable variations within them; (b) the resulting possibility of finely differentiated expression of emotional state, with a multitude of different meanings expressible through vocalization; and (c) the inability to imitate new sounds, in spite of a superior ability to recognize species-specific vocalization. (3) The fixed pattern of phonological development in humans, which is independent of the language spoken by the baby's caregiver, indicates that maturational processes in the central nervous system determine the stages of this development.

If one assumes that certain stages in ontogeny recapitulate certain stages in evolution, a morphogenetic hypothesis seems plausible: The first vocal expressions of the human newborn infant are generated and controlled by brain stem mechanisms. During the cooing and babbling stages – comparable to the nonhuman primate's vocal behavior – the limbic system together with subcortical feedback loops comes into play, and, with the molding of phonemes and words, the neocortex becomes the dominant structure.

A second result emerges from the evolutionary / ontogenetic comparison, based on morphogenetic and functional facts: Evolutionary and ontogenetic development points clearly to vocal rather than to gestural behavior as man's primordial language. The selection pressure on vocal communication, accompanied by amazing morphological and functional changes in the sound-producing apparatus and in the central nervous system, has lasted over many millions of years. The temporal pattern in the ontogeny of human vocal behavior supports the idea that the phonatory gestures of speech were the first to appear in the evolution of language, whereas body gestures, from the beginning, had a secondary, supportive function.

The central receiving system

From the production part of the audiovocal system we turn to the receiving part of the four-partite communication system. Here the vocal signal is perceived and transformed into a message which may or may not produce a modification of behavior on the receiver's part. Whether it is the decoding system of anurans or monkeys, by coevolutionary processes it is tuned to the production system so that the animal is innately responsive to the acoustic features of species-specific vocal signals. Such a template may be genetically determined, for it is found predominantly in nonhuman primates (Herzog & Hopf, 1983, 1984; Ploog, Hupfer, Jürgens, & Newman, 1975; Talmage-Riggs, Winter, Ploog, & Mayer, 1972; Winter, 1969; Winter et al., 1973), or may require auditory experience during early development, for example, as in songbirds or humans (Marler, 1976; Marler & Mitani, 1988).

Two lines of research strategies have been employed to study these features (Newman, 1988): the neurophysiological approach (Müller-Preuss, 1981, 1986; Müller-Preuss & Maurus, 1985; Müller-Preuss & Ploog, 1981; Newman & Wollberg, 1973; Winter & Funkenstein, 1973; Wollberg & Newman, 1972) and the behavioral approach (Hopf, Hartmann-Wiesner, Kühlmorgen, & Mayer, 1974; Jürgens, 1979; Maurus & Ploog, 1984; Ploog, Hopf, & Winter, 1967; Schott, 1975; Winter et al., 1966). Only the latter approach will be referred to, since it seems to be more relevant to the topics of this book.

For some years it was thought that catalogs of the vocal repertoire of various primate species would be helpful in establishing the function of certain calls. This was only partly successful, since the vocal units of these catalogs were based on sound spectrograms and human percept of a monkey call. From an evolutionary point of view, the most recent approach to the question of specifying the salient features in a monkey call is more interesting. The question to be asked is, How do the monkeys perceive their own sounds? Symmes and Newman (1974) were the first to demonstrate that squirrel monkeys could discriminate between variants in the isolation peep. Other investigators, using an operant conditioning paradigm, studied the discrimination of different forms of the coo call in Japanese macaques and demonstrated that other species had a much more difficult time discriminating between the various coo calls of the Japanese macaque. From this and other tests in the pitch dimension, they concluded that the Japanese macaque has a specific feature detector for its own vocalization, so that the discrimination on the "phonetic" dimension is species-specific (Petersen, 1982; Zoloth et al., 1979).

Playback experiments in the laboratory and in the field were also helpful in establishing the function of primate calls. Winter et al. (1966) found two alarm calls in squirrel monkeys: The "alarm peep" warns against aerial predators, the "yap" against terrestrial predators. The former causes immediately immobility in a group of animals; the latter induces flight to higher places and yapping (mobbing) against the suspicious object. The two different behavioral responses to the two species-specific warning calls were experimentally studied in infant squirrel monkeys reared from birth in social isolation. It turned out that the naïve animals responded innately to both calls. The response to yapping, however, habituated, unless the playback of yapping was combined with the presentation of a reference model (cat, snake). The results indicated a rapid and selective learning process in connection with the innate responsiveness to the terrestrial predator alarm call (Herzog & Hopf, 1983, 1984; Hopf et al., 1985).

Seyfarth and Cheney did playback studies in the field and found that vervet monkeys could discriminate between three different forms of alarm calls and four different forms of grunts (Cheney & Seyfarth, 1982; Seyfarth et al., 1980). Similar studies have been completed on New World primates in captivity, which all show that each can discriminate between subtly different forms of calls with different functions. Bauers and Snowdon (1984), for instance, have shown that cottontop tamarins can discriminate between subtle variations of the chirp call. Only 50–70 ms in length and similar in structure, these calls were used in quite different situations.

From the evolutionary point of view, the similarities and differences between nonhuman and human primates in the perception of vocalizations are of great interest. Are there antecedents of the human speech-decoding mechanisms in the nonhuman primate? Several studies, which achieved remarkably similar results, were carried out. In the first study, Morse and Snowdon (1975) tested rhesus monkeys in a heart rate habituation–dishabituation paradigm. Synthetic stimuli varying in place of articulation (/ ba /, / da /, / ga /) were used in a design which is similar to the study of Eimas, Siqueland, Jusczyk, & Vigorito (1971) on 4-week-old human infants. Morse and Snowdon found that the monkeys can discriminate / ba / from / da / and / ba / from / ga /. However, the monkeys also did well on within-category changes. Sinnott, Beecher, Moody, and Stebbins (1976) found that the monkeys were inferior to the human listeners with regard to discriminating between small changes in the formant transitions of the synthetic syllables. But they could perform this task whether the stimuli were eight tokens of each syllable or single synthetic tokens. In addition, a study was conducted with rhesus monkeys on the voice onset time (VOT) with synthetic tokens of labial consonants that vary in VOT. When VOT is varied in the region of a short-voicing lag, monkeys behave in an operant situation as if there is a perceptual change, that is, in a humanlike fashion (Waters & Wilson, 1976).

In my opinion, the experiments reported so far have not conclusively answered the question of whether or not there is a categorical perception similar to the human kind in nonhuman primates. Actually, the monkeys do fairly well in the within-category distinctions and not strikingly better in the between-category distinctions, which is also the case in human infants under 1 year of age. In principle, the monkeys behave similarly to certain mammals (dogs, cats, chinchillas) which can successfully discriminate labial voiced-plosive consonants from alveolar voiced-plosive consonants when these occur in syllable-initial position. However, Kuhl and Miller (1975) have shown that chinchillas respond as though an abrupt qualitative change occurs in the region of the VOT continuum where voicing lags release by a short time of 20–40 ms, that is, the place where many languages separate voiced from voiceless phonemes (Miller, 1977).

All this raises the question on what properties monkeys and some other vocal mammals based their discrimination. Discrimination based on purely acoustic properties of spectral energy transitions, rather than on the phonetic mode of perception, appears to be typical only for humans (Liberman & Pisoni, 1977). On the other hand, one could argue that slow transitions in form and function are common in evolutionary processes, for example, in regard to morphological and functional differences between the cerebral hemispheres. Since monkeys do better on the perception tasks than chinchillas, cats, and dogs, their auditory mode of perception may be a precursor for the evolution of the phonetic mode of perception.

I want to conclude this discussion of categorical perception with a reference to a set of experiments of a different kind, namely, the search for categories of species-specific sounds within a given species. To test whether monkeys discriminate between their sounds categorically requires synthetic versions of the sounds, so that they can be varied along the critical acoustic parameter by which the vocal variants are distinguished. Snowdon and Pola (1978), in their study on pygmy marmosets, found that two versions of the monkeys' trills were used in very different circumstances, namely, as a contact call and as an agonistic call. The two calls differed from each other only in the dimension of duration. In a subsequent study it was found that the duration boundary that separated the two calls was not precisely fixed but depended on previous experience with a familiar individual (Snowdon, 1986). This example shows that certain boundaries are crucial but not fixed. Idiosyncratic behavior is taken into account by the listener, just as the human listener adapts variations in VOT, tempo of speech, and the accompanying coarticulation. In a second study of categorization it was found that Goeldi's monkeys, like squirrel monkeys, had two similarly structured alarm calls which elicited two different responses, namely, freezing reactions and alarm calls. Masataka (1983) found a clear categorical distinction on the dimension of frequency range. A frequency range of 1.6–2.4 kHz produced warning-call responses, and a range of 2.6–5.6kHz elicited freezing responses. Systematic variation of the synthetic calls on other dimensions produced no similar categorical function.

A methodologically new approach to the question of categorical perception in nonhuman primates was taken by Maurus and his coworkers (1984, 1988). Based on experiments using four calls without distinct frequency modulation, they showed that the animals emit calls containing categorical amplitude changes. The amplitude changes within one call are either very small or very large. Different positions of large amplitude leaps within a call carry different functions and depend on the social situation (Maurus, Streit, Barclay, Wiesner, & Kühlmorgen, 1986). Since positions of amplitude modulations within one phoneme or word are part of the prosodic features of language and can also carry semantic functions, I suggest that this categorical vocal behavior may be another forerunner of linguistic faculties.

Although I cannot go into the fascinating neurophysiological aspects of auditory perception of primate vocal communication (e.g., Müller-Preuss, 1986), I want to bring up one example which may have evolutionary significance. It is concerned with the difference between the perception of self-produced calls and their playbacks at varying intensities. The experiments are based on the assumption that the complex nature of acoustic communication requires control circuits between structures involved in the production of calls and structures involved in the perception of calls. To gain experimental access to this question, the action potentials of single neurons were recorded extracellularly. Neurons in the auditory cortex, in the medial geniculate body (MGB), and in the inferior colliculus (IC) of the midbrain were recorded during self-produced vocalizations and during playbacks of the same vocalizations from tape (Fig. 1.7). More than half of several hundred cells in the auditory cortex and the MGB responded weakly or not at all to the self-produced call, but they responded reliably and independently of intensities to the playback of the same call. At midbrain level (IC) the situation is strikingly different. The neurons respond consistently to both stimuli, the self-produced and the playbacks (Müller-Preuss & Ploog, 1981; Ploog, 1981).

This audiovocal mechanism has considerable adaptive value, in two respects. First, since a certain cell population in the cortex and thalamus appears to receive full neuronal information about the animal's own vocal output, comparable to information it receives about foreign calls, it may assist the animal in comparing and modifying vocal patterns. Although, in the case of the squirrel monkey, we have shown that most of

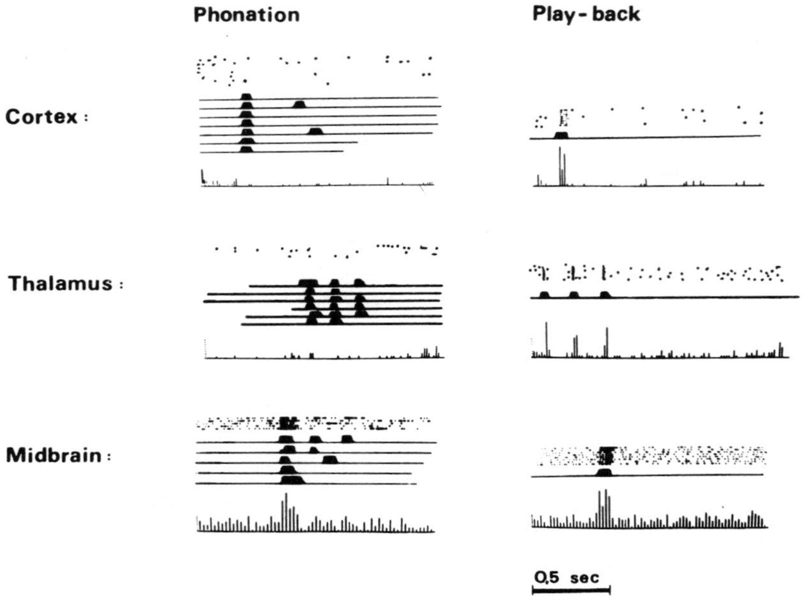

Figure 1.7. Cell responses at cortical, thalamic, and midbrain level during self-produced calls and their playbacks. Dot displays in the upper part of the diagrams represent several action-potential sequences of single neurons during self-produced vocalization and playback, respectively. Traces in the middle part show the envelopes of the calls. Lowest trace represents peri–stimulus time histogram, that is, cumulated neuronal activity across several calls.

the vocal repertoire is preprogrammed at birth (Winter et al., 1973), recent studies indicate that certain modifications are possible (Lieblich, Symmes, Newman, & Shapiro, 1980). This flexibility might be even greater in more advanced primates. Second, another fraction of the cell population is inhibited during phonation but open to the processing of signals coming from the environment while the animal is vocally active. This permits immediate recognition of essential acoustic information as well as a rapid mode of audiovocal communication, for example, in "dialogues" (Maurus, Kühlmorgen, Wiesner, Barclay, & Streit, 1985). The audiovocal selective inhibitory mechanism is certainly only one part of a higher complex integrative system with feedback and feedforward loops at various levels of the central nervous system, (e.g., cortico-ponto-cerebello-thalamo-cortical or nigro-striato-nigral). However, from our behavioral studies on infant monkeys (Herzog & Hopf, 1983, 1984; Ploog, 1969; Ploog et al., 1967), one can infer that this selective mechanism is already operating at birth. In this regard the monkey does not differ from the human neonate. It can be assumed that both are equipped to make the distinction between their own vocalizations and vocal input from others at a very early stage of their development. Why the human infant can use this control mechanism for vocal play in babbling and the monkey does not is an open question.

Cerebral asymmetries

The last issue which I want to raise in the context of the evolution of vocal communication is concerned with cerebral morphological and functional asymmetries. Morphological asymmetries are present in the brains of Old World and New World monkeys, apes, fossil man, and modern man (LeMay, 1985; Heilbroner & Holloway, 1988). The significance of the asymmetries in the nonhuman primates is still obscure. Most reviews of laterality or hemispheric dominance indicate that functional asymmetries, similar to those found in humans, are not evident (Beaton, 1986; Warren, 1977). More recently, however, primate handedness has been reconsidered (MacNeilage, Studdert-Kennedy, & Lindblom, 1987). Studies on handedness of rhesus monkeys, baboons, gorillas, and chimpanzees suggest that it might be useful to distinguish between handedness when simply reaching for an object (food) and its manual specialization for novel and complex tasks. Reach tasks may not be sensitive enough measures to produce reliable hand preferences (Fagot & Vauclair, 1988a,b; Hopkins & Morris, 1989; Hopkins, Washburn, & Rumbaugh, 1989). In the evolution of lateralized functions, selection for different lateralized processes may have occurred. The results obtained by refined testing may advance current theories on the evolution of laterality and its relation to linguistic functioning.

It has been assumed that some of the asymmetries, especially in the superior temporal gyrus (STG) and the Sylvian fissure, may be located in areas that subserve functions that are forerunners of language (Heilbroner & Holloway, 1988; LeMay, 1985). However, in regard to function, only a few studies point in this direction. They all are concerned with the role of the auditory cortex in primate hearing (e.g., Dewson, 1977; Pohl, 1984). The effects of STG lesions on the recognition of species-specific calls were studied by us in squirrel monkeys (Hupfer, Jürgens, & Ploog, 1977). Subjects were trained to perform a categorical discrimination between a group of structurally variable species-specific vocalizations with 60 tokens and a group of equally variable sounds from other natural sources with 75 tokens of varying degrees of similarity to species-specific calls. Neither unilateral nor bilateral small lesions produce a significant effect. The animals with bilateral (but not unilateral), medium-sized lesions showed a significant retention deficit for both categories of sounds. With the largest and most complete bilateral ablations they were unable to discriminate between sounds at all. They never did relearn the task. Moreover, they were even incapable of discriminating between the yapping call and white noise, while they could still recognize whether there was a sound or no sound. Precisely this inability to discriminate among complex auditory stimuli of any kind is known in humans and is called *auditory agnosia*. Large, bilateral lesions of the auditory cortex cause this specific impairment. The patients are neither able to understand spoken language nor to identify sounds or noises of any other kind (Ploog, 1979). We concluded that the monkey needs the auditory cortex for the discrimination of complex acoustic stimuli but can do equally well with either the right or the left.

Bilateral ablation of the STG in Japanese macaques rendered them unable to discriminate between two distinct categories of coo calls. Unilateral ablation of the left STG, including the auditory cortex, resulted in an initial impairment in discrimination, but similar unilateral ablation of the right STG had no effect (Heffner & Heffner, 1984). Petersen et al. (1984) came to a comparable result. Japanese macaques were also trained to discriminate between two variations of coo calls which differ in the relative temporal position of the peak frequency. The animals could easily discriminate between early peak and late peak vocalizations. However, when the calls to be discriminated were presented to the right ear, the Japanese macaques performed better. Comparison monkeys, two other species of macaques, for whom the phonetic discrimination is not relevant, did not show a lateralization effect. The outstanding feature of these studies is the special design of the stimulus presentation, in which the influence of the acoustic structure of the calls is disassociated from the communicatively significant feature of the vocal signal. The comparison monkeys attended to the same acoustic dimension of the signals in performing the discrimination as the Japanese macaques. This demonstrates that all the monkeys tested have the sensory capacities for making this discrimination. However, the comparison monkeys did not employ lateralized mechanisms when doing so. Petersen and his colleagues suggest the possibility that a lateralized network is activated when species-specific call features are detected. This means that the communicative valence of the signals is more important than their purely acoustic nature in producing the lateralization effects.

From here, it seems, a bridge can be built to a lateralized species-specific speech-perceiving subsystem in the human, where the phonetic message is encoded in the physical signal of the sound (Liberman & Pisoni, 1977). This is about as far as one can go in accounting for the evolution of animal vocal perception capacities at present.

Conclusions

The purpose of this essay has been to point out evolutionary processes in audiovocal communication, describing them as adaptive transformations which eventually led to an optimization of this form of communication. In primates, the final product of this development is the ability to speak and comprehend phonological gestures. Having compared phylogenetic with ontogenetic aspects of the audiomotor and the other somatomotor processes, our answer to the old question whether humans used gestures to make themselves understood before they used the voice is that vocal sounds must have formed the primordial language.

To grasp the full evolutionary significance of audiovocal communication, the coevolutionary processes of the whole system should be considered. We therefore described the transformations of the peripheral apparatus which generates the species-specific signals, the evolution of the cerebral system which does the patterning and controlling of the signal, and the cerebral decoding mechanism which tranforms the signal into a message. The key to the understanding of audiovocal communication is the way in which the subsystems, especially the cerebral motor patterning and decoding systems, are linked together. Recent morphological, functional, and behavioral data on laterality, as well as comparative ontogenetic studies of vocal behavior in nonhuman primates and preverbal communication in human infants, contribute to current theories on the evolution of language and speech. We are still far from having resolved the issue.

References

Amorosa, H. (1982). The timing of speech and hand motor coordination in language delayed children. *Journal of the Acoustical Society of America, 71*(Suppl. 1), 22.

Amorosa, H., von Benda, U., Dames, M., & Schäfersküpper, P. (1986). Deficits in fine motor coordination in children with unintelligible speech. *European Archives of Psychiatry and Neurological Sciences, 236*, 26–30.

Armstrong, E. (1986). Enlarged limbic structures in the human brain: The anterior thalamus and medial mamillary body. *Brain Research, 362*, 394–397.

Bauers, K. A., & Snowdon, C. T. (1984). Perceptual discrimination between chirp vocalizations of cotton-top tamarins: A play-back study. *American Journal of Primatology, 6*, 398.

Beaton, A. (1986). *Left side, right side: A review of laterality research.* New Haven: Yale University Press.

Benda, C. E. (1969). *Down's syndrome, mongolism and management.* New York: Grune & Stratton.

Capranica, R. R. (1968). The vocal repertoire of the bullfrog (*Rana catesbeiana*). *Behaviour, 31*, 301–325.

Cheney, D. L., & Seyfarth, R. M. (1982). How vervet monkeys perceive their grunts: Field playback experiments. *Animal Behaviour, 30*, 739–751.

Darwin, C. (1859 / 1964). *On the origin of species.* (Facsimile ed.). Cambridge, Mass.: Harvard University Press.

Dewson, J. H. (1977). Preliminary evidence of hemispheric asymmetry of auditory function in monkeys. In S. R. Harnad, R. W. Doty, L. Goldstein, J. Jaynes, & G. Krauthamer (Eds.), *Lateralization in the nervous system* (pp. 63–71). New York: Academic Press.

Eimas, P. D., Siqueland, E. R., Jusczyk, P., & Vigorito, J. (1971). Speech perception in infants. *Science, 171*, 303–306.

Fagot, J., & Vauclair, J. (1988a). Handedness and manual specialization in the baboon. *Neuropsychologia, 26*, 795–804.

(1988b). Handedness and bimanual coordination in the lowland gorilla. *Brain, Behavior and Evolution, 32*, 89–95.

Harnad, S. R., Steklis, H. D., & Lancaster, J. (Eds.). (1976). *Origins and evolution of language and speech* (Annals of the New York Academy of Sciences, Vol. 280). New York: New York Academy of Sciences.

Harré, R., & Reynolds, V. (Eds.). (1984). *The Meaning of Primate Signals.* Cambridge: Cambridge University Press.

Heffner, H. E., & Heffner, R. S. (1984). Temporal lobe lesions and perception of species-specific vocalizations by macaques. *Science, 226*, 75–76.

Heilbroner, P. L., & Holloway, R. L. (1988). Anatomical brain asymmetries in New World and Old World monkeys: Stages of temporal lobe development in primate evolution. *American Journal of Physical Anthropology, 76*, 39–48.

Herzog, M., & Hopf, S. (1983). Effects of species-specific vocalizations on the behaviour of surrogate-reared squirrel monkeys. *Behaviour, 86*, 197–214.

(1984). Behavioral responses to species-specific warning calls in infant squirrel monkeys reared in social isolation. *American Journal of Primatology, 7*, 99–106.

Hines, M. (1940). Movements elicited from precentral gyrus of adult chimpanzees by stimulation with sine wave currents. *Journal of Neurophysiology, 3*, 442–466.

Hopf, S., Hartmann-Wiesner, E., Kühlmorgen, B., & Mayer, S. (1974). The behavioral repertoire of the squirrel monkey (*Saimiri*). *Folia Primatologica, 21*, 225–249.

Hopf, S., Herzog, M., & Ploog, D. (1985). Development of attachment and exploratory behavior of infant squirrel monkeys under controlled rearing conditions. *International Journal of Behavioral Development, 8*, 55–74.

Hopkins, W. D., & Morris, R. D. (1989). Laterality for visual-spatial processing in two language-trained chimpanzees (Pan troglodytes). Behavioral Neuroscience, 103, 227–234.

Hopkins, W. D., Washburn, D. A., Rumbaugh, D. M. (1989). Note on hand use in the manipulation of joy sticks by rhesus monkeys (Macaca mulatta) and chimpanzees (Pan troglodytes). Journal of Comparative Psychology, 103, 91–94.

Hupfer, K., Jürgens, U., & Ploog, D. (1977). The effects of superior temporal lesions on the recognition of species-specific calls in the squirrel monkey. Experimental Brain Research, 30, 75–87.

Ingvar, D. H. (1983). Serial aspects of language and speech related to prefrontal cortical activity: A selective review. Human Neurobiology, 2, 177–189.

Jürgens, U. (1974). On the elicitability of vocalization from the cortical larynx area. Brain Research, 81, 564–566.

(1979). Vocalization as an emotional indicator: A neuroethological study in the squirrel monkey. Behaviour, 69, 88–117.

(1982). Afferents to the cortical larynx area in the monkey. Brain Research, 239, 377–389.

Jürgens, U., & Ploog, D. (1976). Zur Evolution der Stimme. Archiv für Psychiatrie und Nervenkrankheiten, 222, 117–137.

Kelemen, G. (1963). Comparative anatomy and performance of the vocal organ in vertebrates. In R.-G. Busnel (Ed.), Acoustic behaviour of animals (pp. 489–521). Amsterdam: Elsevier.

Kuhl, P. K., & Miller, J. D. (1975). Speech perception by the chinchilla: Voiced–voiceless distinction in alveolar plosive consonants. Science, 190, 69–72.

Larsen, B., Skinhöj, E., & Lassen, N. A. (1978). Variation in regional cortical blood flow in the right and left hemispheres during automatic speech. Brain, 101, 193–209.

LeMay, M. (1985). Asymmetries of the brains and skulls of nonhuman primates. In S. D. Glick (Ed.), Cerebral lateralization in nonhuman species (pp. 233–245). Orlando, Fla.: Academic Press.

Lenneberg, E. H. (1967). Biological foundations of language. New York: Wiley.

Levelt, W. J. M. (1989). Speaking: From intention to articulation. Cambridge, Mass.: MIT Press.

Liberman, A. M., & Pisoni, D. D. (1977). Evidence for a special speech-perceiving subsystem in the human. In T. Bullock (Ed.), Dahlem workshop on recognition of complex acoustic signals. Life Sciences Research Report, 5, 59–76. Berlin: Abakon.

Lieberman, P. (1973). On the evolution of language: A unified view. Cognition, 2, 59–94.

(1984). The biology and evolution of language. Cambridge, Mass.: Harvard University Press.

Lieblich, A. K., Symmes, D., Newman, J. D., & Shapiro, M. (1980). Development of the isolation peep in laboratory-bred squirrel monkeys. Animal Behaviour, 28, 1–9.

MacNeilage, P. F., Studdert-Kennedy, M. G., & Lindblom, B. (1987). Primate handedness reconsidered. Behavioral and Brain Sciences, 10, 247–303.

Marler, P. (1976). Sensory templates in species-specific behavior. In J. Fentress (Ed.), Simpler networks: An approach to patterned behavior and its foundations (pp. 314–329). New York: Sinauer.

Marler, P., & Mitani, J. (1988). Vocal communication in primate and birds: Parallels and contrasts. In D. Todt, P. Goedeking, & D. Symmes (Eds.), Primate vocal communication (pp. 3–14). Berlin: Springer.

28   Detlev W. Ploog

Masataka, N. (1983). Categorical responses to natural and synthesized alarm calls in Goeldi's monkeys (*Callimico goeldii*). *Primates, 24*, 40–51.

Maurus, M., Kühlmorgen, B., Wiesner, E., Barclay, D., & Streit, K.-M. (1985). "Dialogues" between squirrel monkeys. *Language and Communication, 5*, 185–191.

Maurus, M., & Ploog, D. (1984). Categorization of social signals as derived from quantitative analyses of communication processes. In R. Harré & V. Reynolds (Eds.), *The meaning of primate signals* (pp. 226–241). Cambridge: Cambridge University Press.

Maurus, M., Streit, K.-M., Barclay, D., Wiesner, E., & Kühlmorgen, B. (1986). Interrelations between structure and function in the vocal repertoire of *Saimiri*. *European Archives of Psychiatry and Neurological Sciences, 236*, 35–39.

(1988). A new approach to finding components essential for intraspecific communication. In D. Todt, P. Goedeking, & D. Symmes (Eds.), *Primate vocal communication* (pp. 69–87). Berlin: Springer.

Maurus, M., Streit, K.-M., Geissler, B., Barclay, D., Wiesner, E., & Kühlmorgen, B. (1984). Categorical differentiation in amplitude changes of squirrel monkey calls. *Language and Communication, 4*, 195–208.

Mayr, E. (1942). *Systematics and the origin of species.* New York: Columbia University Press.

Miller, J. D. (1977). Perception of speech sounds in animals: Evidence for speech processing by mammalian auditory mechanisms. In T. Bullock (Ed.), *Dahlem workshop on recognition of complex acoustic signals. Life Sciences Research Report, 5*, 49–58. Berlin: Abakon.

Morse, P. A., & Snowdon, C. T. (1975). An investigation of categorical speech discrimination by rhesus monkeys. *Perception and Psychophysics, 17*, 9–16.

Müller-Preuss, P. (1981). Acoustic properties of central auditory pathway neurons during phonation in the squirrel monkey. In S. Syka & L. Aitkin (Eds.), *Neuronal mechanisms of hearing* (pp. 311–315). New York: Plenum.

(1986). On the mechanisms of call coding through auditory neurons in the squirrel monkey. *European Archives of Psychiatry and Neurological Sciences, 236*, 50–55.

Müller-Preuss, P., & Jürgens, U. (1976). Projections from the cingular vocalization area in the squirrel monkey. *Brain Research, 103*, 29–43.

Müller-Preuss, P., & Maurus, M. (1985). Coding of call components essential for intraspecific communication through auditory neurons in the squirrel monkey. *Naturwissenschaften, 72*, 437.

Müller-Preuss, P., & Ploog, D. (1981). Inhibition of auditory cortical neurons during phonation. *Brain Research, 215*, 61–76.

Negus, V. E. (1949). *The comparative anatomy and physiology of the larynx.* New York: Hafner.

Newman, J. D. (1988). Primate hearing mechanisms. In H. D. Steklis & J. Erwin (Eds.), *Comparative primate biology: Vol. 4. Neuroscience* (pp. 469–499). New York: Liss.

Newman, J. D., & Wollberg, Z. (1973). Multiple coding of species-specific vocalizations in the auditory cortex of squirrel monkeys. *Brain Research, 54*, 287–304.

Pandya, D. N., Van Hoesen, G. W., & Mesulam, M. M. (1981). Efferent connections of the cingulate gyrus in the rhesus monkey. *Experimental Brain Research, 42*, 319–330.

Paulsen, K. (1967). *Das Prinzip der Stimmbildung in der Wirbeltierreihe und beim Menschen.* Frankfurt: Akademische Verlagsgesellschaft.

Petersen, M. R. (1982). The perception of species-specific vocalization in primates: A conceptual framework. In C. T. Snowdon, C. H. Brown, & M. R. Petersen (Eds.), *Primate communication* (pp. 171–211). Cambridge: Cambridge University Press.

Petersen, M. R., Zoloth, S. R., Beecher, M. D., Green, S., Marler, P. R., Moody, D. B., & Stebbins, W. C. (1984). Neural lateralization of vocalizations by Japanese macaques: Communicative significance is more important than acoustic structure. *Behavioral Neuroscience, 98,* 779–790.

Ploog, D. (1969). Early communication processes in squirrel monkeys. In R. J. Robinson (Ed.), *Brain and early behaviour development in the fetus and infant* (pp. 269–298). London: Academic Press.

(1979). Phonation, emotion, cognition, with reference to the brain mechanisms involved. In *Brain and Mind* (Ciba Foundation Series No. 69, pp. 79–98). Amsterdam: Excerpta Medica.

(1981). Neurobiology of primate audio-vocal behavior. *Brain Research Review, 3,* 35–61.

(1988). Neurobiology and pathology of subhuman vocal communication in human speech. In D. Todt, P. Goedeking, & D. Symmes (Eds.), *Primate vocal communication* (pp. 195–212). Berlin: Springer.

Ploog, D., Hopf, S., & P. Winter (1967). Ontogenese des Verhaltens von Totenkopfaffen (*Saimiri sciureus*). *Psychologische Forschung, 31,* 1–41.

Ploog, D., Hupfer, K., Jürgens, U., & Newman, J. D. (1975). Neuroethological studies of vocalization in squirrel monkeys with special reference to genetic differences of calling in two subspecies. In M. A. B. Brazier (Ed.), *Growth and development of the brain* (pp. 231–254). New York: Raven Press.

Pohl, P. (1984). Ear advantages for temporal resolution in baboons. *Brain and Cognition, 3,* 438–444.

Schott, D. (1975). Quantitative analysis of the vocal repertoire of squirrel monkeys (*Saimiri sciureus*). *Zeitschrift für Tierpsychologie, 38,* 225–250.

Seyfarth, R. M., Cheney, D. L., & Marler, P. (1980). Monkey responses to three different alarm calls: Evidence for predator classification and semantic communication. *Science, 210,* 801–803.

Sinnot, J. M., Beecher, M. D, Moody, D. B., & Stebbins, W. C. (1976). Speech sound discrimination by monkeys and humans. *Journal of the Acoustical Society of America, 60,* 687–695.

Snowdon, C. T. (1986). Vocal communication. In G. Mitchell & J. Erwin (Eds.), *Comparative primate biology: Behavior, conservation, and ecology* (Vol. 2A, pp. 495–530). New York: Liss.

Snowdon, C. T., & Pola, Y. V. (1978). Interspecific and intraspecific responses to synthesized pygmy marmoset vocalizations. *Animal Behaviour, 26,* 192–206.

Symmes, D., & Newman, J. D. (1974). Discrimination of isolation peep variants by squirrel monkeys. *Experimental Brain Research, 19,* 365–376.

Talmage-Riggs, G., Winter, P., Ploog, D., & Mayer, W. (1972). Effects of deafening on the vocal behavior of the squirrel monkey (*Saimiri sciureus*). *Folia Primatologica, 17,* 404–420.

Warren, J. M. (1977). Handedness and cerebral dominance in monkeys. In S. R. Harnad, R. W. Doty, L. Goldstein, J. Jaynes, & G. Krauthamer (Eds.), *Lateralization in the nervous system* (pp. 151–172). New York: Academic Press.

Waters, R. S., & Wilson, W. A., Jr. (1976). Speech perception by rhesus monkeys: The voicing distinction in synthesized labial and velar stop consonants. *Perception and Psychophysics, 19,* 285–289.

Wilson, E. O. (1975). *Sociobiology: The new synthesis.* Cambridge, Mass.: Harvard University Press (Belknap Press).

Winter, P. (1969). Dialects in squirrel monkeys: Vocalization of the Roman arch type. *Folia Primatologica, 10,* 216–229.

Winter, P., & Funkenstein, H. H. (1973). The effect of species-specific vocalization on the discharge of auditory cortical cells in the awake squirrel monkey. *Experimental Brain Research, 18,* 489–504.

Winter, P., Handley, P., Ploog, D., & Schott, D. (1973). Ontongeny of squirrel monkey calls under normal conditions and under acoustic isolation. *Behaviour, 47,* 230–239.

Winter, P., Ploog, D., & Latta, J. (1966). Vocal repertoire of the squirrel monkey *(Saimiri sciureus),* its analysis and significance. *Experimental Brain Research, 1,* 359–384.

Wollberg, Z., & Newman, J. D. (1972). Auditory cortex of squirrel monkey: Response patterns of single cells to species-specific vocalization. *Science, 175,* 212–214.

Zoloth, S. R., Petersen, M. R., Beecher, M. D, Green, S., Marler, P., Moody, D. B., & Stebbins, W. C. (1979). Species-specific perceptual processing of vocal sounds by monkeys. *Science, 204,* 870–872.

2. On the neurobiology of vocal communication

UWE JÜRGENS

Vocal communiation can take place on different levels of complexity. Accordingly, the brain structures involved in its control vary. The lowest level, from an evolutionary point of view, is represented by a completely genetically determined vocal reaction. An example is pain shrieking in humans. In this reaction, both the elicited vocal motor pattern as well as the eliciting stimulus do not have to be learned. A heavy blow against the body, for instance, will elicit shrieking from birth on. An infant does not need prior experience with this stimulus in the form of a pairing with another, unconditioned stimulus. It also does not need to hear shrieking from other humans in order to be able to produce this cry. This is evident not only from the fact that shrieking appears immediately after birth but also from the observation that shrieking occurs even in congenitally deaf infants (Eibl-Eibesfeldt, 1973). The shrieking reaction to a painful stimulus thus corresponds to what ethologists call an *innate releasing mechanism*.

The brain structures responsible for the control of such vocal innate releasing mechanisms seem to be limited, at least in some cases, to the brain stem. Support for this conclusion comes essentially from two observations. One derives from so-called anencephalic infants, that is, infants born without a forebrain, having only a more or less intact brain stem (Fig. 2.1). Such infants, despite the fact that they lack the whole cortex as well as the basal ganglia and the thalamus, nevertheless react to painful stimuli with shrieking (Monnier & Willis, 1953). The other observation comes from systematic brain transection experiments in cats. In these experiments, it has been found that as long as the transection is rostral to the mesencephalon, the cats still react to caressing with purring and to tail pinching with meowing and growling. If the transection is made caudal to the midbrain, vocalization can no longer be obtained (Bazett & Penfield, 1922). Both observations suggest (1) that for a num-

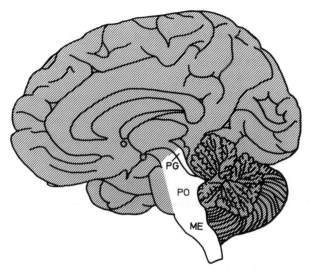

Figure 2.1. Sagittal section of the human brain. The hatched areas represent brain structures lacking in an anencephalic infant described by Monnier and Willis (1953) that was still able to utter shrieking sounds. Abbreviations: ME, medulla oblongata; PG, periaqueductal gray; PO, pons.

ber of innate vocal reactions the forebrain, that is, telencephalon and
diencephalon, is dispensable; (2) that the mesencephalon represents the
highest level of the neuraxis indispensable for vocalization. Systematic
lesioning experiments in the squirrel monkey and the cat have revealed
that the critical structure within the mesencephalon is the periaqueductal gray and the laterally bordering tegmentum. The destruction of this
area alone is sufficient to produce mutism (Adametz & O'Leary, 1959;
Jürgens & Pratt, 1979a; Skultety, 1958). This not only holds for the cat
and the squirrel monkey; there is a case report in the neurological literature describing a patient who, after a small lesion restricted to the periaqueductal gray and bordering tegmentum, became completely mute
until his death 2 months later. This patient did not show a general aki-
nesia but was able to walk around and to take his meals without help
(Botez & Carp, 1968).

The periaqueductal region is necessary but, of course, not sufficient
for the production of vocalization; vocalization requires an input from
sensory brain structures and an output to those motor nuclei innervating the laryngeal, oral, and respiratory muscles involved in phonation.
In the case of pain shrieking, the sensory input comes via collaterals of
the spinothalamic tract which transmits, among others, pain informa-

tion from the trunk and extremities to the brain (Harmann, Carlton, & Willis, 1988). The fibers ascend within the spinal cord and terminate mainly in the ventroposterior nucleus of the thalamus and the periaqueductal gray (Yezierski, Sorkin, & Willis, 1987). Pain fibers from the head region enter the brain directly via the trigeminal nerve and, after a relay in the spinal trigeminal nucleus, end in the same areas as the spinothalamic tract (Brodal, 1969). If this input of pain fibers is interrupted, pain shrieking is abolished (Hassler, Kaemmerer, Dieckmann, Christ, & Riverson, 1968). But this is a modality-specific abolition of vocalization, not a general loss of voice. The periaqueductal region receives an input not only from pain fibers; it also receives an input from the visual system via the overlying superior colliculus, from the auditory system via the adjacent inferior colliculus, and from the tactual system via the spino- and quintothalamic tract (Beitz, 1982; Mantyh, 1982; Meller and Dennis, 1986). These inputs are independent of each other. In the squirrel monkey, we were able, by making small lesions in the periaqueductal region, to block one input, leaving others intact. More specifically, we were able to block the vocal alarm reaction to a visual stimulus (in this case, a dummy leopard), leaving intact the vocal alarm reaction in response to a tactile stimulus, namely, grasping the animal (Jürgens & Pratt, 1979a).

As for the output, neuroanatomical studies have shown that not all motor nuclei involved in phonation receive their information directly from the periaqueductal region (Holstege, Kuypers, & Dekker, 1977; Travers & Norgren, 1983). All phonatory motor nuclei, however, get an input from the lateral reticular formation of the lower brain stem, which, in turn, is directly connected with the periaqueductal region (Thoms & Jürgens, 1987). Small lesions within the lateral reticular formation, unlike those in the periaqueductal region, do not abolish specific vocal reactions but cause a deterioration of the acoustic structure of all types of vocalization (Kirzinger and Jürgens, 1985). This suggests that the lateral reticular formation of the lower brain stem represents a crucial relay station within the vocalization-control system. Its function seems to be to coordinate the activity of the different muscles involved in phonation, that is, laryngeal, articulatory, and respiratory ones. In contrast, the periaqueductal region serves a triggering function, that is, it couples specific external stimuli with specific vocal patterns coordinated in the lower brain stem reticular formation.

Let us consider now a higher level of vocal behavior: the level of voluntary vocalization control; or more specifically, voluntary control with respect to the initiation and inhibition of innate vocal reactions. Shrieking, as we have seen, is an innate vocal reaction to painful stimuli. Everybody knows, however, that human shrieking also can be produced without pain – for instance, on the stage by an actor mimicking pain – and that it can be suppressed even if pain is severe. This holds not only for humans but, to some extent, also for subhuman primates. Rhesus monkeys, for instance, can be trained, in a vocal operant conditioning task, to increase their vocalization rate if each vocalization is rewarded with food (Sutton, Larson, Taylor, & Lindeman, 1973). Rhesus monkeys even learn to utter one specific call type ("coo") during the presentation of a colored stimulus light, utter a second call type ("bark") during the presentation of a differently colored light, and refrain from vocalizing during presentation of a third stimulus light (Sutton, 1979). Another, more naturalistic example is described by Cheney and Seyfarth (1985). These authors observed the warning behavior of vervet monkeys in their natural environment in East Africa. They found that adult females are more likely to utter alarm calls in the presence of their own infants than in the presence of non-kin. Furthermore, adult males utter warning calls more often in the presence of adult females than adult males. These observations indicate that monkeys do have at least some voluntary control over vocalization initiation.

Brain-lesioning studies in the rhesus monkey have shown that this voluntary control depends upon an intact anterior limbic cortex. Destruction of that region abolishes the capability to master a vocal operant conditioning task (Aitken, 1981; Sutton, Larson, & Lindeman, 1974). Such a lesion, however, does not affect unconditioned vocal reactions to external stimuli – for instance, alarm calling in the presence of a predator (Kirzinger & Jürgens, 1982). We made corresponding observations of a human patient in our clinic (Jürgens & von Cramon, 1982). This patient, due to the occlusion of the ascending branches of both anterior cerebral arteries, suffered bilateral destruction of the anterior limbic cortex. When this patient was asked to mimic different emotional vocal expressions – for instance, to produce joyful exclamations, angry curses, or pain outcries – it turned out that all utterances showed a very flat intonation curve, sounding more or less monotonous. Thus both, humans and monkeys, have in common that lesions within the anterior limbic cortex are followed by a deficit in voluntary control of emotional vocal utterances.

The anterior limbic cortex represents a higher level within the vocalization control system than the periaqueductal region. This holds not only anatomically – the limbic cortex is part of the forebrain, the peri-

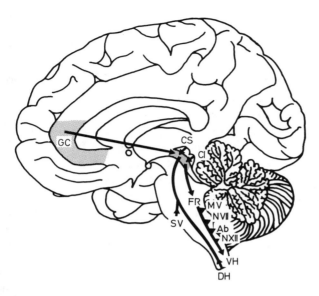

Figure 2.2. Sagittal section of the human brain, showing pathways involved in the control of nonverbal emotional vocal utterances. Abbreviations: Ab, nucleus ambiguus; CI, colliculus inferior; CS, colliculus superior; DH, dorsal horn of the spinal cord; FR, reticular formation; GC, cingulate gyrus; MV, trigeminal motor nucleus; N VII, facial nucleus; N XII, hypoglossal nucleus; SV, sensory trigeminal nucleus; VH, ventral horn of spinal cord.

aqueductal region lies in the brain stem; it also holds functionally. Combined lesioning and electrical brain stimulation experiments in the monkey have shown that electrical stimulation of the anterior limbic cortex yields vocalization, which is abolished after periaqueductal lesions are made (Jürgens & Pratt, 1979b). On the other hand, vocalizations elicited by electrical stimulation of the periaqueductal region are not abolished by lesions in the anterior limbic cortex. This finding is in agreement with the pure lesioning studies mentioned earlier, which show that periaqueductal lesions can cause a complete mutism, while anterior limbic lesions affect only one aspect of vocal behavior, namely, the volitional initiation of emotional vocal utterances. Neuroanatomical studies have revealed that the anterior limbic cortex is directly connected with the periaqueductal region; it thus is in a position to exert direct control over the more elementary periaqueductal vocalization center (Jürgens & Müller-Preuss, 1977; Müller-Preuss and Jürgens, 1976). A schematic representation of the anatomical relationships just described is given in Figure

2.2. The most complex level of vocal behavior, finally, is that involving voluntary control over the acoustic structure of vocal utterances. This includes the capability to learn vocal patterns by imitation as well as the production of new patterns by invention. Both capabilities exist in a well-developed form only in humans and certain birds. Because birds have a brain anatomy very different from that of mammals and produce their sounds with a different peripheral organ (the syrinx rather than the larynx), I shall restrict the following discussion to the vocal behavior of humans in comparison to that of other mammals.

At present, there is not a single well-documented case in the literature to demonstrate that vocal learning by imitation takes place in mammals below humans. There have been reports of changes in the vocal repertoire during ontogeny, but in no case could it be demonstrated that such changes are due to learning, rather than to maturational factors (Snowdon, French, & Cleveland, 1987). Even our closest relative, the chimpanzee, turned out to be unable to acquire even a rough approximation of spoken words (Hayes & Hayes, 1951; Kellogg, 1968). The complete failure of such speech-teaching attempts, in view of the chimpanzee's well-developed capacity for the acquisition of nonvocal communication signals, such as American Sign Language (Gardner & Gardner, 1969), as well as the capacity for highly differentiated facial movements (van Hooff, 1962), points again to a genetic determination of vocal behavior in nonhuman primates – more specifically, to genetically determined limitations of vocal motor learning.

From this the question arises, what differences exist in the brain anatomy between humans and the other primates which could explain the differences in vocal learning capability? Our own neuroanatomical studies have shown that monkeys (and the same probably holds for all nonhuman mammals) lack a direct connection between the primary motor cortex and the nucleus ambiguus, that is, the site of the laryngeal motoneurons (Jürgens, 1976). Such a direct connection does exist in humans (Kuypers, 1958a). As the primary motor cortex plays a crucial role in voluntary motor control in general, the lack of a direct connection in the monkey fits with the monkey's poor capacity for voluntary vocal control. This interpretation gets further support from another observation. While monkeys lack a direct connection between motor cortex and laryngeal motoneurons, they do have a direct connection between motor cortex and jaw muscle motoneurons, which lie in the trigeminal motor nucleus (Kuypers, 1958b; Sirisko & Sessle, 1983). Conditioning experiments show that monkeys are able to learn a controlled sensible jaw movement, namely, to exert a predetermined constant biting force for a fixed period (Luschei & Goodwin, 1975). Correspondingly, this holds for finger movements. Monkeys are able to perform delicate learned finger movements (Hepp-Reymond & Wiesendanger, 1972). Again, there is a direct connection between the motor cortex and those motoneurons in the cervical spinal cord innervating the finger muscles – a connection lacking, for instance, in the cat, which also lacks delicate finger movements (Kuypers, 1981; Wiesendanger, 1981). These observations suggest than an improved capability for voluntary fine motor control is paralleled by the formation of direct fiber connections between motor cortex and corresponding motoneurons.

The crucial role of the primary motor cortex for voluntary motor control is also exemplified by the effect of a lesion in this area. Bilateral destruction of the motor cortex in a human completely abolishes the capacity to produce learned vocal utterances, such as speech or the humming of melodies (Foerster, 1936; Groswasser, Korn, Groswasser-Reider, & Solzi, 1988; Leicester, 1980). Bilateral destruction of the same area in the monkey has no effect at all on the animal's genetically determined vocalizations (Jürgens, Kirzinger, & von Cramon, 1982). The same holds for those brain structures which serve as the main input and output structures of the primary motor cortex. The primary motor cortex receives its information mainly from the cerebellum via the ventrolateral thalamus and sends its information predominantly to the putamen, a part of the basal ganglia (Fig. 2.3). Lesions in all three structures cause severe disturbances in speech production but do not affect the acoustic structure of monkey calls (Andrew, Fowler, & Harrison, 1983; Bell, 1968; Gurd, Bessel, Bladon, & Bamford, 1988; Kent, Netsell, & Abbs, 1979; Kirzinger, 1985; Kirzinger & Jürgens, 1985; Krayenbühl, Siegfried, & Yasargil, 1963; Lechtenberg & Gilman, 1978; Metter et al., 1986; Samra et al., 1969). This means that a number of brain structures participate in the voluntary control of vocal patterns which are dispensable for the production of genetically determined vocal patterns.

In conclusion, we may say that the neural control of vocal utterances is brought about by essentially three subsystems (Fig. 2.4). One subsystem consists of the reticular formation and phonatory motor and sensory nuclei in the lower brain stem and spinal cord. This subsystem is responsible for the motor coordination of the different muscles involved in vocalization; it probably also contains the subroutines necessary for the production of genetically preprogrammed vocal patterns. This subsystem, however, is not by itself capable of producing vocal utterances.

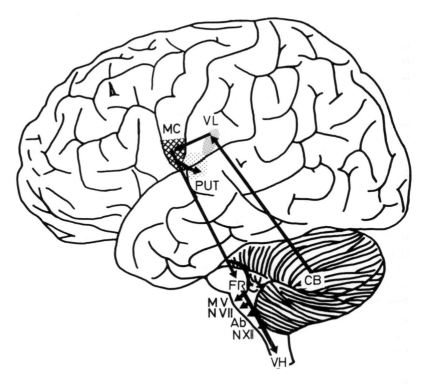

Figure 2.3. Lateral view of the human brain, showing pathways indispensable for speech production but dispensable for nonverbal emotional vocal
utterances. Abbreviations: Ab, nucleus ambiguus; CB, cerebellum; FR, reticular formation; MC, facial representation of motor cortex; MV, trigeminal motor nucleus; N VII, facial nucleus; N XII, hypoglossal nucleus; PUT,
putamen; VH, ventral horn of spinal cord; VL, nucleus ventralis lateralis
thalami.

It needs a facilitating input from a second subsystem, a group of brain
structures involved in motivation control. This second subsystem provides the driving force necessary to initiate a vocal utterance. It also
decides which types of fixed vocal patterns are initiated. The subsystem
in itself is hierarchically organized. Its lowest level is represented by the
periaqueductal gray and the laterally bordering tegmentum. This area
receives a direct input from sensory systems and thus is in a position to
couple directly specific external stimuli with specific call types. The next-
highest level is represented by a number of subcortical limbic structures,
such as the hypothalamus, midline thalamus, amygdala, bed nucleus of
stria terminalis, preoptic region, and septum, which take part in the

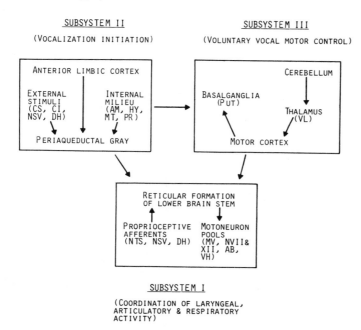

SUBSYSTEM II
(VOCALIZATION INITIATION)

SUBSYSTEM III
(VOLUNTARY VOCAL MOTOR CONTROL)

ANTERIOR LIMBIC CORTEX

EXTERNAL STIMULI (CS, CI, NSV, DH)

INTERNAL MILIEU (AM, HY, MT, PR)

PERIAQUEDUCTAL GRAY

CEREBELLUM

BASALGANGLIA (PUT)

THALAMUS (VL)

MOTOR CORTEX

RETICULAR FORMATION OF LOWER BRAIN STEM

PROPRIOCEPTIVE AFFERENTS (NTS, NSV, DH)

MOTONEURON POOLS (MV, NVII& XII, AB, VH)

SUBSYSTEM I
(COORDINATION OF LARYNGEAL, ARTICULATORY & RESPIRATORY ACTIVITY)

Figure 2.4. Schema of the three subsystems involved in the neural control of phonation. Abbreviations: AB, nucleus ambiguus; AM, amygdala; CI, colliculus inferior; CS, colliculus superior; DH, dorsal horn of spinal cord; HY, hypothalamus; MT, midline thalamus; MV, trigeminal motor nucleus; NSV, sensory trigeminal nucleus; NTS, solitary tract nucleus; N VII, facial nucleus; N XII, hypoglossal nucleus; PR, preoptic region; PUT, putamen; VH, ventral horn of spinal cord; VL, nucleus ventralis lateralis thalami.

generation of emotional states by relating external stimuli to internal motivation–relevant stimuli. The highest level within this hierarachy is represented by the anterior limbic cortex, which seems to be responsible for the voluntary control of emotional states. The third subsystem, finally, consists of the motor cortex and its main input and output structures (cerebellum, ventrolateral thalamus, primary somatosensory cortex, putamen, nucleus ruber, and pyramidal tract). This subsystem is engaged in the voluntary fine control of vocal patterns. All three subsystems converge in the reticular formation of the lower brain stem; in other words, there is a direct connection between primary motor cortex as well as periaqueductal region with the reticular formation of Subsystem I. Subsystems II and III, that is, motivational and fine motor control systems, in addition, can communicate via a direct connection between primary motor cortex and limbic cortex.

References

Adametz, J., & O'Leary, J. L. (1959). Experimental mutism resulting from periaqueductal lesions in cats. *Neurology, 9*, 636–642.

Aitken, P. G. (1981). Cortical control of conditioned and spontaneous vocal behavior in rhesus monkeys. *Brain and Language, 13*, 171–184.

Andrew, J., Fowler, C. J., & Harrison, M. J. G. (1983). Stereotaxic thalamotomy in 55 cases of dystonia. *Brain, 106*, 981–1000.

Bazett, H. L., & Penfield, W. G. (1922). A study of the Sherrington decerebrate animal in the chronic as well as the acute condition. *Brain, 45*, 185–265.

Beitz, A. J. (1982). The organization of afferent projections to the midbrain periaqueductal gray of the rat. *Neuroscience, 7*, 133–159.

Bell, D. S. (1968). Speech functions of the thalamus inferred from the effects of thalamotomy. *Brain, 91*, 619–638.

Botez, M. I., & Carp, N. (1968). Nouvelles données sur le problème de mécanisme de déclenchement de la parole. *Revue Roumaine de Neurologie, 5*, 153–158.

Brodal, A. (1969). *Neurological anatomy.* New York: Oxford University Press.

Cheney, D. L., & Seyfarth, R. M. (1985). Vervet monkey alarm calls: Manipulation through shared information? *Behaviour, 94*, 150–166.

Eibl-Eibesfeldt, I. (1973). The expressive behaviour of the deaf-and-blind-born. In M. von Cranach & J. Vine (Eds.), *Social communication and movement* (pp. 163–194). London: Academic Press.

Foerster, O. (1936). Motorische Felder und Bahnen. In O. Bumke & O. Foerster (Eds.), *Handbuch der Neurologie* (pp. 1–448). Berlin: Springer.

Gardner, R. A., & Gardner, B. T. (1969). Teaching sign language to a chimpanzee. *Science, 165*, 664–672.

Groswasser, Z., Korn, C., Groswasser-Reider, J., & Solzi, P. (1988). Mutism associated with buccofacial apraxia and bihemispheric lesions. *Brain and Language, 34*, 157–168.

Gurd, J. M., Bessell, N. J., Bladon, R. A. W., & Bamford, J. M. (1988). A case of foreign accent syndrome, with follow-up clinical, neuropsychological and phonetic descriptions. *Neuropsychologia, 26*, 237–251.

Harmann, P. A., Carlton, S. M., & Willis, W. D. (1988). Collaterals of spinothalamic tract cells to the periaqueductal gray: A fluorescent double-labeling study in the rat. *Brain Research, 441*, 87–97.

Hassler, R., Kaemmerer, E., Dieckmann, G., Christ, J. F., & Riverson, A. E. (1968). Die Trigeminusneuralgie, Pathophysiologie und Aetiologie. *Acta Neurochirurgica, 18*, 129–169.

Hayes, K. J., & Hayes, C. (1951). The intellectual development of a home-raised chimpanzee. *Proceedings of the American Philosophical Society, 95*, 105–109.

Hepp-Reymond, M.-C., & Wiesendanger, M. (1972). Unilateral pyramidotomy in monkeys: Effect on force and speed of a conditioned precision grip. *Brain Research, 36*, 117–131.

Holstege, G., Kuypers, H. G., & Dekker, J. J. (1977). The organization of the bulbar fibre connections to the trigeminal, facial and hypoglossal motor nuclei: 2. An autoradiographic tracing study in cat. *Brain, 100*, 265–286.

Jürgens, U. (1976). Projections from the cortical larynx area in the squirrel monkey. *Experimental Brain Research, 25*, 401–411.

Jürgens, U., Kirzinger, A., & von Cramon, D., (1982). The effects of deep-reaching lesions in the cortical face area on phonation: A combined case report and experimental monkey study. *Cortex, 18,* 125–140.

Jürgens, U., & Müller-Preuss, P. (1977). Convergent projections of different limbic vocalization areas in the squirrel monkey. *Experimental Brain Research, 29,* 75–83.

Jürgens, U., & Pratt, R. (1979a). Role of the periaqueductal grey in vocal expression of emotion. *Brain Research, 167,* 367–378.

(1979b). The cingular vocalization pathway in the squirrel monkey. *Experimental Brain Research, 34,* 499–510.

Jürgens, U., & von Cramon, D. (1982). On the role of the anterior cingulate cortex in phonation: A case report. *Brain and Language, 15,* 234–248.

Kellogg, W. N. (1968). Communication and language in the home-raised chimpanzee. *Science, 162,* 423–427.

Kent, R. D., Netsell, R., & Abbs, J. H. (1979). Acoustic characteristics of dysarthria associated with cerebellar disease. *Journal of Speech and Hearing Research, 22,* 627–648.

Kirzinger, A. (1985). Cerebellar lesion effects on vocalization of the squirrel monkey. *Behavioral Brain Research, 16,* 177–181.

Kirzinger, A., & Jürgens, U. (1982). Cortical lesion effects and vocalization in the squirrel monkey. *Brain Research, 233,* 299–315.

(1985). The effects of brain stem lesions on vocalization in the squirrel monkey. *Brain Research, 358,* 150–162.

Krayenbühl, H., Siegfried, J., & Yasargil, M. G. (1963). Résultats tardifs des opérations stéréotaxiques dans le traitement de la maladie de Parkinson. *Revue Neurologique, 108,* 485–494.

Kuypers, H. G. (1958a). Corticobulbar connexions to the pons and lower brain stem in man. *Brain, 81,* 364–388.

(1958b). Some projections from the pericentral cortex to the pons and lower brain stem in monkey and chimpanzee. *Journal of Comparative Neurology, 110,* 221–255.

(1981). Anatomy of the descending pathways. In J. M. Brookhart, V. B. Mountcastle, V. B. Brooks & S. R. Geiger (Eds.), *Handbook of physiology:* Vol. 2. *The nervous system.* Pt. 1, *Motor control* (pp. 597–666). Bethesda, Md.: American Physiological Society.

Lechtenberg, R., & Gilman, S. (1978). Speech disorders in cerebellar disease. *Annals of Neurology, 3,* 285–290.

Leicester, J. (1980). Central deafness and subcortical motor aphasia. *Brain and Language, 10,* 224–242.

Luschei, E. S., & Goodwin, G. M. (1975). Role of monkey precentral cortex in control of voluntary jaw movements. *Journal of Neurophysiology, 38,* 146–157.

Mantyh, P. W. (1982). The ascending input to the midbrain periaqueductal gray of the primate. *Journal of Comparative Neurology, 211,* 50–64.

Meller, S. T., & Dennis, B. J. (1986). Afferent projections to the periaqueductal gray in the rabbit. *Neuroscience, 19,* 927–964.

Metter, E. J., Jackson, C., Kempler, D., Riege, W. H., Hanson, W. R., Mazziotta, J. C., & Phelps, M. E. (1986). Left hemisphere intracerebral hemorrhages studied by (F-18)-fluorodeoxyglucose PET. *Neurology, 36,* 1155–1162.

Monnier, M., & Willis, H. (1953). Die integrative Tätigkeit des Nervensystems beim meso-rhombo-spinalen Anencephalus (Mittelhirnwesen). *Monatsschrift für Psychiatrie und Neurologie, 126,* 239–273.

Müller-Preuss, P., & Jürgens, U. (1976). Projections from the "cingular" vocalization area in the squirrel monkey. *Brain Research, 103,* 29–43.

Samra, K., Riklan, M., Levita, E., Zimmerman, J., Waltz, J. M., Bergmann, L., & Cooper, I. S. (1969). Language and speech correlates of anatomically verified lesions in thalamic surgery for parkinsonism. *Journal of Speech and Hearing Research, 12,* 510–540.

Sirisko, M. A., & Sessle, B. J. (1983). Corticobulbar projections and orofacial and muscle afferent inputs of neurons in primate sensorimotor cerebral cortex. *Experimental Neurology, 82,* 716–720.

Skultety, F. M. (1958). The behavioral effects of destructive lesions of the periaqueductal gray matter in adults cats. *Journal of Comparative Neurology, 110,* 337–365.

Snowdon, C. T., French, J. A., & Cleveland, J. (1987). Ontogeny of primate vocalizations: Models from bird song and human speech. In D. M. Taub & F. A. King (Eds.), *Current perspectives in primate social dynamics* (pp. 389–402). New York: Van Nostrand Reinhold.

Sutton, D. (1979). Mechanisms underlying learned vocal control in primates. In H. D. Steklis & M. J. Raleigh (Eds.), *Neurobiology of social communication in primates: An evolutionary perspective.* New York: Academic Press.

Sutton, D., Larson, C., & Lindeman, R. C. (1974). Neocortical and limbic lesion effects on primate phonation. *Brain Research, 71,* 61–75.

Sutton, D., Larson, C., Taylor, E. M., & Lindeman, R. C. (1973). Vocalization in rhesus monkeys: Conditionability. *Brain Research, 52,* 225–231.

Thoms, G., & Jürgens, U. (1987). Common input of the cranial motor nuclei involved in phonation in the squirrel monkey. *Experimental Neurology, 95,* 85–99.

Travers, J. B., & Norgren, R. (1983). Afferent projections to the oral motor nuclei in the rat. *Journal of Comparative Neurology, 220,* 280–298.

van Hooff, J. A., (1962). Facial expressions in higher primates. *Symposia of the Zoological Society of London, 8,* 97–125.

Wiesendanger, M. (1981). The pyramidal tract: Its structure and function. In A. L. Towe & E. S. C. Luschei (Eds.), *Handbook of behavioral neurobiology:* Vol. 5. *Motor coordination* (pp. 401–491). New York: Plenum.

Yezierski, R. P., Sorkin, L. S., & Willis, W. D. (1987). Response properties of spinal neurons projecting to midbrain or midbrain-thalamus in the monkey. *Brain Research, 437,* 165–170.

3. Vocal affect expression as symptom, symbol, and appeal

KLAUS R. SCHERER

Lending strong support to Darwin's insistence on the importance of the vocal organs as a means of communicating emotion (1872/1965), recent research on vocal affect expression has established not only that a variety of emotional states differentially affect vocalizations and their acoustic parameters in both animals and humans but also that conspecifics are reliably able to use this information to infer the state of the sender. Having recently reviewed both the methodology for research in this area and the results of past studies on both animals and humans (see Scherer, 1985, 1986a, 1989), I shall concentrate in this essay on issues related to vocal affect signaling that have so far been neglected. Most research to date has focused on what could be called expressive signs as *symptoms* of sender state. Just like a symptom of an illness, a particular vocal expression externalizes a more general underlying syndrome, in this case an affect state, and is more or less reliably used by conspecifics as an index to this underlying state. It is in fact no accident that the Brunswikian lens model which I have repeatedly suggested as a useful paradigm for theory and research in this area (Scherer, 1978, 1982) has been extensively used as a model for diagnostic procedure in a variety of medical settings and for diagnostic judgment in general. Given the obvious symptomatic function of vocal expression in relation to affective state, it is often overlooked that any expressive sign, just like any language sign, may have two additional functions, as postulated in the organon model proposed by Karl Bühler (1933, 1934): representation, that is, functioning as a symbol of objects or facts; and social influence or appeal, that is, functioning as a signal to others. The diagram in Figure 3.1 depicts a slightly modified version of the organon model.

It would be fair to say that just as the *symptom* expression of *linguistic* signs has received comparatively little attention in linguistics or psycholinguistics, the *symbol* aspect of *nonlinguistic* vocal expression has been

43

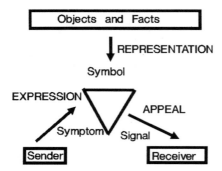

Figure 3.1. Bühler's organon model (slightly modified).

largely overlooked in the nonverbal communication literature. So far, the appeal function, the induction of a particular attitude or action in the receiver, has been neglected altogether (with the possible exception of speech act theory). In this essay I shall focus on these two neglected functions of vocal expression, symbol and appeal. In the absence of prior empirical work, the argument is somewhat speculative. I hope that the claims I make will serve to provoke healthy controversy and foster empirical research to investigate vocal affect expression in a more comprehensive manner than has been done to date. Before turning to vocal signs as symbols and appeals, to situate the reader in this somewhat incoherent field of research I will briefly summarize what I take to be our current information concerning vocal expression as a symptom of affect.

Vocal affect expression as symptom

Given the strong likelihood of major phylogenetic continuity of vocal affect expression (see Jürgens & Ploog, 1976; Ploog, 1980, 1988; Scherer, 1985; Scherer & Kappas, 1988), it may be useful to briefly survey the literature on the communication of emotion in animals. Obviously, any investigation of the vocal auditory communication system of a particular species provides evidence on vocal cues of motivational-affective state. Unfortunately, two problems prevent the systematic use of this literature: (1) the fact that vocalizations studied in the field are often described only by the use of more or less appropriate verbal labels, sometimes supplemented by spectrographic illustration of single cases. This makes it difficult to determine the nature of the acoustic cues involved. (2) Calls are generally studied within the confines of the particular behavioral repertoire of the respective species, which renders generalization difficult. A few authors, notably Morton (1977) and Tembrock (1975), have attempted to identify some general principles concerning the relationship between broad motivational-affective states and particular acoustic patterns of the accompanying vocalizations. Table 3.1 shows an attempt at integrating their findings across several species. In addition, Jürgens (1979), in careful experimental work with squirrel monkeys, has provided a complete inventory of the affect vocalizations for that species that can be usefully compared with the human case. Unfortunately, so far there has been no direct attempt at a comparative study of human and animal affect vocalizations using comparable motivational-affective states, induction procedures, and acoustic measurement.

As for the animal work, some of the research on humans suffers from the fact that the acoustic characteristics of the vocalizations studied cannot be reliably assessed, given the use of verbal labels as voice-quality descriptors (see Scherer, 1986a, p. 145). However, the number of studies which have investigated vocal correlates of emotional states using electroacoustic equipment or advanced digital analysis procedures, yielding objective acoustic parameters, is constantly increasing. The results published to date allow us to establish a reasonably coherent inventory of the acoustic patterns that have been repeatedly found for particular emotional states (see Table 3.2).

In spite of this encouraging development, research methodology in this area is still rather inadequate, particularly as far as the comparability of results is concerned. This is due to major differences among studies with respect to the emotional states studied, the induction procedures used, the subjects observed, the speech or vocalization samples obtained, the measurements applied, and the parameters reported (see Scherer, 1986a). However, it is to be hoped that current advances in digital signal processing on a microcomputer basis will lead to a higher degree of standardization of research methodology in this field. Furthermore, a growing convergence of opinions concerning the definition of emotional states and the operationalization of emotion induction may help to overcome the problem of widely varying criterial states.

Space does not permit us to deal with research on the vocal expression of stress and other affective disturbances in humans. However, work conducted in both our own and other laboratories has shown that there are reliable vocal cues of stress (Scherer, 1986b) and emotional disorder such as depression or schizophrenia (Darby, 1981; Scherer, 1987). However, these results must still be regarded as preliminary, given the many difficulties in identifying a unitary stress pattern or in obtaining homo-

Table 3.1. *Acoustic correlates of affective-motivational states across different species of animals*

Affective-motivational state	Acoustic characteristics
Relaxation, contentment, comfort, play	Repeated short sounds with relatively low frequencies
Dominance, hostility, agonistic intention	Low frequency sounds, harshness, falling frequency
Defense, fear	Short, tonelike calls with rising frequency, high-amplitude onset, and broad-frequency spectrum
Submission, resignation	High-frequency, tonelike sounds with repeated frequency shifts

Source: Based on Tembrock, 1975, and Morton, 1977; see Scherer, 1985, pp. 191–195.

geneous groups of patients with clearly defined syndromes of affect disorders.

In an effort to lay the basis for a theory-guided approach to research in this area, I have attempted to develop detailed predictions for future studies in this area, using a component process model of emotion and current knowledge about emotion-related changes in the autonomic nervous system and the striated musculature (somatic nervous system) with respect to their effect on vocalization and the accompanying acoustic parameters (Scherer, 1986a, 1989).

"Externalization" of an underlying emotion, "sending" or "encoding," is one component of the vocal affect communication process in humans. "Receiving," "decoding" or "attribution of sender state," is the other. A survey of vocal affect decoding studies published in the last few years has shown that most major affect states are recognized with higher-than-chance accuracy by naïve judges on the basis of vocal cues alone (Scherer, 1981, 1986a). There can be little doubt, then, that vocal affect expressions are extensively used in social communication to infer speaker states such as moods, emotions, and attitudes.

Since most recognition studies have used material with content-free vocalizations or standard text, it is safe to assume that the affect-state information is carried by vocal cues independent of verbal information – in particular, voice quality and prosodic cues. Using a large number of naturalistic utterances, Scherer, Ladd, and Silverman (1984) were able to demonstrate that little information remains when judges are asked to

Table 3.2. *Patterns of replicated empirical findings on acoustic correlates of emotional states in humans*

Emotional state	Acoustic correlates
Boredom / indifference	< mean F0, < mean intensity
Irritation / cold anger	> mean F0, > mean intensity, > high-frequency energy, downward-directed F0 contours
Rage / hot anger	> mean F0, > mean intensity, > F0 range and variability, > high-frequency energy
Sadness / dejection	< mean F0, < F0 range, downward-directed F0 contours, < mean intensity, < high-frequency energy, < precision of articulation
Worry / anxiety	> mean F0
Fear / terror	> mean F0, > F0 range and variability, > high-frequency energy
Joy / elation	> mean F0, > F0 range and variability, > mean intensity

Abbreviations: F0 = fundamental frequency; > = increased, rising; < = decreased, falling.
Source: See Scherer (1989, pp. 180–184) for a detailed report and references for the relevant studies.

rate speaker state on the basis of verbal transcripts. We used a variety of speech masking and filtering techniques in this study in order to establish which cues are responsible for the ability of judges to recognize the underlying emotional state. While some interesting patterns emerged – for example, the relatively great importance of voice-quality cues (in particular the energy distribution in the spectrum) compared with the lesser importance of sequential prosodic cues – the study showed that we need more refined techniques to tease out the respective role of the various voice-quality and prosodic cues in communicating emotional-state information.

In a series of studies using linear predictive coding (LPC)–based resynthesis (Markel & Gray, 1976), we systematically varied a number of acoustic features, keeping the remaining signal constant. In this fashion we were able to demonstrate, for example, that the attribution of emotional arousal varies directly and continuously with $F0$ (fundamental frequency) range, independent of speaker identity and verbal content (Ladd, Silverman, Tolkmitt, Bergmann, & Scherer, 1985; Bergmann, Goldbeck, & Scherer, 1988). It would seem that this technique, while costly and time-consuming, is the only one that permits the experimental demonstration of the role of particular vocal cues in affect-state inferences by human observers.

Vocal affect expression as symbol

My attention was drawn to this aspect of vocal affect expression by the minor revolution in the study of animal communication launched by Peter Marler and his collaborators D. Cheney, R. Seyfarth, S. Gouzoules, and H. Gouzoules (Gouzoules, Gouzoules, & Marler, 1984; Marler, 1984; Seyfarth & Cheney, 1982). Briefly, these researchers have shown in field studies of vervet monkeys that the animals' alarm calls are specific to certain types of predators. Furthermore, a tendency toward overgeneralization in the use of these calls by infant monkeys suggests that the production and appropriate use of the alarm calls is learned. These results were taken as evidence that treating animal vocalizations exclusively as symptoms of underlying motivational-affective states may be mistaken and that, on the contrary, at least some types of alarm calls are highly symbolic in nature and serve cognitive-representational functions.

The results reported by these researchers leave little doubt as to the specificity of the vervet alarm calls with respect to classes of predators. While it is understandable that this newly documented symbolic function has provoked much attention and interest, it would be mistaken to now deemphasize the expressive function of the calls as symptom of the underlying affective and motivational states of the animal. In line with Bühler's organon model, it is quite consistent to argue that a vervet monkey alarm call serves all three of Bühler's functions: as a symptom of the fear state of the animal, as a symbol of the type of predator that provoked the call, and as an appeal to the other members of the group to run away (using the mode of escape appropriate to the respective predator) or to be alert.

Obviously, then, we can make a case for the claim that most animal vocalizations serve three functions at the same time: They are a symptom of the state of the animal; they are a symbol for the object or situation that produced this state; and they act as an appeal to conspecifics to behave in a way that is appropriate with respect to the state of the vocalizer. One might argue that this trifunctionality of affect vocalizations is limited to animal calls, since they are the only means of vocal communication for these species. Obviously, human language is a much more powerful tool for conveying symbolic-representational content as well as for transmitting specific appeals or commands to others. Language can also be used to describe internal affective states in a detailed, evocative fashion (as exquisitely demonstrated by Flaubert). In addition, one could point to the fact that human emotions are generally produced by a large variety of highly complex situations, rather than by the fairly limited and somewhat stereotyped range of objects and situations that tend to elicit affect states in animals (e.g., the different types of predators in the vervet monkey example). This would seem to limit the possibility of human affect vocalizations serving as symbolic-representational signals, since there might be no clear link between an iconically signaled state and the object or situation that has produced this state. From this perspective, human affect vocalizations would be seen as limited to a symptom function.

However, given the phylogenetic continuity of vocal affect signaling and the fact that spoken language is based on vocalizing, one is tempted to investigate potential symbolic functions of vocal expression. In a recent essay (Scherer, 1988a), I presented a case for the symbolic function of nonlinguistic vocal affect expression. The argument goes as follows: There must be a close relationship between features of objects or situations and their relevance for the individual in the differentiation of the resulting emotional states. If so, it should be possible to infer (although obviously only in an approximate and global manner) some of the features of the eliciting situation from the nature of the differentiated affect state of the individual. If, in addition, the differentiated affect state is accompanied by specific physiological reactions, which, in turn, through their effect on respiration, phonation, and articulation, produce affect-specific vocalizations, the latter would seem to have at least a limited representational function.

Let us examine this argument in greater detail. Many emotion theorists agree on the notion that the elicitation and the differentiation of discrete emotional states can be explained by assuming an appraisal process based on a limited number of evaluative criteria or dimensions (see Scherer, 1988b). Table 3.3 shows an example of how, from such a perspective, one can attempt to predict discrete emotional states on the basis of particular patterns of outcomes of these appraisal processes. It

Table 3.3. *Predicted appraisal patterns for some major emotions*

	ELA/JOY	DISP/DISG	SAD/DEJ	FEAR	RAGE/HOA	BOR/IND	SHAME
Novelty							
Suddenness	hi/med	open	low	high	high	v low	low
Familiarity	open	low	low	open	low	high	open
Predictability	low	low	open	low	low	v high	open
Intrinsic pleasantness	open	v low	open	low	open	open	open
Goal significance							
Concern relevance	self/rela	body	open	body	order	body	self
Outcome probability	v high	v high	v high	high	v high	v high	v high
Expectation	open	open	open	dissonant	dissonant	consonant	open
Conduciveness	v con	open	obstruct	obstruct	obstruct	open	open
Urgency	low	medium	low	v high	high	low	high
Coping potential							
Cause: agent	open	open	open	oth/nat	other	open	self
Cause: motive	cha/int	open	cha/neg	open	intent	open	int/neg
Control	open	open	v low	open	high	medium	open
Power	open	open	v low	v low	high	medium	open
Adjustment	medium	open	medium	low	high	high	medium
Compatibility standards							
External	open	open	open	open	low	open	open
Internal	open	open	open	open	low	open	v low

Abbreviations: ELA/JOY, elation/joy; DISP/DISG, displeasure/disgust; SAD/DEJ, sadness/dejection; RAGE/HOA, rage/hot anger; BOR/IND, boredom/indifference; v, very; med, medium; rela, relationships; nat, nature; con, condusive; cha, chance; neg, negligence; intent, intention; oth, other. Open: Evaluation outcome does not determine type of emotion.

should be stressed that while the term *appraisal*, as well as the labels given to the evaluation criteria, sound highly cognitive, it is in fact assumed that emotion-eliciting appraisal operates in a more or less elaborate fashion, depending on the role of subcortical processing and the level of central nervous system sophistication in phylogeny and ontogeny (for further details, see Scherer, 1984; Leventhal & Scherer, 1987).

The next link in the argument concerns the specificity of the physiological reactions for each discrete emotional state and, in consequence, through the effect of autonomic nervous system and somatic nervous system changes on the voice production process, a differentiated pattern of acoustic characteristics. While the empirical evidence for physiological specificity for the emotions is rather scarce (Wagner, 1989), this seems mostly due to the dearth of relevant studies. From a biological, functional point of view, which is adopted by many authors in the field of emotion, it would seem crucial that the organismic responses to a particular emotion-eliciting situation should be tailored to the respective requirements for adaptation and thus specific to each emotional state (see Darwin, 1872/1965; Frijda, 1986). In trying to derive more concrete predictions concerning the physiological and expressive reactions in a functional perspective, I have attempted to show that it might be promising to adopt the level of individual appraisal mechanisms for this purpose – under the assumption that each evaluation of external or internal demands might entail a specific organismic reaction to cope with the respective state of affairs. For example, a novel, sudden stimulus is known to evoke a highly structured orientation response (Siddle, 1983). Expectation violation and frustration of goal-directed behavior are likely to elicit sympathetic nervous system activation, and preparation to fight in a situation appraised to require the use of physical force also seems to produce a variety of physiological adjustments (Henry & Stephens, 1977; Van Toller, 1979; Wagner, 1989). Using this line of argument, I have developed a set of predictions concerning the physiological and, in turn, vocal consequences of particular results of emotion-antecedent appraisal or stimulus evaluation checks (summarized in Table 3.4). Table 3.5 shows examples of how these predictions concerning voice type and the corresponding acoustic characteristics are combined for individual emotions following the logic indicated in Table 3.3.

To return to the symbolic function of nonlinguistic affect vocalization: Given the suggested relationship between cognitive and subcognitive appraisal processes and particular physiological and vocal reactions described in Table 3.4, it is assumed that a listener should be able to infer

Table 3.4. *Voice type changes and their acoustic correlates as effects of emotion-antecedent event evaluation*

Event appraised as:	Voice type	Acoustic correlates
Novel, sudden change		Interruption of ongoing vocalization, noiselike inhalation sounds
Intrinsically pleasant	Wide	> low-frequency energy, <$F1$, >$F1$ bandwidth
Intrinsically unpleasant	Narrow	> high-frequency energy, >$F1$, <$F1$ bandwidth, <$F2$ and $F3$
Relevant and consistent with expectations	Relaxed	$F0$ at lower end of range, < high-frequency energy, pronounced formant differences
If conducive to reaching goal or satisfying need	+ Wide	> low-frequency energy, <$F1$, >$F1$ bandwidth
If obstructive to reaching goal or satisfying need	+ Narrow	> high-frequency energy, >$F1$, <$F1$ bandwidth, <$F2$ and $F3$
Relevant and discrepant with expectations	Tense	> mean $F0$, > mean intensity, jitter and shimmer > high-frequency energy, <$F1$ bandwidth, pronounced formant differences
If conducive to reaching goal or satisfying need	+ Wide	> low-frequency energy, <$F1$, >$F1$ bandwidth
If obstructive to reaching goal or satisfying need	+ Narrow	> high-frequency energy, >$F1$, <$F1$ bandwidth, <$F2$ and $F3$
Impossible to control by human force	Lax	< mean $F0$, <$F0$ range, < mean intensity, < high-frequency energy, >$F1$ bandwidth, spectral noise, formants approaching neutral setting
Possible to master with own coping ability/power	Full	< mean $F0$, > mean intensity, strong energy in entire frequency range
Impossible to influence with own coping potential/power	Thin	> mean $F0$, widely spaced harmonics with little energy

Abbreviations: $F0$ = fundamental frequency, > = increased, rising, < = decreased, falling.
Source: See Scherer (1986, pp. 155–159) for a more detailed description of the predictions.

Table 3.5. *Predicted acoustic changes for four major emotions*

Emotion	Event evaluation	Voice type	Changes in acoustic parameters
Anger	Discrepant Obstructive	Tense Narrow	Tense + narrow + full: > mean $F0$, > mean intensity, jitter and shimmer
	Control	Tense	> $F1$, < $F1$ bandwidth, < $F2$ and $F3$,
	High power	Full	Strong energy in entire frequency range, > high-frequency energy
Fear	Novel Discrepant	Tense	Tense + narrow + thin: > mean $F0$, > $F0$ range and variability, jitter and shimmer
	Obstructive	Narrow	> $F1$, < $F2$ and $F3$, < $F1$ bandwidth,
	Low power	Thin	> high-frequency energy, widely spaced harmonics with little energy
Sadness	Obstructive No control	Narrow Lax	Tense + narrow + lax: < mean $F0$, < $F0$ range, < mean intensity, > $F1$, < $F2$ and $F3$, spectral noise formants approaching neutral setting
Joy	Discrepant Conducive	Tense Wide	Tense + wide: > mean $F0$, > mean intensity, jitter and shimmer < $F1$, pronounced formant differences

Abbreviations: $F0$ = fundamental frequency; > = increased, rising; < = decreased, falling
Source: See Scherer (1986, 1989) for details of the argument.

or reconstruct the emotion-antecedent cognitive appraisal processes of the vocalizer (and thereby the eliciting features of the object or situation) on the basis of the differentiated reaction patterns resulting from the outcomes of the evaluation checks. For example, if a listener is exposed to the acoustic characteristics shown in the last column of Table 3.5, he or she should be able to reconstruct the results of the cognitive appraisals listed in the second column and thus be able to infer some of the characteristics of the eliciting object or event (as well as label the emotion that was elicited). While this may be a less specific symbolic-representational function than the representation of predator groups by vervet monkeys, it would seem nevertheless possible to argue for a rudimentary representational symbol function in the sense of Bühler, for human nonlinguistic affect vocalizations.

Vocal affect expression as appeal

While it is obvious that we can use verbal means to command, cajole, or seduce others to do what we would like them to do, little effort has been spent on identifying a possible appeal function of nonlinguistic aspects of vocal behavior. A possible exception is the speech act literature, in which the implicit demands conveyed by particular lexical choices, but also by intonation contours, have been made a topic of study (see Levinson, 1983, for an overview and a critique).

Yet, just as vervet alarm calls have the obvious function of inducing flight – or at least attention and caution – in conspecifics, we can assume that human affect vocalizations have a similar appeal function in that they inform all those overhearing such a sound of the possible or desirable courses of action in the respective situation. I have argued this point in using disgust vocalizations as an example. The equivalent of a "yuck" sound is likely to induce hesitation, if not avoidance, toward food that is responsible for such a vocalization in all those overhearing it (see Scherer, 1988a, pp. 82–84). I believe that research efforts to explore this highly neglected function of affect vocalizations would constitute a major contribution to the study of vocal communication (see Scherer, 1988a, p. 93).

My special interest in this essay concerns a particular aspect of the appeal function, namely the induction of an emotion in the listener in the service of persuasion. Ancient manuals of rhetoric emphasized the importance of inducing emotion in the audience to facilitate persuasion and to influence attitudes and behavior. This, in fact, was regarded as the strongest form of appeal. Famous teachers of rhetoric such as Aristotle, Cicero, and Quintilian stressed the major role of the vocal expression of affect by the orator in evoking an appropriate emotion in the listener. Catharsis is one such mechanism of emotion induction in an audience.

In spite of the venerable age of the concern with the role of the expression of emotion in persuasion, we know little of the mechanism or of its functioning and effect. In recent social psychological work on attitude change (Petty & Cacioppo, 1986), there are some first attempts to explore the role of emotion in the persuasion process. While the way in which the induction of emotion in the audience facilitates persuasion is still largely unknown, it is highly likely that emotional arousal helps to sway an audience because of the following mechanisms (see also Clark & Williamson, 1989):

- directing attention to the message and the communicator; direction of cognitive arousal
- reducing the span of apprehension and focusing attention on particular issues
- reducing information-processing capacity, in particular critical-rational thinking; strengthening of unconscious automatic processing mechanisms
- activation of memory elements congruent with the emotion; activation of appropriate cognitive schemata
- changes in inference and judgment processes, particularly in the area of social cognition
- increasing ego involvement
- focusing cognitive processes on emotion-congruent behavioral scripts
- increasing the readiness for action; lowering of behavioral inhibition
- eliciting phylogenetically preprogrammed behavioral action patterns

The issue of interest in the present context concerns the question of how one could imagine the process whereby vocal affect expression of an orator will induce the same or other appropriate emotions in the listener. In a somewhat speculative vein, we can return to a hypothesis that was formulated by the German philosopher and sociologist Theodor Lipps. Lipps assumed the existence of two fundamental instincts: one concerning the expression of internal processes via motor behavior, and one of external motor mimicry of observed expressions. It seems useful to quote Lipps verbatim to render his thoughts with some precision:

> Once I was sad. While being sad, I experienced the tendency to produce the [facial] expressions of sadness. Yet I did not experience it as something *external* to the sadness, but as an integral part of it. I followed this tendency and generated the gesture through "instinctive" action. If I now see someone produce such an expression of sadness, my perception, or rather my "apperception" of it contains the tendency to produce the same expression. Yet, this is the *same* tendency which was an indissociable part of my *sadness*. This means that the elicitation of the tendency to produce the expression implies the reproduction of sadness, which in fact constitutes a single, indivisible experience. (Lipps, 1913, pp. 229–230; emphasis added, my translation)

Thus, Lipps believed that the automatic tendency toward motor mimicry of observed expressive behavior serves as the mechanism for emotion transfer. In other words, the observation of someone else's expressed emotion will, at least in a rudimentary fashion, evoke the same emotion in us, the observers. It is obvious that the theory sounds rather farfetched and contrary to intuition or everyday experience. In consequence, it has not had much success in psychology.

It is quite striking, however, that the theory keeps reappearing under different guises. A recent book on empathy (Eisenberg & Strayer, 1987) makes a rather strong point concerning the role of motor mimicry in the sense of Lipps as a possible basis for the undeniable phenomenon of empathy. While the evidence is still spotty, it does not seem excluded that the observation of emotional expression does in fact elicit a congruent motor innervation in the observer, although the strength of this innervation is obviously much lower. The intensity differential could in fact be the reason why this effect so far has not been empirically demonstrated in a convincing fashion. It seems reasonable to assume that motor mimicry of facial emotional expression might be restricted to slight innervations of the facial musculature such as can be demonstrated with the use of facial electromyographic measurement but which do not result in visually observable facial signals.

In fact, the influential tradition of facial feedback notions in the psychology of emotion (Tomkins, 1962, 1963; Laird, 1974; Buck, 1980) seems to be quite consistent with Lipps's original idea. It constitutes a logical extension, since it argues for emotion induction on the basis of proprioceptive feedback from the striated musculature. Though I am fairly skeptical with regard to the strong form of the facial feedback hypothesis (in line with much recent criticism: Manstead, 1988; Tourangeau & Ellsworth, 1979), I would not want to exclude that the hypothesized feedback processes do in fact exist, albeit with fairly low-intensity effects. Combined with Lipps's notion of motor mimicry, this would provide a fairly coherent notion of how one could imagine emotion induction to work on the basis of the observation of facially expressed emotions.

Since much of the past work has focused on facial expression, one might wonder to what extent vocal expression can be expected to serve similar functions. In fact, Theodor Lipps was convinced that motor mimicry would work in the same fashion in the vocal modality: "In the same manner as one gains sympathetic understanding [*Einfühlung*] of the other individual through the perception of visual movements and other forms of the material appearance, one perceives affective vocalizations, leading to the sympathetic understanding of their meaning" (Lipps, 1913, p. 321). What is more, we can even adduce evidence from another, rather different theoretical perspective: the motor theory of speech perception. In this tradition (Liberman, Cooper, Shankweiler, & Studdert-Kennedy,

1967), it was argued that we understand speech because of subliminal motor mimicry of the articulatory movements of the speaker. Obviously, if we were to transpose this theory to vocal affect expression, we could argue that the "understanding" of the affect of the other person should be largely facilitated by motor mimicry of the physiologically induced specific affect vocalization characteristics. Again, if we couple Lipp's motor mimicry idea with an afferent feedback notion, we would arrive at an explanation of how affect could be induced via vocal communication.

I obviously do not want to push this speculative hypothesis too far. Clearly, we often experience the opposite affect when being exposed to the emotional expression of an orator to whom, or to whose opinion, we are violently opposed. We are able to control affect arousal to a large extent. In any one situation, there are many factors that would seem to have affect-eliciting potential. In spite of all these factors, one could assume that under particularly suitable circumstances the exposure to vocal emotion expression of a persuasive communicator could in fact produce a rudimentary emotion of the same kind and thus facilitate persuasion and induce behavioral tendencies. Thus, as far as this particular domain is concerned, one could assume that vocal affect expression may in fact serve an appeal function in the sense that Bühler indicated.

Outlook

Peter Marler and his associates have been very influential in changing the focus of work on animal vocalizations away from an exclusive emphasis on the symptom function. What I have been trying to do in this essay is to demonstrate that a similar reorientation of research and theorizing on human vocal communication might be equally fruitful. Both the symbol and the appeal functions of nonlinguistic vocal behavior have been much neglected so far. This may be partly due to the fact that it is difficult to deny that for affect vocalizations, the symptom function does in fact dominate the others in terms of overall importance. Furthermore, it is obvious that the empirical study of the symbol and appeal functions is extremely complex in comparison with research on the symptom function, which in itself has proven a most difficult phenomenon to study experimentally. Yet the availability of powerful methodological tools for the analysis of vocal encoding and decoding (see Scherer, 1982, 1989), as well as the appearance of congenial theories on both the elicitation and the expression of emotion, would seem to encourage future attempts in the direction indicated.

References

Bergmann, G., Goldbeck, T., & Scherer, K. R. (1988). Emotionale Eindruckswirkung von prosodischen Sprechmerkmalen. *Zeitschrift für experimentelle und angewandte Psychologie, 35,* 167–200.

Buck, R. (1980). Nonverbal behavior and the theory of emotion: The facial feedback hypothesis. *Journal of Personality and Social Psychology, 5,* 811–824.

Bühler, K. (1933). *Ausdruckstheorie.* Jena: Fischer.

(1934). *Sprachtheorie.* Jena: Fischer.

Clark, M. S., & Williamson, G. M. (1989). Moods and social judgments. In H. L. Wagner & A. S. R. Manstead (Eds.), *Handbook of psychophysiology: Emotion and social behavior* (pp. 347–370). Chichester: Wiley.

Darby, J. (Ed.) (1981). *Speech evaluation in psychiatry.* New York: Grune & Stratton.

Darwin, C. (1872/1965). *The expression of the emotions in man and animals.* Chicago: University of Chicago Press. (Original work published 1872)

Eisenberg, N., & Strayer, J. (1987). *Empathy and its development.* Cambridge: Cambridge University Press.

Frijda, N. (1986). *The emotions.* Cambridge: Cambridge University Press.

Gouzoules, S., Gouzoules, H., & Marler, P. (1984). Rhesus monkey (*Macaca mulatta*) screams: Representational signalling in the recruitment of agonistic aid. *Animal Behavior, 32,* 182–193.

Henry, J. P., & Stephens, P. M. (1977). *Stress, health, and the social environment: A sociobiologic approach to medicine.* New York: Springer.

Jürgens, U. (1979). Vocalization as an emotional indicator: A neuroethological study in the squirrel monkey. *Behaviour, 69,* 88–117.

Jürgens, U., & Ploog, D. (1976). Zur Evolution der Stimme. *Archiv für Psychiatrie und Nervenkrankheiten, 222,* 117–137.

Ladd, D., Silverman, K., Tolkmitt, F., Bergmann, G., & Scherer, K. (1985). Evidence for the independent function of intonation contour type, voice quality, and F0 range in signalling speaker affect. *Journal of the Acoustical Society of America, 78,* 435–444.

Laird, J. D. (1974). Self-attribution of emotion: The effect of expressive behavior on the quality of emotional experience. *Journal of Personality and Social Psychology, 29,* 475–486.

Leventhal, H., & Scherer, K. R. (1987). The relationship of emotion to cognition: A functional approach to a semantic controversy. *Cognition and Emotion, 1,* 3–28.

Levinson, S. C. (1983). *Pragmatics.* Cambridge: Cambridge University Press.

Liberman, A. M., Cooper, F. S., Shankweiler, D. P., & Studdert-Kennedy, M. (1967). The perception of the speech code. *Psychological Review, 74,* 431–461.

Lipps, T. (1913). *Leitfaden der Psychologie.* Leipzig: Engelmann.

Manstead, A. S. R. (1988). The role of facial movement in emotion. In H. L. Wagner (Ed.), *Social psychophysiology: Theory and clinical application* (pp. 105–129). Chichester: Wiley.

Markel, J. D., & Gray, A. H., Jr. (1976). *Linear prediction of speech.* Berlin: Springer.

Marler, P. (1984). Animal communication: Affect or cognition? In K. R. Scherer & P. Ekman (Eds.), *Approaches to emotion* (pp. 345–368). Hillsdale, N.J.: Erlbaum.

Morton, E. S. (1977). On the occurrence and significance of motivational-structural rules in some bird and mammal sounds. *American Naturalist, 111,* 855–869.

Petty, R. E., & Cacioppo, J. T. (1986). The elaboration-likelihood model of persuasion. In L. Berkowitz (Ed.), *Advances in experimental social psychology* (Vol. 19, pp. 123–205). New York: McGraw-Hill.

Ploog, D. (1980). Der Ausdruck der Gemütsbewegungen bei Mensch und Tier. In *Jahrbuch der Max-Planck-Gesellschaft 1980* (pp. 66–97). Munich: Vandenhoeck & Ruprecht.

(1988). Neurobiology and pathology of subhuman vocal communication and human speech. In D. Todt, P. Goedeking, & D. Symmes (Eds.), *Primate vocal communication* (pp. 195–212). Heidelberg: Springer.

Scherer, K. R. (1978). Personality inference from voice quality: The loud voice of extroversion. *European Journal of Social Psychology, 8,* 467–487.

(1981). Speech and emotional states. In J. Darby (Ed.), *Speech evaluation in psychiatry* (pp. 189–220). New York: Grune & Stratton.

(1982). Methods of research on vocal communication: Paradigms and parameters. In K. R. Scherer & P. Ekman (Eds.), *Handbook of methods in nonverbal behavior research* (pp. 136–198). Cambridge: Cambridge University Press.

(1984). On the nature and function of emotion: A component process approach. In K. R. Scherer & P. Ekman (Eds.), *Approaches to emotion* (pp. 293–317). Hillsdale, N.J.: Erlbaum.

(1985). Vocal affect signalling: A comparative approach. In J. Rosenblatt, C. Beer, M.-C. Busnel, & P. J. B. Slater (Eds.), *Advances in the study of behavior* (Vol. 15, pp. 189–244). New York: Academic Press.

(1986a). Vocal affect expression: A review and a model for future research. *Psychological Bulletin, 99,* 143–165.

(1986b). Voice, stress, and emotion. In M. H. Appley & R. Trumbull (Eds.), *Dynamics of stress* (pp. 159–181). New York: Plenum.

(1987). Vocal assessment of affective disorders. In J. D. Maser (Ed.), *Depression and expressive behavior* (pp. 57–82). Hillsdale, N.J.: Erlbaum.

(1988a). On the symbolic functions of vocal affect expression. *Journal of Language and Social Psychology, 7,* 79–100.

(1988b). Criteria for emotion-antecedent appraisal: A review. In V. Hamilton, G. H. Bower, & N. H. Frijda (Eds.), *Cognitive perspectives on emotion and motivation* (pp. 89–126). Dordrecht: Nijhoff.

(1989). Vocal correlates of emotion. In H. L. Wagner & A. S. R. Manstead (Eds.), *Handbook of psychophysiology: Emotion and social behavior* (pp. 165–197). Chichester: Wiley.

Scherer, K. R., & Kappas, A. (1988). Primate vocal expression of affective states. In D. Todt, P. Goedeking, & D. Symmes (Eds.), *Primate vocal communication* (pp. 171–194). Heidelberg: Springer.

Scherer, K. R., Ladd, D. R., & Silverman, K. (1984). Vocal cues to speaker affect: Testing two models. *Journal of the Acoustical Society of America, 76,* 1346–1356.

Seyfarth, R. M., & Cheney, D. L. (1982). How monkeys see the world: A review of recent research on East African vervet monkeys. In C. T. Snowdon, C. H. Brown, & M. R. Petersen (Eds.), *Primate communication* (pp. 239–252). Cambridge: Cambridge University Press.

Siddle, D. A. T. (1983). *Orienting and habituation: Perspectives in human research.* Chichester: Wiley.

Tembrock, G. (1975). Die Erforschung des tierlichen Stimmausdrucks (Bioakustik). In F. Trojan (Ed.), *Biophonetik* (pp. 51–68). Mannheim: Bibliographisches Institut.

Tomkins, S. S. (1962). *Affect, imagery, consciousness:* Vol. 1. *The positive affects.* New York: Springer.

   (1963). *Affect, imagery, consciousness:* Vol. 2. *The negative affects.* New York: Springer.

Tourangeau, R., & Ellsworth, P. (1979). The role of facial response in the experience of emotion. *Journal of Personality and Social Psychology, 37,* 1519–1531.

Van Toller, C. (1979). *The nervous body: An introduction to the automatic nervous system and behaviour.* New York: Wiley.

Wagner, H. (1989). The peripheral physiological differentiation of emotions. In H. L. Wagner & A. S. R. Manstead (Eds.), *Handbook of psychophysiology: Emotion and social behavior* (pp. 77–98). Chichester: Wiley.

Noncategorical and categorical signals in primate communication

Introduction and review

KIM A. BARD

Part II deals with three main issues: First, the categorical nature of vocalization; second, the meaningfulness of the communication; third, a
recurrent theme of this entire volume, development – specifically, the
influence of learning on vocal communication. All four chapters present
important information on primate vocalization, both human and nonhuman, but the main focus is on nonhuman primate vocalization.

The categorical nature of vocalization is the overarching topic for debate. Our understanding of vocal communication appeared to increase
when we first conceptualized primate vocalization as consisting of discrete categories. As a beginning point, stimulating considerable research
and continuing controversy, categorization of vocalization was useful.
Whether it is valid as a true reflection of all primate communication is
discussed by all the authors in part II.

The meaning of the message is a second theme. The issue is discussed
directly by Marler, Evans, and Hauser, but it is an inherent part of each
of the four chapters. Questions addressed by the authors include: Do
primate vocalizations convey a communicative message, and, if so, what
type of message is communicated? The debate is over the type of message, that is, whether the message is referential or emotional. The dichotomy appears to be partly a reflection of the type of vocalization
studied. An oversimplified referential example is alarm calls which appear to refer to predator types. A prototypical motivational example is
distress calls, which appear to refer to intensity of emotional response.
A single nonverbal vocalization can convey a variety of meanings to a
receiver. To emphasize a point made in different forms by all the au-

Partial support was provided by a National Research Service Award from NICHD,
HD-07105, from NIH grants RR-03591 to R. B. Swenson and RR-00165 to the Yerkes
Regional Primate Research Center, and from the generous contribution of the Max
Planck Institute for Research in Psychiatry.

thors, the typical adult human is an extraordinarily good receiver, rarely at a loss in attaching meaning. The onus on scientists, however, is to attach only the "appropriate" meaning. It is interesting to contemplate what each of the authors would consider appropriate. From my perspective, that of a developmental psychologist specializing in great apes, I might characterize each chapter in the following way: Marler, Evans, and Hauser consider attaching a referential meaning without attributing underlying mental processing; Newman and Goedeking consider the search for underlying physiological processes a reflection of the appropriate meaning; Owren, Seyfarth, and Hopp consider the acoustic processing ability of each species as a precursor to attaching any meaning to a vocalization; and Symmes and Biben consider developmental history as the appropriate path to learning the meaning of a vocalization.

The main issue dealt with in the chapter by Marler, Evans, and Hauser is the debate over the meaning of vocalization, that is, motivation versus reference, which is the proximate cause of vocal production. They advocate an ethologist's approach to the study of communication that can provide an understanding of the function of vocal production. Rather than dichotomize vocalizations – those resulting from emotional reaction versus those that hold meaningful information about the world – Marler, Evans, and Hauser propose to rigorously investigate the relative contributions of each characteristic. The characteristics are clearly not mutually exclusive, and the authors present a strong argument that both human speech and animal vocalizations fall along a continuum anchored with the rare instance of purely emotionally based vocalizations, at one end, and pure forms of referentially based vocalizations at the other end.

Newman and Goedeking propose that both ultimate and proximate factors be considered when analyzing vocalizations. In their theory-driven chapter, they argue for "splitting" the components of vocalizations, since each structural component or attribute may have an independent communicative function. As the terms used in observational methodology imply, "splitting" always leaves open the possibility of "lumping" at a later time, whereas the reverse is not possible. The goals of Newman and Goedeking are to elucidate the factors contributing to variability in vocalizations, in order to provide evidence for the action of natural selection on these attributes and to link vocalizations with physiological changes.

The chapter by Owren, Seyfarth, and Hopp presents a change in perspective, from vocal production to reception, in other words, acoustic processing. This perspective is enlightening and challenging. Data are presented which contradict conclusions drawn from studies of vocal production. Dramatic differences between primate species are evident in the processing of acoustic parameters. They propose that routine psychoacoustic examinations be included in all studies of vocalization. It would appear that researchers and theoreticians alike could benefit by heeding their proposal.

The final chapter in part II, by Symmes and Biben, concerns the issue of flexibility in vocal production. In it we recapture the flavor of the nature–nurture controversy and again conclude on a note of compromise, acknowledging the interaction of both variables. Symmes and Biben argue for the influence of learning, both in the production aspect of vocalizations and in the referential aspect. They plead for rigorously controlled experiments to investigate the role of learning and development in nonverbal vocal communication.

Each of these four chapters deals with an important issue. Each represents the leading edge of research in the subject area, and all advocate an exchange of ideas and communication of findings among disciplines. Marler, Evans, and Hauser propose that the rigor of their approach be applied to studies of vocal production by human children. This position is also advanced by Symmes and Biben. Newman and Goedeking encourage integration with evolutionary considerations. Owren, Seyfarth, and Hopp strongly suggest the necessity of evaluating vocal production in parallel with vocal reception, that is, audition. Symmes and Biben argue that development of vocal production must be studied directly, in rigorously controlled experiments. All suggest, to me, that the distinction between categorical and noncategorical vocalizations has been useful but is an oversimplified version of the complex variables responsible for vocal production in nonhuman primates. Moreover, the dichotomy does not allow for the consideration of other variables, such as the appeal to answer suggested by Scherer.

4. Animal signals: Motivational, referential, or both?

PETER MARLER, CHRISTOPHER S. EVANS, AND MARC D. HAUSER

Scholars in several disciplines are concerned with problems of meaning. The approaches are as varied as the number of concerned participants. As an illustration of the diversity, consider Ogden and Richard's semiotic book *The Meaning of Meaning* and Hilary Putnam's philosophical essay with the same title (Ogden & Richards, 1923; Putnam, 1975). The first lays out in detail how the meaning of particular signs or symbols can be derived from associations set up during interactions with the external world; the second is primarily concerned with the intricacies of intentionality and the truthfulness of difference propositions.

Ethologists approaching the problem of meaning in nonhuman signals have gone in two directions. There are those who have avoided philosophicolinguistic interpretations and looked only at the relationship between the signal produced, the environmental context, and the caller's motivational state. This "motivational" perspective has led to the conclusion that signal repertoire size is strictly limited in animals and that, as a consequence, subtle nuances in call meaning can be derived only from changes in contextual parameters. According to this account, therefore, animal signals lack a key characteristic of human words, widely viewed as a diagnostic feature of speech, namely the capacity to function referentially, by encoding precise information about objects and events, independently of the speaker's motivational state. For purposes of the present discussion, we identify these two viewpoints as "motivational" and "referential" interpretations of signal production. The presumption in many quarters has been that animal signals are all of the motivational type and that only humans possess referential signals. Studies of the neurophysiological bases of nonhuman primate vocal behavior, conducted on squirrel monkeys by Ploog and his colleagues, also emphasize motivational factors and the involvement of limbic mechanisms in their control (Jürgens, 1979a,b, 1988; Ploog, 1981, 1988).

Some ethologists have attempted to grapple with the terminology of philosophers and linguists and to determine directly what, if any, is the relationship between the natural signals of nonhuman animals and words used in human language. This approach has led to the conclusion that the inherent meaning of animal signals, independent of contextual factors, is sometimes more rich than has been supposed and that some nonhumans make use of referential signaling. According to this interpretation, certain nonhuman signals are, in some respects, functionally equivalent to some human words. In this essay we reopen the question of what nonhuman animal signals mean, concentrating especially on issues of reference and motivation. The impetus for our effort to refine and combine the two contrasting approaches to this issue derives from the conviction that by approaching the study of animal communication from a position that retains the concept of referentiality yet remains neutral about the underlying mental processes, we may uncover more common ground with those who study language acquisition and cognitive development in children. We envision the prospect both of attracting their interest and of eliciting their cooperation in what could become a mutually productive endeavor.

Our position is that the problems of the psycholinguist studying the ontogeny of communication in preverbal and verbal children are similar to those confronting the ethologist studying communication in frogs, birds, dolphins, or monkeys. Even though we know that most humans ultimately will develop language, young children, like nonhuman animals, cannot be directly interrogated about what they think, mean, or intend. Thus there are common methodological and theoretical obstacles facing linguists and ethologists interested in establishing the precise meaning or referent of a vocal utterance.

First, the linguist must avoid the temptation of seeing each of the child's vocal utterances simply as a precursor to words in the native language (Hauser & Marler, in press; Studdert-Kennedy, 1986). Similarly, the ethologist must avoid the temptation to infer complex mental underpinnings for a given utterance, based solely on behavioral evidence which "looks" like adult human behavior in similar situations (Cheney & Seyfarth, 1990).

Second, up to a certain age children cannot be interrogated with the expectation of obtaining interpretable verbal responses. Although researchers working with prelinguistic infants recognize this methodological constraint, we feel that those working with apparently verbal children (e.g., the one- and two-word stages) could sometimes be more critical of the verbal responses provided during both naturalistic and experimental conditions. Specifically, because young children clearly have a different perspective of the world than older children (e.g., children up to the age of 4 fail on appearance–reality distinctions; Flavell, Green, & Flavell, 1986), their labels or names for things may not always accurately reflect adult usage (e.g., MacNamara, 1982).

Third, because ethologists and developmental psycholinguists must rely primarily on nonlinguistic behavioral response assays for establishing meaning, both disciplines would benefit from more sophisticated experimental paradigms, allowing such behaviors to be unambiguously interpreted. Both sets of researchers also need to recognize that a sophisticated treatment of the problem of meaning (e.g., Dretske, 1988; Grice, 1957; Quine, 1973) is unlikely to be attainable through nonlinguistic behavioral responses alone, since these will provide only inferential conclusions about intentionality, a pivotal issue from a philosophical perspective. However, if we are clear about our theoretical aspirations and thorough with our analytic procedures, we may achieve a more firmly circumscribed set of possible referential targets or features for a given utterance, to which further questions about intended meaning can then be addressed.

Our approach to the general problem of meaning is to focus on the issue of reference by empirically establishing correlations between adult signal production and observed environmental objects or events, eschewing complex mental inferences. This functional sense of the word *reference*, which differs from that of most philosophers (e.g., Devitt & Sterelny, 1987), is compatible with its use by a number of psycholinguists (e.g., Smith, 1988).

Our use of the term *reference* is thus avowedly reductionist. We adopt this usage in order to facilitate a more rigorous treatment of animal signals and to provide for more insightful comparisons between the communication systems of nonhuman and human animals. Whatever the outcome, such comparisons, properly conducted, can only enrich our understanding of the biological bases of language.

Putative referential signals in animals

In contrast with traditional analyses of animal communication, which have emphasized the dependence of signal morphology upon the state of the sender (e.g., Darwin, 1872; Morton, 1982; Smith, 1977), it has become clear that some animals are capable of encoding and transmitting information about external events that is in some degree independent of their motivational state (e.g., Struhsaker, 1967). There is also evidence that companions can decode the information that such signals convey (Cheney & Seyfarth, 1990; Gouzoules, Gouzoules, & Marler, 1984; Seyfarth, Cheney, & Marler, 1980a,b; Seyfarth & Cheney, 1984; reviews in Gouzoules, Gouzoules, & Marler, 1985; Marler, 1985; Seyfarth & Cheney, 1984; Snowdon, 1987; see also Scherer, chapter 3 in the present volume).

In contrast with the mode of signal functioning, labeled variously as "affective," "emotional," and "non-symbolic," which we identify here under the blanket term *motivational*, this second signaling mode has been characterized as "symbolic" (Marler, 1977), "semantic" (e.g., Seyfarth et al., 1980a), "referential" (e.g., Gouzoules et al., 1985), or "representational" (e.g., Cheney and Seyfarth, 1982; Marler, 1985). Despite this nomenclatural diversity, it appears that members of the latter class, which we identify here under the blanket term of *referential* signals, have the common property of external designata, all of which are relatively specific in nature.

While the practice of identifying communicative events as either "motivational" or "referential" (or some equivalent dichotomous terminology) may be a convenient shorthand, it fails to capture the full complexity of the phenomena being studied. In this essay, we seek to make the case that no animal signal that has been identified as referential is devoid of motivational content and that, as naturally employed, the same is true of human speech.

The first animal signals to be specified as referential were the alarm calls of the vervet monkey (*Cercopithecus aethiops*), which are given to different classes of predators (Seyfarth et al., 1980a,b; Struhsaker, 1967). But, while motivational interpretations alone cannot explain the properties of vervet alarm calls for senders and receivers, it seems probable, as the authors of these studies originally noted, that these vocalizations do possess motivational content, apparently mediated by such vehicles as call loudness and rate of delivery and perhaps by other signal properties as yet unstudied. We suggest that the same is likely to be true of vervet grunts (Cheney & Seyfarth, 1982; Seyfarth & Cheney, 1984), the agonistic recruitment calls of rhesus monkeys (*Macaca mulatta*) (Gouzoules et al., 1984), and the food calls of toque macaques (*Macaca sinica*) and chimpanzees (*Pan troglodytes*) (Dittus, 1984; Goodall, 1986; Hauser & Wrangham, 1987; Marler & Tenaza, 1977), all of which have been interpreted as referential signals. It seems inconceivable to us that these calls do not also possess motivational content, even though this has yet to be explicitly investigated in most cases. Similarly, a rich literature attests to the presence in speech of motivational information about affect, emotion, and other internal states, encoded in such attributes as loudness, stress, and variations in fundamental frequency (Ohala, 1983, 1984; Scherer, chapter 3 in the present volume; Tarter, 1980).

Conversely, we suggest that there is a sense in which signals viewed traditionally as "motivational" also effectively encode referential information about those external events which engender particular states of affect or emotion. This information is typically less specific than that encoded in traditional "referential" signals (Marler, 1975; Premack 1975). However, even in the least specific cases, as when stimuli engender different degrees of generalized arousal, which is then encoded in a signal, some inferences can always be drawn about the nature of the eliciting stimuli, even if only that some are stronger than others (e.g., Schneirla, 1959).

There is every reason to assume that such referential information as is encoded in "motivational" signals, unspecific though it may be, can also be decoded by companions, especially if they have access to the context in which signaling takes place (Premack, 1975). For example, infant crying, typically viewed as a motivational signal, can also provide referential information, especially to a mother familiar with the special predispositions of her own infant (Lester, 1985). We shall return to this theme later.

Models of referentiality and motivation

As we are using them, the terms *motivational* and *referential* each implies a model of the multidimensional relationship between the acoustic characteristics of signals, the properties of the classes of stimuli with which signals are associated, and motivational state at the time of signal production. We can represent these factors in three-dimensional space (Fig. 4.1). To display a vocal signal in such a schematic plot, several simplifying assumptions are necessary. Within a given class of vocal signals, individual exemplars will differ, often varying independently along several acoustic dimensions (e.g., dominant frequency, bandwidth, amplitude, duration). For purposes of this graphic representation, we have assumed an ideal signal set and have represented the variation in acoustic structure along a single dimension.

Second, the range of external stimuli associated with production of a

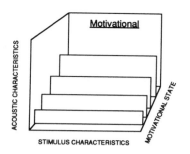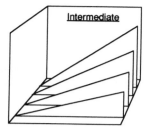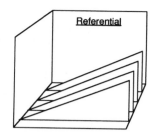

Figure 4.1. A continuum of signal classes. At one extreme, the structure of "motivational" signals is determined entirely by the sender's motivational state and is independent of stimulus characteristics. At the opposite pole, "referential" signal morphology is wholly dependent on stimulus characteristics and is unaffected by variation in motivational state. Signals occupying intermediate positions on the continuum have both referential and motivational components. Most, and perhaps all, vocal signals belong to this latter category, although the relative contributions of motivational and referential factors in determining acoustic characteristics, and hence the precise position of the signal on the continuum, will vary widely.

given class of signals (e.g., shape, size, and apparent speed of a raptor) rarely lend themselves to a unidimensional representation, as we have done here. Finally, it is clear that multiple dimensions often are required to represent qualitative variations of motivational state. For the purposes of this model, these dimensions are reduced to a single index, such as might be adequate to portray levels of generalized arousal. The object of these simplifications is to focus attention on the relative contributions of stimulus properties and of motivational variables in determining call morphology, hence the reduction of the three factors each to a single dimension.

It has been suggested previously that referential and motivational signals can be placed at opposite ends of a continuum of stimulus and motivation specificity (Marler, 1977). In the ideal "motivational" case, signal structure will approach independence from specific stimulus characteristics and can be predicted largely, if not solely, from knowledge of the sender's motivational state. In fact, as already suggested, some minimal degree of stimulus specificity must be present even in the most prototypic of "motivational" signals, since variations in motivational state will be associated with different kinds of external stimulation. This remains true despite the involvement of several sensory modalities, and even when the relevant stimulus parameters must be defined in terms of intensity rather than quality. The primary consideration here is not independence of generalized motivational states from stimulus characteristics but rather dependence upon stimuli with minimal degrees of specificity. By contrast, signals traditionally thought of as referential are typically associated with external stimuli that are highly specific, forming a limited set, with relatively uniform characteristics. Similarly, the degree to which signal structure can be predicted solely from the sender's motivational state will be minimal in the ideal case of a purely "referential" signal.

The aim of this method of representing the factors governing signal structure and its variations is to emphasize the positioning of those particular signals which reflect both motivational state and specific environmental events at intermediate positions on these continua. It is our contention that in animal communication and in natural speech behavior, pure examples of polar extremes along any of these dimensions are rare. Rather, norms are to be found among intermediate positions, with the relative emphasis upon specific environmental events and upon specific motivational states varying according to such factors as the functional demands of a communicative situation, motor limitations on signal production, and constraints on sensory and perceptual processing.

Examples of motivational signals that fall at one end of the stimulus specificity continuum are the "distress" and "contentment" calls of many precocial birds (e.g., Abraham, 1974; Collias & Joos, 1953) and the cries of human infants (reviewed in Lester, 1985; Lester & Boukydis, chapter 8 in the present volume), both of which are potentiated by pain, discomfort, or hunger. At the highly specific end of the same continuum, human speech is clearly composed of a stream of referential signals, although always accompanied, in natural speech behavior, with an undercurrent of motivational information (Ohala, 1983, 1984; Scherer, chapter 3 in the present volume; Tarter, 1980). The "alarm" calls of California ground squirrels (Leger, Owings, & Boal, 1979; Leger & Owings, 1978; Owings & Hennessey, 1984; Owings & Virginia, 1978), black-tailed prairie dogs (Owings & Loughry, 1985), Gunnisons's prairie dogs (C. N. Slobodchikoff, personal communication), and black-capped chickadees (Ficken, 1990) all display acoustic variation that is correlated with predator attributes, even though they are viewed as operating primarily in a motivational mode. Signals of nonhuman primates that function in a social context, such as grunts and agonistic screams, operating largely in motivational fashion (Rowell, 1962; Rowell & Hinde, 1962), also convey information about rank and group membership in a referential manner, in both vervet monkeys (Cheney & Seyfarth, 1982) and macaques

(Gouzoules et al., 1984; Gouzoules & Gouzoules, 1989). Food calls of animals, whether used by chimpanzees, macaques, or chickens, appear to encode information about food quantity and quality (Dittus, 1984; Hauser & Wrangham, 1987; Marler, Dufty, & Pickert, 1986). In the macaque example, however, Dittus has clearly indicated that, on rare occasions, food calls are also associated with general euphoria, as when warm sunlight breaks through the forest canopy after a rainstorm.

Although it is now clear that a number of animal signals have a significant referential component, we find it difficult to conceive of any natural vocalization that does not contain a motivational component, however small. The artificial quality of much machine-generated speech seems attributable to the absence of motivational information that is normally present (Fant, 1989; Klatt & Klatt, 1990). Indeed, a compelling case can be made that most, and perhaps all, natural vocal signals have both referential and motivational characteristics, even though the proportional contributions of these factors vary widely (cf. Gouzoules et al., 1985; Marler, 1977, 1978, 1984).

A motivational-to-referential continuum?

This review of the information encoded in animal vocalizations leads us to conclude that many, and perhaps all, signals can, in principle, be placed along a motivational-to-referential continuum, although the current dearth of information about the motivational state of signalers during call production is a significant obstacle. Most recent investigators have also studied signal decoding, concentrating on whether the information inherent in the signal is sufficient for playbacks of the call alone to elicit an appropriate response from social companions. An experimental design is typically used in which the putative referent is absent and contextual information is either systematically varied or kept constant. This approach, which incorporates criteria for both sender and receiver, effectively posits a threshold at some point on the continuum depicted in Figure 4.1, above which calls may be considered predominantly referential and below which they must be considered predominantly motivational.

For example, Seyfarth et al. (1980b) conducted playbacks of vervet monkey alarm calls and were able to demonstrate that each of three types of call elicited by three major classes of predator, carnivores, raptors, and snakes evoked appropriate and qualitatively different responses. In a subsequent experiment, the motivational and referential models were effectively pitted against each other; call duration and amplitude were both manipulated, representing acoustic parameters that were believed to vary with the motivational state of the signaler. Variations in duration over a tenfold range did not affect the type of response elicited by playback of any of the call types, lending support to a referential interpretation.

Naturalistic observation of rhesus macaques indicates that juveniles produce five types of screams during agonistic encounters; each scream type is associated with a particular class of opponent in terms of dominance rank, matrilineal relatedness, and likely severity of aggression (Gouzoules et al., 1984). Different predictions of maternal responsiveness to playbacks are obtained when these calls are ranked either by putative signaler motivation (i.e., probability of receiving injury) or by whether the interaction involves a rank-challenge (the latter possibility would have implications for the rank status of call receivers in the same matrilineage as the sender). In playback experiments, acoustic cues believed to reflect generalized signaler motivation, such as call amplitude and duration, were controlled, and the responsiveness of mothers to their infant's calls was examined. Strong responses were obtained to classes of calls characteristic of rank-challenge interactions, even though the risk of infant injury was slight. Thus, a ranking of call salience based on a referential model, suggesting that screams encode information about the type of interaction in which an infant is engaged, predicted maternal responses better than a ranking based upon a motivational interpretation, as inferred from the likelihood of injury to the sender.

If animals respond to vocalizations at least in part according to the referential information they convey, then subjects given the opportunity to compare two vocalizations should base their comparison more on the calls' external referents than on some other factor – for example, the calls' acoustic properties. This result emerged from experiments conducted on vervet monkeys. Cheney and Seyfarth (1988) found that vervets who had learned to ignore one type of call subsequently also ignored an acoustically different call given by the same signaler, but only if the calls had similar referents. After habituating to repeated presentation of one individual's intergroup "chutter," for example, subjects transferred their habituation to the same individual's intergroup "wrr." In contrast, subjects who had habituated to an individual's leopard alarm did not transfer habituation to the same individual's eagle alarm. Similarly, vervets who had habituated to the eagle alarm of a starling transferred habituation to a vervet's eagle alarm but not to a vervet's leopard alarm (Seyfarth & Cheney, 1990). Such results provide a further indication that vervet alarm calls function referentially.

California ground squirrels have a repertoire of alarm calls. It includes a graded series of broadband "chatter-chats," typically evoked by terrestrial predators, and a whistle, principally evoked by low-flying raptors but which also occurs during aggressive interactions between squirrels (Owings & Virginia, 1978). Hence, although call structure can be to some degree mapped onto the characteristics of the eliciting stimulus, ground squirrel alarm calls seem to lack the high degree of referential specificity demonstrated by vervet alarm calls and rhesus screams. In a subsequent series of playback experiments, within-class variation (i.e., changes in the number of notes or bandwidth of a chatter-chat sequence) had reliable effects on behavior (Leger et al., 1979; Leger & Owings, 1978). This suggests that receivers are attentive to acoustic information that encodes information about the sender's motivational state. Further experiments revealed that squirrels are also attentive to variation in the number of "whistle" alarm calls played back (Leger et al., 1979). Since most animals produce only a single whistle in response to a raptor, these playback stimuli effectively mimicked varying numbers of vocalizing conspecifics. The results of this study suggest that the contextual information accessible to a signal receiver is important in increasing the specificity of the behavioral response to this class of alarm calls.

The importance of signal context

With effects of context factored out, both vervet alarm calls and rhesus macaque screams exceed the threshold for functional referentiality, in the sense that the signal alone appears to encode sufficient information about referent characteristics to allow conspecific receivers to respond appropriately (Cheney & Seyfarth, 1982; Gouzoules et al., 1984; Seyfarth et al., 1980a,b). Current indications are that ground squirrel alarm calls do not exceed this threshold. However, although contextual information does not appear to be strictly necessary for interpretation of signals such as vervet alarm calls and rhesus screams, which fall near the referential end of the continuum (Fig. 4.1), it is clear that contextual cues, when available, nevertheless enrich the information content of these calls (e.g., Cheney & Seyfarth, 1982; Green & Marler, 1979).

Note that call context includes not only environmental factors, such as vulnerability to predation and availability of suitable refuges (such as burrows or dense brush) but also information about the identity, age,

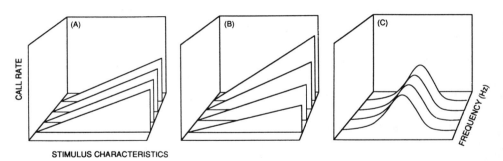

Figure 4.2. Models of the way in which motivational and referential information might be reflected in the acoustic characteristics of a hypothetical food call. The temporal pattern of calling is assumed to vary monotonically with food characteristics; highly preferred foods elicit higher rates. Similarly, motivational state is reflected in spectral characteristics, with higher levels of arousal producing higher dominant frequencies. (A) Food characteristics and motivational state have independent effects on call structure. The relationship between stimulus attributes and call rate is constant over a wide range of motivational state (frequency) values; consequently, the signal is referential and ambiguity is minimal. (B) Food characteristics and motivational state interact to determine call structure. The function relating call rate and stimulus attributes varies with the motivational state of the sender. Signals of this type have greater ambiguity but may still function referentially, since motivational state is encoded in spectral characteristics and the appropriate call rate/stimulus characteristics function can be selected by the receiver. (C) The relationship between food characteristics and call rate is nonmonotonic. Signals of this type are not functionally referential, since low call rates are characteristic of two different classes of stimuli.

and sex of the caller (e.g., Owings & Loughry, 1985; Seyfarth & Cheney, 1980). Context will play a proportionally more crucial role in the process of decoding signals placed toward the motivational end of the continuum (Green & Marler, 1979; Smith, 1965, 1969, 1977). It is also likely that the information gleaned from call morphology, and from nonvocal signals, together with other aspects of call context, often is sufficient to allow specific behavioral responses, even when the information content of the call alone does not exceed the threshold for functional referentiality (e.g., Leger et al., 1979). Indeed, accounts of experiments in which putatively referential calls are played to conspecific listeners typically describe behavioral responses, such as looking toward the loudspeaker and scanning in other directions (Seyfarth et al., 1980b) or climbing boulders and assuming a bipedal posture (Leger et al., 1979) that suggest attempts to obtain cues about the sender's nonvocal behavior and about the environmental situation in which vocalizations were emitted. Any further information that can be gleaned about the motivational state of the sender will play a role analogous to that of call context, supplementing the referential component of signals in efforts to determine meaning (Green & Marler, 1979; Marler, 1977; Premack, 1975).

A receiver's knowledge about sender motivational state and call context potentially increases the amount of information that can be extracted from a signal; however, the importance of these factors is, in part, determined by environmental conditions. For example, even signals at the referential end of the continuum may be sufficiently degraded when noise levels are high (e.g., windy conditions, masking from other vocalizing animals, extensive reverberation) as to be uninterpretable without the additional cues provided by the signaler's nonvocal behavior, such as fixation of its gaze upon the call referent.

Note that, under these conditions, signals that otherwise would be placed above the "referential threshold" now fall below it; that is, the degraded signal reaching the receiver no longer encodes sufficient information about referent characteristics to allow a specific response. A correlate of this argument is that signals at the referential end of the continuum will be more "robust," remaining functional, without contextual supplementation, under a wider range of environmental conditions than signals that are displaced toward the motivational end of the continuum. This increased tolerance of poor transmission conditions may be one of the selection-pressures for the evolution of referential signals.

Relationships between motivational and referential signal components

There are many ways in which motivational and referential information might be encoded in call morphology (Fig. 4.2). As an example, consider a call given in the context of food, such as has been described in chickens (Marler et al., 1986), in which some acoustic parameter (e.g., call rate) has been found to covary with the quality of food items (i.e., preference expressed in a simultaneous choice test). Thus, highly preferred foods elicit higher call rates than less-preferred foods. There may also be a degree of redundancy in the signal, so that a number of highly correlated call parameters all vary with stimulus quality, though this has yet to be thoroughly investigated (Marler et al., 1986). If this proves to be the case, then call rate may be thought of as representing such a cluster of acoustic features.

Call features that independently encode signaler motivation have yet to be explored with chicken food calls, but let us assume hypothetically that the signaler's motivational state (i.e., "hunger" or level of food deprivation) is reflected in some other call characteristic, say dominant frequency. The constraints of a three-dimensional representation of an n-dimensional set of relationships require simplifying assumptions; in this case, we postulate a simple, monotonic, relationship between motivational state and call characteristics, with increasing levels of food deprivation reflected in higher call frequencies. Thus the z-axis (Fig. 4.2) could be labelled "Hunger" instead of "Dominant Frequency." This is an important assumption, with different implications for signal ambiguity than when the relationship between either stimulus or motivation and acoustic properties is curvilinear.

The simplest relationship between motivation, stimulus characteristics, and call morphology is that of independence (Fig. 4.2A). Increments in food "quality" are reflected in matched increases in call rate, while the effect of food deprivation is to increase call frequency (Hz), with no effect on temporal characteristics. Note that the function depicting the relationship between call rate (y-axis) and food characteristics (x-axis) is identical at all frequency values (z-axis).

This model appears to fit several of the extant descriptions of referential signaling. Investigators have typically assumed that, in these signals, motivation is encoded separately from referential information and have accordingly arranged their playbacks to control for likely affective signal components, such as duration and amplitude (e.g., Gouzoules et al., 1984; Seyfarth et al., 1980a). Other acoustic parameters thought to reflect the motivational state of the signaler include call bandwidth (e.g., Owings & Loughry, 1985), frequency modulation (Goedeking, 1988), and "jitter" (Cox, Ito, & Morrison, 1989). While we have referred to the class of signals described by this model as "referential," this term is, in effect, a shorthand description of the finding that a particular subset of acoustic parameters is associated with a suite of stimulus characteristics and elicits a particular response set, and that varying this subset can elicit qualitatively distinctive responses from conspecific receivers. It seems probable that playbacks concentrating on "motivational" features (e.g., amplitude) would reveal sensitivity to this type of acoustic information, not only in signals traditionally viewed as motivational but also in those usually placed at the "referential" end of the continuum.

Although the "motivational" parameters examined in studies so far do not appear to determine response type, they may modulate the probability of occurrence or intensity of behavior within a response class. Different assays, more sensitive than those used in playback studies to date, will be needed to detect effects of this sort; it will perhaps be profitable to employ physiological as well as behavioral measures (e.g., heart rate; Evans and Gaioni, 1990).

A second possibility is that call morphology is determined by a simple interaction between motivational state and stimulus characteristics (Fig. 4.2B). The function relating call rate (y-axis) to food characteristics (x-axis), is different at each value of frequency (Hz). Recall that, in this hypothetical example, frequency is assumed to encode motivational state; in this model, call rates elicited by a particular food item are higher when the sender is more food-deprived. Signals of this type have some inherent ambiguity, since a large number of functions, each corresponding to a particular motivational state, is required to relate call characteristics to stimulus properties. This ambiguity may be resolved, however, so long as motivation is also coded independently (e.g., in spectral information), allowing the correct call-rate / food quality function to be selected by the receiver. Note that one test for referential function, in which motivational parameters are held constant while referential parameters are manipulated (Gouzoules et al., 1984), does not discriminate between this model and the previous one, since the acoustic "titrations" are all performed along a single call-characteristic-vs.-stimulus-characteristic function (i.e., at a single z-axis value, Fig. 4.2B).

In contrast, calls in which the acoustic morphology is determined by a complex interaction between stimulus attributes and motivation have a degree of ambiguity that cannot be resolved on the basis of signal characteristics alone. If call rate and dominant frequency are each functions of both motivational state and stimulus parameters, as when the stimulus determines the signaler's state directly, then similar calls could be evoked under a wide range of conditions and would encode a large number of possible meanings.

For example, calls produced at a high rate and with a high dominant frequency would be produced both by a food-deprived animal encountering a low-quality food item and by a satiated animal encountering a highly preferred food item. Vocalizations of this type have reduced stimulus specificity and would consequently fail a critical test of referential function. However, even "motivational" signals of this type potentially encode a great deal of information, which can be decoded by receivers with access to contextual cues provided by the environment or by the nonvocal behavior of the sender (Smith, 1977). Note that contextual information thus functions to facilitate the selection of appropriate responses to "motivational" signals in the same way that independently encoded information about motivational state allows resolution of the ambiguity present in one class of referential signals.

A second class of signals with inherent ambiguity, that cannot be resolved on the basis of acoustic information alone, consists of calls in which the relationship between either motivation or stimulus characteristics and acoustic structure is not monotonic (as has been assumed in all of the models discussed so far) but curvilinear. For example, if the function relating call rate and stimulus attributes is nonmonotonic (Fig. 4.2C), then this signal will also fail to meet the criterion of high referential specificity, since low rates of calling are elicited by two different classes of stimuli. A nonmonotonic relationship between motivation and call characteristics does not impede referential function when the effects of motivational state and stimulus variation are independent (Fig. 4.2A) but produces unresolvable ambiguity in calls modeled by a simple interaction (Fig. 4.2B). This problem results from the inability of the receiver, in this case, to select the appropriate call-rate / stimulus characteristics function.

Empirical studies are needed to establish which models of the relationships between stimulus characteristics, motivational state, and call morphology best describe natural communicative systems, both animal and human.

Strategies for analyzing the meaning of animal signals

An essential first step for determining the meaning of a signal is an investigation of the correspondence between acoustic characteristics and external events. Such an analysis allows us to determine whether the vocalization meets the criterion of high referential specificity (e.g., Marler, 1984). Ideally, this process involves detailed characterization of the stimulus characteristics necessary for call production and of the relationship between call structure and stimulus attributes (e.g., Gyger et al., 1987). Note that quantitative analyses sometimes reveal discrete categories in signals previously thought to be graded (e.g., Gouzoules et al., 1984; Seyfarth & Cheney, 1984).

Procedures for establishing the necessary and sufficient attributes of a given signal-stimulus pair have been effectively used in studies of the development of concepts (Carey, 1985) and vocabularies in children (reviewed in Smith, 1988). However, as pointed out in a number of studies, although it is difficult to determine the conditions that must be satisfied for category membership, both humans and nonhumans appear to tolerate loose sound–meaning associations (e.g., Nelson & Marler, 1989; Roberts & Horowitz, 1986).

As a further step, playbacks may be conducted to determine whether certain call parameters encode sufficient information to determine receiver response. This must be explored in the absence of the putative referent and with full control of contextual cues from the environment and from nonvocal behaviors of the signaler. Demonstrations of referential functionality are most compelling when a comparative dimension is available, as when two or more call types, with no overlap in acoustic space, are shown to elicit qualitatively different responses (e.g., Seyfarth et al., 1980a,b). A correlate of this argument is that a motivational counterinterpretation of signal function is more credible and parsimonious when the alternative evidence for referentiality is based on variation within a single call type, rather than on contrasting reference in two or more call types.

In order to demonstrate that motivational variation in the acoustic structure of a signal does not determine receiver response, it is important to incorporate in the design of playback experiments a number of call variants, chosen to correspond to a range of motivational states in the sender (e.g., differences in observed latency of the caller to flee a predator or in level of food deprivation). These controls effectively allow a test of the extent to which referential and motivational information are encoded independently. Assuming that a signal has some degree of referential functionality, playbacks of exemplars recorded from animals in a variety of motivational states allow the call to be more accurately modeled. Independent assays of motivational state (e.g., heart rate or corticosteroid levels) are also potentially valuable, both for assessing the nature of motivational variation in call morphology and for selecting playback exemplars to test for referential and motivational function. External validity is increased if playbacks include calls emitted by individuals of different sex, age, and social status (e.g., Owings & Loughry, 1985; Seyfarth et al., 1980a,b).

A complementary series of experiments may then be undertaken to evaluate the contribution of motivational factors to call morphology. This will involve an examination of the relationship between behaviors of the sender associated with call production and acoustic characteristics of the signal; again, it may be revealing to employ physiological measures, designed to reveal changes in motivational state not always reflected in overt behavior.

Descriptions of the behavioral antecedents and sequelae of signal production are of potential value in appraising the extent of motivational contributions to signal morphology (e.g., Gouzoules et al., 1984). This approach depends upon correlative inference, however, and is consequently less powerful than direct modification of motivational state, as by experimental or pharmacological manipulations. The latter might be especially illuminating in experiments on predator-elicited calls; alternatively, conditioned fear paradigms could be employed (e.g., Curio, Ernst, & Vieth, 1978; Mineka & Cook, 1988). Food calls are especially tractable, since, under laboratory conditions, food-deprivation can readily be controlled. Further, independent assays of motivational state are available, such as the rate of an operant response performed for access to food. Also, the stimulus characteristics of food are more readily quantifiable than those of a predator or of a social relationship. Experiments of this type would determine to what extent motivational information is encoded independently of referential information, complementing analyses more focused on questions of referentiality.

Subsequent playbacks might then reexamine the extent to which motivational information is extracted by receivers, allowing a comparison with earlier playbacks in which acoustic parameters assumed to be referential vehicles were manipulated. It would be critical to determine whether motivational variation in signal structure elicits the same range of responses as referential variation, militating against referential functionality for the signal, or whether information about motivational state merely modulates behavior within response classes determined by referential information.

The ultimate goal of this series of proposed experiments would be a comprehensive characterization of the way in which environmental events and motivational states are reflected in signal morphology. Such a program of research should reveal whether a given signal exceeds the threshold for referential function, while providing a description of the complex interplay between referential and motivational factors in determining the form of animal vocalizations.

Conclusion

The evidence indicates that the distinction between the terms *referential* and *motivational*, as applied in a categorical fashion to signals and their mode of functioning, cannot be sustained. It is more appropriate to postulate varying degrees of referentiality, viewed as points on a continuum. They range from the highly specific relationship between signal and referent associated with many human words and with some animal signals traditionally thought of as purely "referential" to the lesser degree of specificity associated with human displays of affect and most animal signals, traditionally thought of as "motivational."

The challenge for the future is to develop new approaches to the study of communication, both human and animal, that do full justice both to issues of reference, and also to the contributions to signaling behavior of the various kinds of motivational influence. We believe that both of these factors make crucial contributions to the efficacy of communication. To underestimate either one, even for the pragmatic purposes of research strategy, must lead to a failure to appreciate the degree to which integration of these two modes of encoding information into signal structure enriches the potential of any communicative system, including those employed in human social interactions.

It is also our hope that the framework laid out in this working paper is both theoretically compatible and empirically useful for those studying child language acquisition. In particular the constraints involved in using nonverbal behavior to establish the meaning of an utterance are worth special emphasis (cf. Smith, 1988). We urge linguists tempted by so-called rich interpretations of infant behavior to consider the advisability of withholding assumptions about cognitive capacities until these have been clearly documented.

References

Abraham, R. L. (1974). Vocalizations of the mallard (*Anas platyrhynchos*). *Condor*, 76, 401–410.

Carey, S. (1985). *Conceptual changes in childhood*. Cambridge, Mass: MIT Press.

Cheney, D. L., & Seyfarth, R. M. (1982). How vervet monkeys perceive their grunts: Field playback experiments. *Animal Behaviour, 30,* 739–751.

(1988). Assessment of meaning and the detection of unreliable signals by vervet monkeys. *Animal Behaviour, 36,* 477–486.

(1990). *How monkeys see the world: Inside the mind of another species.* Chicago: University of Chicago Press.

Collias, N. E., & Joos, M. (1953). The spectrographic analysis of sound signals in domestic fowl. *Behaviour, 5,* 175–188.

Cox, N. B., Ito, M. R., & Morrison, M. D. (1989). Quantization and measurement errors in the analysis of short-time perturbations in sampled data. *Journal of the Acoustical Society of America, 86,* 42–54.

Curio, E., Ernst, U., & Vieth, W. (1978). Cultural transmission of enemy recognition: One function of mobbing. *Science, 202,* 899–901.

Darwin C. (1872). *The expression of the emotions in man and animals.* London: Murray.

Devitt, M., & Sterelny, K. (1987). *Language and reality.* Cambridge, Mass.: MIT Press.

Dretske, F. (1988). *Explaining behavior*. Cambridge, Mass.: MIT Press.

Dittus, W. (1984). Toque macaque food calls: Semantic communication concerning food distribution in the environment. *Animal Behaviour, 32,* 470–477.

Evans, C. S., & Gaioni, S. J. (1990). Conspecific calls evoke characteristic cardiac responses in mallard ducklings. *Animal Behaviour, 39,* 785–796.

Fant, G. (1989). The speech code. In C. von Euler, I. Lundberg, & G. Lennerstrand (Eds.), *Brain and reading* (pp. 171–182). London: Macmillan.

Ficken, M. S. (1990). Acoustic characteristics of alarm calls associated with predation risk in chickadees. *Animal Behaviour, 39,* 400–401.

Flavell, J. H., Green, F. L., & Flavell, E. R. (1986). Development of knowledge about the appearance–reality distinction. *Monographs of the Society for Research in Child Development, 51,* Issue No. 1, Serial No. 212.

Goedeking, P. (1988). Vocal play behavior in cotton-top tamarins. In D. Todt, P. Goedeking, & D. Symmes (Eds.), *Primate vocal communication* (pp. 33–144). Berlin: Springer.

Goodall, J. (1986). *The chimpanzees of Gombe: Patterns of behavior*. Cambridge, Mass.: Harvard University Press.

Gouzoules, H., & Gouzoules, S. (1989). Design features and developmental modification of pigtail macaque (*Macaca nemestrina*), agonistic screams. *Animal Behaviour, 37,* 383–401.

Gouzoules, S., Gouzoules, H., & Marler, P. (1984). Rhesus monkey (*Macaca mulatta*) screams: Representational signalling in the recruitment of agonistic aid. *Animal Behaviour, 32,* 182–193.

(1985). External reference in mammalian vocal communication. In G. Ziven (Ed.), *The development of expressive behavior: Biology–environment interactions* (pp. 77–101). New York: Academic Press.

Green, S., & Marler, P. (1979). The analysis of animal communication. In P. Marler & J. Vandenberg (Eds.), *Social behavior and communication: Handbook of behavioral neurobiology* (Vol. 3, pp. 73–158). New York: Plenum.

Grice, H. P. (1957). Meaning. *Philosophical Review, 66,* 377–378.

Gyger, M., Marler, P., & Pickert, R. (1987). Semantics of an avian alarm call system: The male domestic fowl, *Gallus domesticus. Behaviour, 102,* 15–40.

Hauser, M. D., & Marler, P. (In press). How do and should studies of animal communication affect interpretations of child phonological development? In C. Ferguson & L. Menn (Eds.), *Child phonological development*. Parkton, Md.: York Press.

Hauser, M. D., & Wrangham, R. (1987). Manipulation of food calls in captive chimpanzees. *Folia Primatologica, 48,* 207–210.

Jürgens, U. (1979a). Vocalization as an emotional indicator: A neuroethological study in the squirrel monkey. *Behaviour, 69,* 88–117.

(1979b). Neural control of vocalization in nonhuman primates. In H. D. Steklis and M. J. Raleigh (Eds.), *Neurobiology of social communication in primates* (pp. 11–44). New York: Academic Press.

(1988). Central control of monkey calls. In D. Todt, P. Goedeking, & D. Symmes (Eds.), *Primate vocal communication* (pp. 162–167). Berlin: Springer.

Klatt, D., & Klatt, L. (1990). Analysis, synthesis and perception of voice quality variations among female and male talkers. *Journal of the Acoustical Society of America, 87* (2), 820–857.

Leger, D., & Owings, D. (1978). Responses to alarm calls by California ground squirrels: Effects of call structure and maternal status. *Behavioral Ecology and Sociobiology, 3,* 177–186.

Leger, D. W., Owings, D. H., & Boal, L. (1979). Contextual information and differential responses to alarm whistles in California ground squirrels. *Zeitschrift für Tierpsychologie, 49,* 142–155.

Lester, B. M. (1985). Introduction: There's more to crying than meets the ear. In B. M. Lester & C. F. Z. Boukydis (Eds.), *Infant crying* (pp. 1–27). New York: Plenum.

MacNamara, J. (1982). *Names for things.* Cambridge, Mass.: MIT Press.

Marler, P. (1975). On the origin of speech from animal sounds. In J. Kavanagh & J. Cutting (Eds.), *The role of speech in language* (pp. 11–37). Cambridge, Mass.: MIT Press.

(1977). Primate vocalization: Affective or symbolic? In G. Bourne (Ed.), *Progress in ape research* (pp. 85–96). New York: Academic Press.

(1978). Affective and symbolic meaning: Some zoosemiotic speculations. In T. Sebeok (Ed.), *Sight, sound and sense* (pp. 113–123). Bloomington: Indiana University Press.

(1984). Animal communication: Affect or cognition? In K. Scherer & P. Ekman (Eds.), *Approaches to emotion* (pp. 345–365). Hillsdale, N.J.: Erlbaum.

(1985). Representational vocal signals of primates. *Fortschritte der Zoologie, 31,* 211–221.

Marler, P., Dufty, A., & Pickert R. (1986). Vocal communication in the domestic chicken. 1. Does a sender communicate information about the quality of a food referent to a receiver? *Animal Behaviour, 34,* 188–193.

Marler P., & Tenaza, R. (1977). Signalling behavior of apes, with special reference to vocalization. In T. Sebeok (Ed.), *How animals communicate* (pp. 965–1033). Bloomington: Indiana University Press.

Mineka, S., & Cook, M. (1988). Social learning and the acquisition of snake fear in monkeys. In T. Zentall & B. G. Galef, Jr. (Eds.), *Social learning* (pp. 51–73). Hillsdale, N.J.: Erlbaum.

Morton, E. S. (1982). Grading, discreteness, redundancy and motivational-structural rules. In D. E. Kroodsma & E. H. Miller (Eds.), *Acoustic communication in birds* (Vol. 1, pp. 183–210). Academic Press: New York.

Nelson, D. A., & Marler, P. (1989). The perception of birdsong and an ecological concept of signal space. In M. Berkley & W. Stebbins (Eds.), *Comparative perception* (pp. 443–478). New York: Wiley.

Ogden, C. K., & Richards, I. A. (1923). *The meaning of meaning.* London: Routledge & Kegan Paul.

Ohala, J. J. (1983). Cross-language use of pitch: An ethological view. *Phonetica, 40,* 1–18.

(1984). An ethological perspective on common cross-language utilization of F0 of voice. *Phonetica, 41,* 1–16.

Owings, D. H., & Hennessey, D. F. (1984). The importance of variation in sciurid visual and vocal communication. In J. O. Murie & G. R. Michener (Eds.), *The biology of ground-dwelling squirrels* (pp. 169–200). Lincoln: University of Nebraska Press.

Owings, D. H., & Loughry, W. J. (1985). Variation in snake-elicited jump-yipping by black-tailed prairie dogs: Ontogeny and snake specificity. *Zeitschrift für Tierpsychologie, 70,* 177–200.

Owings, D. H., & Virginia, R. A. (1978). Alarms calls of California ground squirrels (*Spermophilus beecheyi*). *Zeitschrift für Tierpsychologie, 46,* 58–70.

Ploog, D. (1981). Neurobiology of primate audio-vocal behavior. *Brain Research Review, 3,* 35–61.

(1988). Neurobiology and pathology of subhuman vocal communication and human speech. In D. Todt, P. Goedeking, & D. Symmes (Eds.), *Primate vocal communication* (pp. 195–212). Berlin: Springer.

Premack, D. (1975). On the origin of language. In M. S. Gazzaniga & C. B. Blakemore (Eds.), *Handbook of psychobiology* (pp. 591–605). New York: Academic Press.

Putnam, H. (1975). The meaning of meaning. In K. Gunderson (Ed.), *Minnesota Studies in the Philosophy of Science, 7,* 125–148. Minneapolis: University of Minnesota Press.

Quine, W. V. (1973). On the reasons for the indeterminacy of translation. *Journal of Philosophy, 12,* 178–183.

Roberts, K., & Horowitz, F. D. (1986). Basic level categorization in seven- and nine-month old infants. *Journal of Child Language, 13,* 191–209.

Rowell, T. E. (1962). Agonistic noises of the rhesus monkey (*Macaca mulatta*). *Symposium of the Zoological Society,* London, *8,* 91–96.

Rowell, T. E., & Hinde, R. A. (1962). Vocal communication by the rhesus monkey (*Macaca mulatta*). *Proceedings of the Zoological Society of London, 138,* 279–294.

Schneirla, T. C. (1959). An evolutionary and developmental theory of biphasic processes underlying approach and withdrawal. In M. R. Jones (Ed.), *Nebraska Symposia on Motivation, 7,* 1–42. Lincoln: University of Nebraska Press.

Seyfarth, R. M., & Cheney, D. L. (1980). The ontogeny of vervet monkey alarm calling: A preliminary report. *Zeitschrift für Tierpsychologie, 54,* 37–56.

(1984). The acoustic features of vervet grunts. *Journal of the Acoustical Society of America, 75,* 1623–1628.

(1990). The assessment by vervet monkeys of their own and another species' alarm calls. *Animal Behaviour, 40,* 477–486.

Seyfarth, R. M., Cheney D. L., & Marler, P. (1980a). Vervet monkey alarm calls: Semantic communication in a free-ranging primate. *Animal Behaviour, 28,* 1070–1094.

(1980b). Monkey responses to three different alarm calls: Evidence for predator classification and semantic communication. *Science, 210,* 801–803.

Smith, M. D. (1988). The meaning of reference in emergent lexicons. In J. L. Locke & M. D. Smith (Eds.), *The emergent lexicon* (pp. 23–50). New York: Academic Press.

Smith, W. J. (1965). Message, meaning and context in ethology. *American Naturalist, 99,* 405–409.

(1969). Messages of vertebrate communication. *Science, 165,* 145–150.

(1977). *The behavior of communicating.* Cambridge, Mass.: Harvard University Press.

Snowdon, C. T. (1987). A comparative approach to vocal communication. In D. W. Leger (Ed.), *Nebraska Symposia on Motivation, 35,* 145–199. Lincoln: University of Nebraska Press.

Struhsaker, T. T. (1967). Auditory communication among vervet monkeys (*Cercopithecus aethiops*). In S. A. Altmann (Ed.), *Social communication among primates* (pp. 281–324). Chicago: University of Chicago Press.

Studdert-Kennedy, M. (1986). Invariance: Functional or descriptive. In J. S. Perkell & D. H. Klatt (Eds.), *Invariance and variability* (pp. 51–54). Hillsdale, N.J.: Erlbaum.

Tarter, V. C. (1980). Happy talk: Perceptual and acoustic effects of smiling on speech. *Perception and Psychophysiology, 27,* 24–27.

5. Noncategorical vocal communication in primates: The example of common marmoset phee calls

JOHN D. NEWMAN AND PHILIPP GOEDEKING

The term *noncategorical vocal communication* is used in this essay to refer to vocalizations that do not readily fall into discrete categories. However, since categories may be created by mental processes imposed upon apparently noncategorical phenomena (cf. Ghiselin, 1981), we will restrict the following presentation to empirically observed or measured consequences of sound production. Our primary focus will be upon those sounds generally referred to as "graded," or continuously variable. Since variability is inherent in all vocalizations, it is useful to distinguish between *parameter variability* (e.g., variation in one or another acoustic dimension, such as pitch, duration, or loudness) and *signal class variability*, in which the existence of intermediate or transitional forms prevents the orderly division into separate categories or subtypes of acoustically distinct vocalizations. Both types of signal variation may either be expressed by a given individual over the course of time or reflect differences within a group of individuals.

Graded vocalizations in nonhuman primates: An overview

We will begin with a brief overview of some of the more frequently cited examples of primate species for which documentation of intergradation in the vocal repertoire has been published. Most of the published work pertains to signal class variability, in that typologies of vocal classes are first constructed; these are then scrutinized for the extent to which class boundaries are blurred by the presence of vocalizations possessing structural attributes intermediate to two or more classes. Until more species are examined across a wide range of contexts, developmental stages, and habitats, the communicative significance of intergradation between acoustically different call types will remain unclear. Even less is known about the significance of graded changes within a particular call type.

Macaques have been shown to use graded vocalizations of several types. Green's field study of the Japanese macaque (*Macaca fuscata*) (Green, 1975) revealed that intergradations exist among all of the major call types recorded. Green observed that points of transition between vocal patterns frequently occurred in the course of long vocal sequences, such as those produced by an unrequited female in estrus or by an infant during weaning tantrums. During these long vocal bouts, there was a progression from calls of one type to transitional forms before switching to calls of another type. Transitions to more noisy and variable vocalizations were associated with an increase in the state of arousal or agitation of the vocalizer. Green also observed that more subtle transitions from one subtype to the next occurred within calls of a given class, such as the Class II coos, again following an orderly association with increased arousal. Rowell (1962), and Rowell and Hinde (1962), found that captive rhesus macaques (*Macaca mulatta*) produced a wide range of intermediate calls. In particular, the "harsh noises" used in agonistic encounters form a graded series (bark, pant-threat, growl, roar) which varies mainly in the number of acoustic units and their duration (Rowell & Hinde, 1962). More intense agonistic noises (screech, geckering screech, scream) also differ in duration but, in addition, vary in the range of frequencies emphasized, a parameter that may be under sympathetic nervous system influence (Rowell, 1962). A more detailed analysis of "screams" revealed that intermediate forms between acoustically and functionally differentiable subtypes were, in fact, rare (Gouzoules, Gouzoules, & Marler, 1984). A study of rhesus macaques trained to vocalize in an operant conditioning paradigm (Larson, Sutton, Taylor, & Lindeman, 1973) demonstrated that the same individual monkey had the capacity to modulate expression of the voiced or tonal "coo" to produce a graded series of calls differing in duration and spectral composition. Whether the species uses this capacity in normal communication has yet to be demonstrated.

Another Old World species, the talapoin (*Miopithecus talapoin*), has been studied both in the field and in captivity by Gautier (1974). The vocal repertoire of the talapoin consists of two systems of graded vocalizations: an aggression–flight system and a cohesion system. Gradations in the former can be correlated with associated graded changes in facial expression and may be related to the excitation level of the vocalizer. In the cohesion system, complete intergradation of structural subtypes is seen only in infants.

Members of the Old World genus *Colobus* have been found to use graded vocalizations extensively. Marler's (1970) analysis of the vocalizations of the red colobus (*Colobus badius*) in the Kibale Forest of Uganda revealed a graded sound system; three call categories were discerned, all connected by intermediate forms, even as part of the same sequence. Marler (1972) subsequently reported that black and white colobus monkeys vary the extent of gradedness according to whether the signals are used primarily in intertroop communication (where more discrete signals are employed) or for signaling within the troop. However, even the intertroop roaring emitted by a given male may vary in number of pulses per syllable, syllables per phrase, and in distribution of energy in the frequency spectrum. "Cawing," a vocalization heard only from adult females, juveniles, and infants, intergrades into "squeaking" and "screaming," with intermediate patterns occurring, even in a continuous sequence of utterances from one individual.

There is also evidence for graded vocalizations in New World monkeys. Squirrel monkeys (*Saimiri*) were initially viewed as having a predominantly discrete vocal repertoire, with few intermediates between call types (Winter, Ploog, & Latta, 1966). Subsequently, evidence has begun to emerge indicating more intergradation within and between call types (Winter, 1969; Winter, Handley, Ploog, & Schott, 1973; Schott, 1975; Newman, 1985; Boinski & Newman, 1988). One study has reported that an infant squirrel monkey separated from its social group increases the duration of the "isolation peep" as the distance from its natal troop increases (Masataka & Symmes, 1986). A study of play in young squirrel monkeys demonstrated that the length of a play bout was positively correlated with duration and number of slope reversals of the "play peeps" regularly emitted during playing (Biben & Symmes, 1986).

Noncategorical vocal communication and emotional expression

Emotion can be defined as "the behavioral response that reflects the interrelationship of the inner feeling tone and its outward expression as modified by the several varieties of affect, by drive, and by cognitive control" (Benson, 1984; p. 32). The view that gradations in voice character are the outward manifestation of graded changes in internal state goes back at least to the writings of Darwin (1872 / 1965). Contemporary thinking on the nature of emotion emphasizes greater flexibility in the motor programs associated with different internal states; the role of the external environment in regulating these motor programs; and emergence of the "emotional signal," rather than "emotional expression," as the relevant frame of reference (Campos, Campos, & Barrett, 1989). Empirical data demonstrating a consistent relationship between the morphology of a particular vocal signal and a particular emotional state are not currently available. A useful goal in the quest for relevant empirical findings would be to identify objective measures of internal state that can be correlated with ongoing vocal behavior in a graded, linear fashion. Some progress in this direction has been made in the study of the physiological correlates of crying in human infants (Porter, Miller, & Marshall, 1986).

An overview of earlier studies of the vocal correlates of emotions indicates a predominant emphasis on proposed associations between the acoustic character of vocalizations and various emotional states. Scherer and Kappas (1988) identified problems with the current approach to classifying vocalizations in terms of which affect systems they are related to: (1) the difficulty of separating specific calls from a stream of vocalization; (2) the difficulty of interpreting the function of each respective call. These authors question whether it is feasible to discover the underlying relationship between acoustic dimensions and characteristics of specific emotional states without being guided by some explicitly conceptualized theoretical assumptions. According to Scherer (1985), Tembrock has concluded that the state of an animal affects intensity, frequency, and temporal patterning of phonation. In Tembrock's view, "comfort" and "play" calls are repeated short sounds, with relatively low frequencies, and are mediated by parasympathetic nervous system mechanisms. Calls used in agonistic encounters and threat calls also exhibit low frequencies. Defense calls are short, with high-amplitude onset and a broad frequency spectrum; they also are mediated by sympathetic nervous system reactions. Morton (1977) also attempted to identify similarities in the relationship between emotional state and the acoustic features of vocalizations. He proposed a "motivation-structural rule" to formalize the relationship between affective state and acoustic structure: "birds and mammals use harsh, relatively low-frequency sounds when hostile and higher frequency, more pure tone-like sounds when frightened, appeasing, or approaching in a friendly manner" (p. 855). This concept hypothesizes a continuum in which the lower and harsher the sound, the more hostile and aggressive the vocalizer; the higher the frequency and the more tonelike, the more fear or friendliness. Also, rising frequency indicates lower hostility and increasing appeasement or fear; falling frequency indicates increasing hostility. Jürgens (1979) used self-stimulation rates to assign varying degrees of aversiveness to brain sites and correlated vocalizations with the site. Within each of five classes of calls, he found correlations between the aversiveness of the call and its total frequency range, as well as between frequency range and the irregularity of the frequency contour. Since there are a number of different call types in the various call groups expressing a highly aversive emotional state, Jürgens assumed that there are different types of aversive states. In general, Jürgens concluded that an increase in aversiveness of the emotional state underlying a call is paralleled by an increase in total frequency range and intensity. In harmonic calls, in addition, he theorized that the higher-pitched variants are more aversive than the lower-pitched (high cawing vs. low cawing; alarm peep vs. chuck); that an irregular frequency course is more aversive than a smooth one (yelling vs. isolation peep); and that a constant or descending frequency course is more aversive than an upward shift of frequency (short peep vs. ascending peep). These relations hold only if all other features remain constant. Lower-pitched calls can be more aversive than higher-pitched ones if the former have a more irregular frequency course. Also, a low-pitched call can be more aversive than a high-pitched call if both have a regular frequency course but belong to different classes (e.g., cawing vs. chirping). Jürgens made the important observation that this apparent paradox may be related to the different laryngeal muscle groups responsible for these calls. This led to the conclusion that aversiveness is more closely related to the degree of global muscular effort required to produce the call than to an association with a particular pitch range. While not directly addressing the issue of correlating vocal behavior with internal state, Malatesta (1981) provided a useful summary of the ontogenetic course of vocal emotional expression in the context of its dynamic relationship to the facial and bodily components of expression. The author concluded that early patterns of infant vocal emotional expression are probably biogenetically determined, and that the transition from raw affect expression in early infancy to a more modulated pattern later on is a product not only of neuromuscular maturation but of maternal coaching in affective expression.

The attribute concept of vocal signals

Intraindividual variability

Investigating noncategorical vocal communication processes in subhuman primates requires methodological access to complex structural variability in vocal patterns. It also requires conceptual models that explain how variable patterns might serve for information transfer, social manipulation, or the acquisition of knowledge (see also Todt, 1986, 1988). Much of the obfuscation in research on noncategorical vocal communication appears to be attributable to underlying differences in the conceptualization of what a *vocalization* is. Two prototypical points of view prevail:

- Conceptualize a vocalization as a discrete entity, the respective communicative functionality of which can be achieved only if all essential structural components are present. This model is labeled the gestalt hypothesis.
- Conceptualize a vocalization as a configuration of a set of potentially independent structural attributes, each of which has the possibility of serving a communicative function. This model is labeled the attribute hypothesis.

The attribute hypothesis is advocated here, for the following three reasons:

1. Conceiving of a vocalization as a configuration of potentially independent structural properties includes the possibility that particular combinations of attributes can function as gestalts, but not vice versa; hence the attribute hypothesis provides a more powerful conceptual approach to analyzing the significance of structural variability in social signals.
2. Internal variables such as arousal or level of affect are known to influence the settings of muscles involved in vocal expression, leading to nondirected changes in different acoustic parameters such as duration and pitch (Scherer, 1985).
3. Acoustic properties of vocal patterns cannot be assumed to be selectively neutral, and the level at which selection operates is not necessarily the vocalization as a whole but rather individual acoustic parameters (Goedeking, 1988).

The attribute hypothesis allows a differentiation of the influences exerted by ultimate and proximate factors on the phenomenon of vocal variability. On the one hand, external (ultimate) factors such as the sound transmission characteristics of the habitat or detection of the vocalizer by predators (termed "pull-factors" by Scherer, 1985) tend to reduce structural variability in vocalizations. On the other hand, however, internal (proximate) factors such as emotional variables ("push-factors," ibid.) tend to impart variability to otherwise structurally stable vocalizations.

Interindividual variability

Studying variability in call structure requires an evaluation of differences between individuals as well as within the same individual. Several primate species have been reported to exhibit individual differences in the

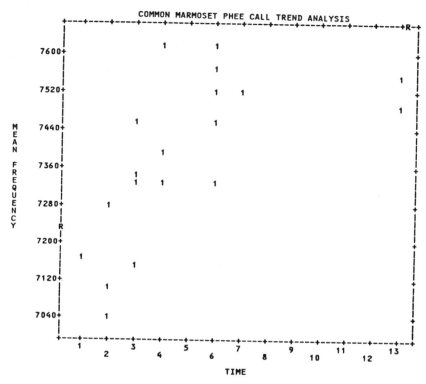

Figure 5.1. Scatter plot relating phee call mean frequency to time since separation, in an adult common marmoset. (Mean frequency is expressed as Hertz, time as minutes.) Note that mean frequency increases with time of separation.

acoustic structure of a particular vocalization (e.g., Cheney & Seyfarth, 1980; Marler & Hobbett, 1975; Snowdon, Cleveland, & French, 1983; Symmes, Newman, Talmage-Riggs, & Lieblich, 1979). The presence of individual differences in the acoustic structure of the same vocalization argues for the importance of recognizing particular individuals in a social group on the basis of voice alone. Recognition of specific individuals by voice alone is an important adaptive character in habitats where genetically related and socially bonded individuals (e.g., parents and their offspring) are likely to be out of visual contact periodically. Selection for stability in acoustic parameters that serves both to promote individual recognition and to optimize transmission properties in a noisy environment is clearly an ultimate factor that may increase the representation of a particular genome in a population.

Empirical evidence for the differentiation of acoustic variables within the same vocalization on the basis of covariation with emotional variables comes from a recent study using the common marmoset, *Callithrix jacchus* (Goedeking & Newman, 1987). In that study, the whistlelike "phee" calls of captive marmosets were studied for variability in acoustic structure when vocalizers were either visually, or both visually and acoustically, separated from familiar conspecifics. Recordings were made over 15 min and automatically analyzed using a minicomputer. Under both experimental conditions, mean frequency and peak frequency of phee calls from the same individual exhibited an increase over time (Fig. 5.1). Conversely, significant trends for call duration showed a mostly negative correlation (Fig. 5.2). These effects were more prominent under combined visual and acoustic separation. The trends are attributed primarily to proximate mechanisms, especially emotional variables. Call parameters for each individual were sufficiently distinctive to permit a high degree of discrimination, using multivariate statistical techniques. We suggest that such interindividual differences may be due primarily to ultimate factors, especially social integration. Since empirical evidence for noncategorical communication observable in a relatively well-defined behavioral context is still rare in the primate literature, these findings deserve discussion in greater detail.

Experimental results concerning intraindividual variability

Experiment 1: Out of 11 individuals, 5 were sufficiently vocal (more than 9 vocalizations / 15 min) to be included for analysis. Since most of the calls were given as a series or sequence of 2 or more closely spaced notes, analysis was confined to these sequential calls. Linear regression analyses for each structural variable were applied to test the existence of trends over time. For several individuals, mean frequency and peak frequency, as well as duration, exhibited significant correlation ($p<.05$) with length of separation. Frequency measures showed a positive correlation (i.e., increasing values) with time of separation, while duration showed predominantly a negative correlation. Thus, for most of the subjects in which phee call structure changed significantly during the 15-min separation, mean frequency and peak frequency increased over this period, while call duration decreased.

The fact that the phee calls of only 3 of the 5 vocal subjects showed significant changes over time and that calls later in a sequence remained structurally stable over the 15-min period of visual separation suggests that maintaining auditory contact with the rest of the colony is adequate

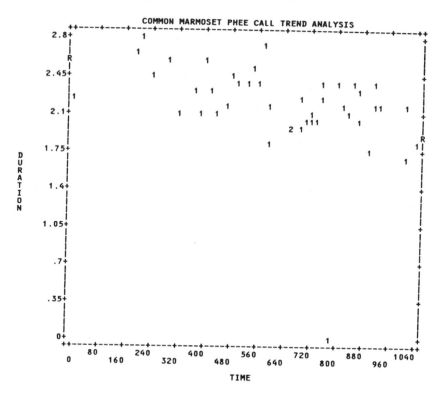

Figure 5.2. Scatter plot relating phee call duration to time since separation, in an adult common marmoset. (Both parameters are expressed as seconds.) Note that call duration decreases with time of separation.

to promote continued production of acoustically stable phee calls, an attribute that would favor consistent transmission of optimal vocal signals. On the other hand, we reasoned that elimination of auditory information arising from the colony (achieved by placing the subject in acoustic as well as visual isolation) would favor emergence of proximate factors related to the emotional state of the vocalizer and, at the same time, reduce the adaptive benefit of maintaining a stable acoustic phee call profile. Therefore, a second experiment was conducted on the same group of subjects.

Experiment 2: More subjects vocalized under the condition of combined acoustic and visual isolation in this experiment than under the conditions used in Experiment 1; a total of 8 subjects were sufficiently vocal to permit analysis of their vocal behavior. As in the first experiment, most phee calls occurred as sequences of closely spaced notes. The same parameters exhibiting significant change over time in Experiment 1 (mean frequency, peak frequency, and duration) were likewise in this experiment the only acoustic parameters showing a significant change with time of separation. The principal result of the increased isolation imposed in this experiment was the greater proportion of subjects for which phee call structure changed significantly over the course of the separation period, and the involvement of all sequential call elements. As was the case with visual isolation alone, the two frequency measures increased in value (became higher in pitch) over time, while duration predominantly decreased (became shorter) over the 15-min separation period. Thus, the acoustic structure of phee calls was less stable under the combined influence of acoustic and visual isolation than with visual isolation alone.

Experimental results concerning interindividual variability

The possible existence of individual differences in phee call structure was addressed by analyzing the same data collected in Experiments 1 and 2. A discriminant function analysis permitted assignment of a predicted caller to each call and produced a summary table of classification results (for methodological details see Smith, Newman, Hoffman, & Fetterly, 1982). Overall, there was correct attribution of each call to its vocalizer with much-higher-than-chance accuracy (Fig. 5.3). This general finding applies to both experiments and is independent of the sequence position of the call. To emphasize the similar contribution of calls first and second in sequence to the discrimination of individual differences in phee call structure, the discriminant scores for each subject's first- and second-call elements were plotted separately. The distribution of discriminant scores are nearly superimposable for the two sequence positions. This suggests that parameters coding for individual differences are expressed redundantly in successive notes of a call sequence. There is also no clear difference in successful attribution between experiments, suggesting that even though certain call parameters changed more dramatically in Experiment 2, this had little influence on the individuality of most vocalizers' calls. One reason for this is that other parameters besides those showing a significant change over time (peak frequency, mean frequency, and duration) were important in discriminating between the calls of different vocalizers.

The study demonstrated the presence of significant trends over time

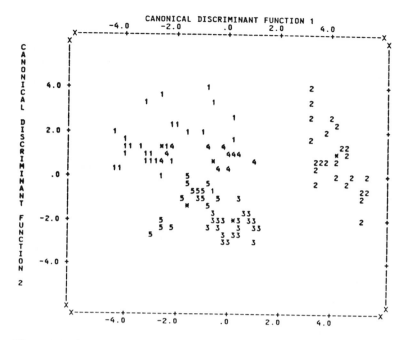

Figure 5.3. Scatter plot of discriminant scores for phee calls from 5 adult common marmosets. The scores were derived from a discriminant function analysis of 6 acoustic parameters measured from each call. Scores for the calls from each individual are plotted as that subject's identifying number (1–5). Asterisks indicate mean score for each subject. Note the small overlap of scores from different animals, indicative of the greater-than-chance successful attribution of calls by vocalizer.

for certain phee call structural parameters. We propose that such trends are manifestations of proximate mechanisms related to the regulation of emotional or arousal state. Elapsed time from initial separation has been shown to correlate positively with plasma cortisol level, reflecting the activation of the pituitary-adrenal axis under the stress of social separation (Coe, Wiener, Rosenberg, & Levine, 1985). Changes in behavior, such as vocalization, may also be correlated with level of distress, which presumably increases with degree of separation. The changes in phee call parameters are consistent with this view, in that structural changes were more evident in the context of combined acoustic and visual separation than with visual separation alone, and the trend toward increased pitch and decreased duration in phee calls later in a session are consistent with the changes reported in human speech with increased level of emotion (Scherer, 1985). While documenting intraindividual variability in phee calls, there is sufficient acoustic consistency in these same vocalizations to result in a high degree of individual distinctiveness. Our argument for the utility of the attribute hypothesis in analyzing vocal signals is supported by the finding that the parameters of greatest value in imparting individual distinctiveness (e.g., start frequency, end frequency, pitch instability) are the most stable over time, whereas other parameters (mean frequency, peak frequency, duration) showing a significant change over the course of a separation experience are inadequate by themselves to encode individual distinctiveness.

Brain substrates mediating emotional expression through phonation

The voluminous nature of this subject requires a focused approach here. A recent collection of essays (Newman, 1988) emphasized the importance of the isolation call in recent studies of the physiology of vocal expression and the anterior limbic cortical component of the frontal lobe (cingulate gyrus) as a neural substrate.

MacLean and Newman (1988) found that bilateral ablation of the cingulate gyrus in squirrel monkeys produced a lasting reduction in the spontaneous emission of the isolation call. In those few cases where isolation calls were produced, the calls exhibited shorter durations and lower peak frequencies, both suggestive of a reduced level of affect. Another recent study (Newman & Bachevalier, 1988) found that bilateral ablation of the amygdala in neonatal rhesus monkeys resulted in subsequent development of isolation calls ("isolation coos") that were deficient in affective quality. One might expect that in the course of exploring the brain with electrodes for electrically eliciting vocalization it would be possible to identify brain substrates where systematic changes in stimulation parameters produced corresponding graded changes in the rhythm, intensity, or acoustic structure of the elicited vocalizations. In a thorough study of this issue, Jürgens and Ploog concluded that "with the exception of the trilling calls from the precommissural fornix and some electrode positions in the substantia innominata, amygdala, medial orbital gyrus, and gyrus cinguli, generally an increase in stimulus intensity is associated with an increase in vehemence of vocalization" (1970, p. 545). This suggests that these particular neuroanatomical structures are involved in aspects of vocal behavior other than noncategorical signaling.

Conclusions

The study of noncategorical vocal communication in primates obviously is still in the early stages of investigation. At the same time, as the grain size with which primate vocalizations are dissected into acoustic components decreases, with the use of ever more sophisticated analytic tools, the likelihood increases that small changes in acoustic structure will be measured. It seems reasonable to conclude that the documentation of noncategorical communication will grow significantly. Whether it continues to be useful to divide species into those with predominantly discrete vocal repertoires and those with predominantly graded repertoires is questionable. Rather, it may be more profitable to emphasize the use of analytic and experimental strategies under controlled conditions, with the goal of linking vocal production and physiological changes in the vocalizer. The concepts of *arousal* and *affective state* require more precise definition, based on physiological measures. Understanding the factors that promote the production of graded calls by an individual within a restricted period of time will be enhanced by manipulating variables internal to the vocalizer (e.g., by the use of drugs). On the other hand, experimental control of external variables, whether they are generated by conspecifics or by other aspects of the environment, will doubtless provide improved understanding of the social and environmental factors influencing vocal variability measured across longer time frames.

References

Benson, D. F. (1984). The neurology of human emotion. *Bulletin of Clinical Neurosciences, 49*, 23–42.

Biben, M., & Symmes, D. (1986). Play vocalizations of squirrel monkeys (*Saimiri sciureus*). *Folia Primatologica, 46*, 173–182.

Boinski, S., & Newman, J. D. (1988). Preliminary observations on squirrel monkey (*Saimiri oerstedi*) vocalizations in Costa Rica. *American Journal of Primatology, 14*, 329–343.

Campos, J. J., Campos, R. G., & Barrett, K. C. (1989). Emergent themes in the study of emotional development and emotion regulation. *Developmental Psychology 25* (3), 394–402.

Cheney, D. L., & Seyfarth, R. M. (1980). Vocal recognition in free ranging vervet monkeys. *Animal Behaviour, 28*, 362–367.

Coe, C. L., Wiener, S. G., Rosenberg, L. T., & Levine, S. (1985). Physiological consequences of maternal separation and loss in the squirrel monkey. In L. Rosenblum & C. L. Coe (Eds.), *Handbook of squirrel monkey research* (pp. 127–148). New York: Plenum.

Darwin, C. (1872 / 1965). *The expression of the emotions in man and animals.* Chicago: University of Chicago Press. (Original work published 1872)

Gautier, J.-P. (1974). Field and laboratory studies of the vocalizations of talapoin monkeys (*Miopithecus talapoin*). *Behaviour, 51,* 209–273.

Ghiselin, M. T. (1981). Categories, life, and thinking. *Behavioral and Brain Sciences, 4* (2), 269–283.

Goedeking, P. (1988). Vocal play behavior in cotton-top tamarins. In D. Todt, P. Goedeking, & D. Symmes (Eds.), *Primate vocal communication* (pp. 133–141). Springer: Berlin.

Goedeking, P., & Newman, J. D. (1987). Intra- and interindividual variability in "phee" calls of captive common marmosets. *American Journal of Primatology, 21,* 344.

Gouzoules, S., Gouzoules, H., & Marler, P. (1984). Rhesus monkey (*Macaca mulatta*) screams: Representational signalling in the recruitment of agonistic aid. *Animal Behaviour, 32,* 182–193.

Green, S. (1975). Variation of vocal pattern with social situation in the Japanese monkey (*Macaca fuscata*). In L. A. Rosenblum (Ed.), *Primate Behavior* (Vol. 4, pp. 1–102). New York: Academic Press.

Jürgens, U. (1979). Vocalization as an emotional indicator: A neuroethological study of the squirrel monkey. *Behaviour, 69,* 88–117.

Jürgens, U., & Ploog, D. (1970). Cerebral representation of vocalization in the squirrel monkey. *Experimental Brain Research, 10,* 532–554.

Larson, C. R., Sutton, D., Taylor, E. M., & Lindeman, R. (1973). Sound spectral properties of conditioned vocalizations in monkeys. *Phonetica, 27,* 100–110.

MacLean, P. D., & Newman, J. D. (1988). Role of midline frontolimbic cortex in production of the isolation call of squirrel monkeys. *Brain Research, 450,* 111–123.

Malatesta, C. Z. (1981). Infant emotion and the vocal affect lexicon. *Motivation and Emotion, 5,* 1–23.

Marler, P. (1970). Vocalizations of East African monkeys: 1. Red colobus. *Folia Primatologica, 13,* 81–91.

(1972). Vocalizations of East African monkeys: 2. Black and white colobus. *Behaviour, 42,* 175–197.

Marler, P., & Hobbett, L. (1975). Individuality in a long-range vocalization of wild chimpanzees. *Zeitschrift für Tierpsychologie, 38,* 97–109.

Masataka, N., & Symmes, D. (1986). Effect of separation distance on isolation call structure in squirrel monkeys (*Saimiri sciureus*). *American Journal of Primatology, 10,* 271–278.

Morton, E. S. (1977). On the occurrence and significance of motivation-structural rules in some bird and mammal sounds. *American Naturalist, 111,* 855–869.

Newman, J. D. (1985). Squirrel monkey communication. In L. A. Rosenblum and C. L. Coe (Eds.), *Handbook of squirrel monkey research* (pp. 99–126). New York: Plenum.

Newman, J. D. (Ed.) (1988). *The physiological control of mammalian vocalizations.* New York: Plenum.

Newman, J. D., & Bachevalier, J. (1988). Acoustic differences in separation calls of rhesus monkeys following neonatal ablation of temporal lobe limbic areas. *Society for Neurosciences Abstracts, 14* (1), 692.

Porter, F. G., Miller, R. H., & Marshall, R. E. (1986). Neonatal pain cries: Effect of circumcision on acoustic features and perceived urgency. *Child Development, 57,* 790–802.

Rowell, T. E. (1962). Agonistic noises of the rhesus monkey (*Macaca mulatta*). *Zoological Society of London Symposia, 8,* 91–96.

Rowell, T. E., & Hinde, R. A. (1962). Vocal communication by the rhesus monkey (*Macaca mulatta*). *Proceedings of the Zoological Society of London, 138,* 279–294.

Scherer, K. R. (1985). Vocal affect signalling: A comparative approach. *Advances in the Study of Behavior, 15,* 189–244.

Scherer, K. R., & Kappas, A. (1988). Primate vocal expression of affective state. In D. Todt, P. Goedeking, and D. Symmes (Eds.), *Primate vocal communication* (pp. 171–194). Berlin: Springer.

Schott, D. (1975). Quantitative analysis of the vocal repertoire of squirrel monkeys (*Saimiri sciureus*). *Zeitschrift für Tierpsychologie, 38,* 225–250.

Smith, H. J., Newman, J. D., Hoffman, H. J., & Fetterly, K. (1982). Statistical discrimination among vocalizations of individual squirrel monkeys (*Saimiri sciureus*). *Folia Primatologica, 37,* 267–279.

Snowdon, C. T., Cleveland, J., & French, J. A. (1983). Responses to context- and individual-specific cues in cotton-top tamarin long calls. *Animal Behaviour, 31,* 92–101.

Symmes, D., Newman, J. D., Talmage-Riggs, G., & Lieblich, A. K. (1979). Individuality and stability of isolation peeps in squirrel monkeys. *Animal Behaviour, 27,* 1142–1152.

Todt, D. (1986). Hinweischarakter und Hinweisfunktion von Verhalten. *Zeitschrift für Semiotik, 8,* 183–232.

(1988). Serial calling as a mediator of interaction processes: Crying in primates. In D. Todt, P. Goedeking, & D. Symmes, (Eds.), *Primate vocal communication* (pp. 88–107). Berlin: Springer.

Winter, P. (1969). Dialects in squirrel monkeys: Vocalizations of the roman arch type. *Folia Primatologica, 10,* 216–229.

Winter, P., Handley, P., Ploog, D., & Schott, D. (1973). Ontogeny of squirrel monkey calls under normal conditions and under acoustic isolation. *Behaviour, 47,* 230–239.

Winter, P., Ploog, D., & Latta, J. (1966). Vocal repertoire of the squirrel monkey (*Saimiri sciureus*), its analysis and significance. *Experimental Brain Research, 1,* 359–384.

6. Categorical vocal signaling in nonhuman primates

MICHAEL J. OWREN, ROBERT M. SEYFARTH, AND
STEVEN L. HOPP

Classifying the vocalizations of nonhuman primates has long occupied researchers interested in understanding the function and significance of such signals. The approach most often used is to produce a taxonomy of physical signals and relate the significant acoustic features that emerge to important aspects of the behavior of the signaler or receiver. The explicit goal or assumption of this approach is that the investigator is ultimately able to determine whether the species in question uses its calls in a categorical manner and, if so, how these categories are constituted. Follow-up experiments involving playback of calls to animals under field or naturalistic captive conditions can then be used to corroborate hypothesized categories and the functions proposed for particular sounds (Snowdon, 1982).

Primate vocal repertoires often exhibit at least two levels of organization, both acoustically and behaviorally. Relatively coarse-grained classification reveals groups of variable but fundamentally similar calls that define overall classes. Call types like "coos," "girneys," "screams," and "alarm barks," in Japanese macaques, that are associated with different behavioral contexts exemplify the first level (Green, 1975). More fine-grained analyses may then reveal that sounds sharing many basic acoustic features exhibit subtle but consistent differences and form subclasses. Within the broad "coo" class, for instance, Green distinguished seven subtypes.

In recent years, studies along these lines have shown that at least some primate species exhibit quite sophisticated vocal communication – testimony to the appropriateness of the investigative approach. Properties like semanticity, syntactic patterning, and deception, once thought

Preparation of this chapter was partially supported by NIH Grant NS 19826 to Michael J. Owren, who was a Postdoctoral Trainee at the National Institute of Child Health and Human Development during much of the preparation.

to be specific to human speech, have now been demonstrated in non-human primates as well (Seyfarth, 1987; Marler, 1982). In each case, the investigator's categorization of acoustic structure or usage has played a central role. For instance, studies showing semantic use of predator alarm calls in vervet monkeys (*Cercopithecus aethiops*) began with the observation that the various sounds could be classified readily by humans either by ear or in spectrographic representations (Seyfarth, Cheney, & Marler, 1980a,b; Struhsaker, 1967). Similarly, acoustic features in vervet "grunt" calls have been linked to specific aspects of the contexts in which these sounds are produced (Cheney & Seyfarth, 1982; Seyfarth & Cheney, 1984), and differentiated rhesus macaque (*Macaca mulatta*) screams produced by juvenile animals have been shown to communicate the severity of aggressive encounters to their mothers (Gouzoules, Gouzoules, & Marler, 1984).

However, acoustic classification of calls and determination of behavioral categories can be quite problematical, particularly as more subtle aspects of signal acoustics and behavioral contexts are examined. Like human speech, primate vocalizations often exhibit great variability in acoustic structure, reflecting a number of levels of communication (Snowdon, 1984). Only some of this variability is likely to be related to the particular aspect of communication that is of immediate interest to an investigator. This problem has been discussed at length elsewhere, for instance by Green and Marler (1979) and by Snowdon (1982). Quite simply, the normal state of affairs is not to find unequivocal correlations between the sound and its behavioral context. Instead, the same sound often occurs in apparently different situations, and a variety of sounds can be found to occur in a given situation. Classification of sounds becomes particularly difficult between hypothesized subclasses and when class boundaries are blurred by intermediate or transitional acoustic forms.

A widely acknowledged caveat is that the receiver's perceptual processing may play a significant role in the relationship between signal and behavior (Green & Marler, 1979; Marler, 1976). In humans, for instance, specialized processing is of great importance in the extraction of "invariant" speech cues from the highly variable speech signal. Recent studies have shown that monkeys may also rely on some perceptual specializations when decoding their own species' vocalizations (discussed in detail later in this essay). Unfortunately, little information is as yet available about complex auditory perception in the vast majority of nonhuman primates. Predominantly, species whose vocal repertoires are well documented have not been subject to careful auditory study, and vice versa. While call perception has been examined in monkeys in a few notable circumstances (e.g., Masataka, 1983a,b; Petersen et al., 1978, 1984; Snowdon & Pola, 1978; Zoloth et al., 1979), psychoacoustic examination has not become a routine part of primate vocal communication studies. Investigators producing field-based classifications of vocal systems and those examining psychoacoustic characteristics frequently work in quite disparate disciplines and have little opportunity to coordinate their efforts.

What may be needed to encourage fuller integration of perceptual, acoustic, and behavioral study is a clear demonstration that detailed data about auditory processing complement, extend, or contradict the proposed vocalization taxonomies. To substantiate this point, we review in this essay some recent results from psychophysical studies of audition in Japanese macaques and the possible implications for categorization of coo calls used by this species. These sounds are of particular interest on several accounts. First, the theory that coo calls are used in a categorical manner by Japanese macaques has become part of accepted primatological lore (e.g., Jolly, 1985), although the existence of categories has not been tested directly, either in the field or laboratory. Second, species-typical coo call processing has been examined in detail, and similarities to some common human speech perception phenomena, including perceptual categorization, have been proposed. Finally, more information is now available about the auditory response in Japanese macaques than in any other nonhuman primate species.

We propose that the overall psychophysical evidence is not necessarily consistent with either field-based interpretations about coo call classification or laboratory-based claims about perceptual categorization underlying such classification. The results of studies of basic hearing functions in these animals set the stage for further investigation of their vocal communication.

Coo calls in Japanese macaques

Field results

Japanese macaques inhabit evergreen and decidous forests throughout the islands of Japan (Eaton, 1976; Takasaki, 1981) and have been intensively studied for many years, both in their natural habitat and in more controlled circumstances involving provisioning or captive settings. These animals exhibit a high rate of calling and routinely use their vocalizations to help coordinate daily social interactions. Following a detailed

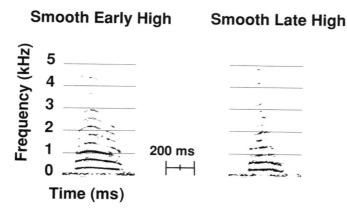

Figure 6.1. Japanese macaque natural calls. Wideband spectrograms of a "smooth early high" *(left)* and a "smooth late high" *(right)* coo call.

study of the entire Japanese macaque vocal repertoire, Green (1975) characterized these animals as exhibiting grading of vocalizations both within and between their major call classes. Green's study focused most intensively on a class of brief, tonal sounds that he dubbed "coos." Within this class, seven similar-sounding but subtlely different coo vocalizations were described; these appeared to be related to different circumstances of calling. The behavioral circumstances reported for the variants concerned affiliative contact between individual members of the Japanese macaque group or between individuals and the group as a whole.

Spectrograms of two coo call types of specific interest are reproduced in Figure 6.1. These calls, referred to as "smooth early high" (SEH) and "smooth late high" (SLH) coos, were distinguished by Green acoustically on the basis of the relative temporal position of peaks in fundamental frequency. The SEH type included coos in which the peak occurs within the first two-thirds of the call, while calls that peak in the last one-third were grouped as SLHs. Peak position is computed by dividing the temporal position of the point of maximum frequency by the total duration of the vocalization (Petersen, 1978). According to this calculation, the category boundary separating SEH and SLH calls lies at 0.67. Two other categories were identified by the presence of one or more local frequency minima, or "dips," preceding or following the larger frequency modulation. These "dip early high" (DEH) and "dip late high" (DLH) calls were hypothesized to be separable on the basis of peak position as well.

Laboratory studies

A collaborative research effort involving personnel from the University of Michigan and Rockefeller University followed up this work in the laboratory. Their studies were based on the hypothesis that if frequency peak position in SEH and SLH calls constitutes a linguisticlike acoustic feature, analogous to phonemic contrasts in human speech, similar perceptual processing might occur in each instance. In conducting the investigations, it was assumed that Green's hypotheses about functional differentiation of coo calls, the importance of peak position, and the location of the category boundary were correct.

Japanese macaques and control monkeys from other species were trained to sort natural exemplars of SEH and SLH coo calls, in an appetitive operant conditioning procedure. Two call categories were specified by the experimenters, defined either on the basis of peak position (early or late) or by overall pitch (high or low). On each trial, the subjects first heard a variable number of stimuli representing one category. They were then rewarded for responding to a stimulus drawn from the other category. One supposition specifically motivating the experiments (e.g., Zoloth & Green, 1979) was that Japanese macaques might make use of a processing strategy referred to as "categorical perception" when decoding coo calls.

Categorical perception exists when two conditions are met. First, a unidimensional acoustic continuum must be partitioned by receivers into two or more functional categories. Second, signals sorted into different categories must be easily discriminated, whereas signals falling within the same category are not well discriminated. Although once thought to be specific to human speech perception, categorical perception has since been found to be much more general (cf. Harnad, 1987). As implied by the definition just stated, two kinds of data are needed to demonstrate this phenomenon, whether in humans (Pisoni, 1978) or animals (Ehret, 1987). An "identification" or "labeling" study must first show that subjects partition the continuum into functionally differentiated regions. A "discrimination" study must then demonstrate that the subjects' sensitivity to variation along the continuum reaches a peak at each partition point, or category boundary.

To perform the coo call labeling task, monkeys categorized field-recorded examples of the SEH and SLH types. Because the calls exhibited variation in peak position, the animals were effectively partitioning a continuum of possible peak positions into two categories. An implicit hypothesis was that Japanese macaques would be predisposed to divide the continuum at the boundary location described by Green, while non-Japanese macaque control subjects would be learning to categorize these sounds and erecting a category boundary *de novo*. A number of outcomes indicated clear parallels between the processing of coo call peak position by Japanese macaques and normative processing of linguistic speech by humans. Descriptions of the studies are available in review chapters (e.g., Beecher, Petersen, Zoloth, Moody, & Stebbins, 1979; Marler, 1982; Petersen, 1982). Briefly, when Japanese macaques sorted coo calls on the basis of relative peak position, they exhibited a right-ear advantage, selective attention for that feature, and perceptual constancy. None of these effects was found when the animals sorted the same set of calls on the basis of overall pitch, ignoring peak position. In general, non-Japanese monkey control subjects did not show a right-ear advantage and attended more easily to the pitch parameter than to peak position when sorting the calls.

A subsequent study by Heffner and Heffner (1984) used cortical lesioning to demonstrate that lateralized processing is occurring in Japanese macaque subjects showing a right-ear advantage. Generalization tests with natural stimuli conducted by Petersen and his coworkers (1984) have also verified that both Japanese monkeys and control subjects do in fact attend to the peak-position feature when the experimental design requires categorization on that basis. Recently, May, Moody, and Stebbins (1988) specifically tested the importance of several covarying aspects of coo calls in the SEH–SLH labeling task and confirmed the preeminence of fundamental frequency peak information for Japanese macaque subjects.

A second study by May and his colleagues (1989) attempted to examine the discriminability of peak positions along the SEH–SLH continuum, thereby testing for the second aspect of the categorical perception phenomenon. Although the authors suggest that the requisite between-category discrimination peak was demonstrated, certain aspects of the procedure they employed seriously weaken the evidence that was obtained. The same Japanese macaques that had already been extensively trained to classify natural stimuli by peak position continued to perform this labeling procedure. However, novel synthetic stimuli were also now presented, in addition to the familiar natural calls, and the subjects were required to execute two rather different tasks simultaneously within each testing session. On the one hand, when a natural pair of standard and target stimuli occurred, sorting continued as before. On the other hand, when the standard and target stimuli were synthetic versions, the subjects were to respond to any detectable peak-position difference between them, regardless of category membership. Thus, synthetic standard-target stimulus pairs sometimes required the same response as an analogous natural pair but often required the opposite response. The animals were found to respond more reliably to the synthetic target stimulus when it did not derive from the same category as the standard stimulus than when both stimuli were drawn from the same category. However, no independent evidence was presented to indicate that the subjects were in fact conforming to the novel contingency in effect during synthetic stimulus presentations (and hence were demonstrating optimal discrimination performance), rather than simply labeling the synthetic sounds in the same manner as the natural calls. No control subjects from other species were tested to indicate that the categorical perception effect claimed by May and his colleagues (1989) was in fact specific to Japanese macaques, as would be expected on the basis of the earlier studies that had inspired these experimenters' work (see Hopp, Sinnott, Owren, & Petersen, in press, for further discussion).

Classifying coo calls

Overall, these studies provided direct confirmation of the importance of peak position as a distinctive acoustic feature in normal perceptual processing of coo calls by Japanese macaques. However, none of the results speak directly to hypotheses about the existence of categories defined by variation in peak position, nor do they specifically test hypotheses about the location of category boundaries. As can be expected in operant conditioning, the animals performing the basic labeling task with these coo calls in the laboratory required extensive training with multiple exemplars of each class before achieving consistently accurate response patterns. Because all the Japanese macaque subjects were specifically rewarded for classifying stimuli into categories defined by peak position, their subsequent ability to do so does not constitute unequivocal evidence of preexisting natural perceptual categorization.

Some of the laboratory evidence is in fact inconsistent with the notion of a single category boundary occurring at the 0.67 peak-position location. Generalization testing conducted with both natural (Petersen et al., 1984) and synthetic (Petersen, 1981) coos indicates that the boundary lies between 0.40 and 0.60. Representative generalization functions from the latter study are shown in Figure 6.2. These functions, virtually identical

NATURAL   COO   GENERALIZATION

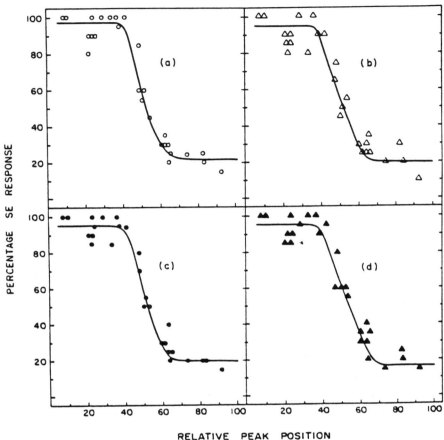

Figure 6.2. Generalization data for six synthetic coo calls obtained from natural coos of two control subjects (a, b) and two Japanese macaques (c, d), in an operant conditioning classification task. Each point represents a single call and shows percent classification as a smooth early high (SEH) coo by relative peak position. The "regression" line in each panel was fitted by eye. (From Aslin, Alberts, & Petersen, 1981. Reprinted with permission.)

for all the species that were tested, have since been replicated in Japanese macaques by May and coworkers (1988), who describe this peak-position region as a transition zone in which both labeling responses can occur. Unfortunately, analogous generalization data for the pitch parameter are not available for comparison.

To date, no nonhuman primate has been shown to exhibit categorical perception of species-typical vocal signals. While May and his colleagues (1989) make such a claim with respect to Japanese macaques, the indirect procedure they employed when testing the relationship between labeling and discrimination of peak-position variation does not provide compelling evidence of categorical perception. Some claims of stepwise labeling functions have been made, based on investigations in which animals' natural responses to playback trials were used (Masataka, 1983a,b; Snowdon & Pola, 1978; critiques in Hopp, 1985; Petersen, 1978), but these experiments did not include discrimination testing at all. As noted, in the studies by Petersen and his colleagues comparison monkeys partitioned the peak-position continuum in the same manner as the Japanese macaques. However, they did so in the absence of selective attention, perceptual constancy, or neural lateralization. On the one hand, this evidence clearly indicates that specialized processing of peak-position information is occurring in the Japanese macaques. On the other hand, while these animals may be predisposed to attend to the peak-position feature, basic auditory mechanisms common to all the monkeys tested appear to play a critical role in any categorization that may occur. This interpretation finds support in the results of psychophysical studies of audition both in macaques and other nonhuman primates.

Auditory processing in Japanese macaques

Studies that attempt to discover the distinctive features of nonhuman primate vocalizations have rarely incorporated information concerning the psychoacoustic response of the species in question. However, in the case of Japanese macaques, a number of relevant data are available. At the most fundamental level, it is of interest to examine their absolute sensitivity for sounds across the audible frequency range. Resulting audiograms reveal the gross shaping of energy at the auditory periphery that both limits and differentially weights the frequencies admitted for detailed processing. Japanese macaques have been found to resemble other Old World species in showing maximal sensitivity to frequencies between approximately 700 Hz and 2 kHz, although macaques in general appear to be less sensitive than other genera to sounds below 1 kHz in frequency (Owren, Hopp, Sinnott, & Petersen, 1988). Japanese macaques are thus more sensitive in the general frequency range of coo calls than elsewhere in the spectrum but give no indication of particular acuity in this region, when compared with other species.

Additional characteristics of the basic auditory response of Japanese macaques are more directly relevant to frequency-peak processing. Sensitivity to energy patterning – for instance in the frequency, temporal, or intensity domains – can play a critical role in determining which aspects of vocalizations form distinctive features. Studies conducted by Sinnott and her colleagues (Sinnott, Petersen, & Hopp, 1985; Sinnott, Owren, & Petersen, 1987a,b) have examined the minimal amount of change in the frequency or duration of pure tone stimuli that can be detected by Japanese macaques as well as by other Old World monkeys and humans. This measurement, called the *difference limen*, is often expressed as the dimensionless Weber fraction: the amount of change required for detection, divided by the size of the standard stimulus against which the change is gauged. The operant testing procedure used in each of Sinnott's studies was similar to that employed in the coo call experiments described earlier. Monkeys were trained to listen to a repeating standard stimulus of fixed frequency or duration and respond to any detectable deviation from this standard.

Frequency discrimination

Detection of discrete frequency change was investigated for both upward and downward shifts. Results for frequency increment discrimination are shown in Figure 6.3a, for the most sensitive Japanese macaque and the least sensitive human subject tested by Sinnott and her colleagues (1985, 1987a). All four Old World monkey species exhibited difference limens at least seven to ten times greater than those of the humans. Calculated as Weber fractions, the results shown in the graph reflect a fraction of .003 for the human subject and .026 for the monkey. Discrimination by the Japanese macaques, however, was the most sensitive of the nonhuman primates tested. Differences between humans and nonhumans were also approximately one order of magnitude in size with respect to frequency decrements, but in that task the various monkey species performed comparably. In other words, the Japanese macaques tested were less sensitive to downward than upward frequency shifts.

The human–monkey discrepancy was not due to differences in testing conditions, as the animals and humans performed the task under similar response contingencies in the same apparatus. For comparison, tests of sensitivity to intensity increments conducted in the same manner showed virtually no difference, with mean monkey difference limens falling within

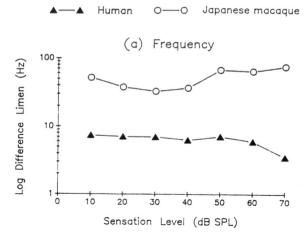

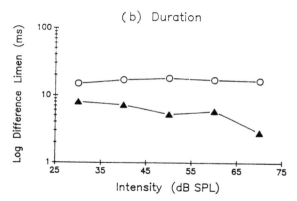

Figure 6.3. (a) Frequency discrimination difference limens at 2 kHz from the most sensitive Japanese macaque and least sensitive human subject tested by Sinnott et al. (1987a). (b) Duration discrimination difference limens from the most sensitive Japanese macaque and least sensitive human subject tested by Sinnott et al. (1987b), using a 25-ms standard.

1 dB SPL of the human results and resulting Weber fractions of .034 and .026, respectively (Sinnott et al., 1985). These studies involve discrete frequency changes, rather than the continuously modulated sweeps that are characteristic of coo calls. Nonetheless, the relevance of data like these has been demonstrated by Moody, May, Cole, and Stebbins (1968), who found that macaques listening for frequency sweeps at near-threshold levels appear to recode this information as discrete frequency steps.

Duration discrimination

Discrepancies between responses from Japanese macaques and humans are less dramatic with respect to sensitivity to small duration differences, but are substantial nonetheless. In studies reported by Sinnott and her colleagues (1987b), subjects again listened to a background tone, this time of constant duration, and responded to target sounds that were either longer or shorter. Temporal increment results from the most sensitive Japanese macaque and the least sensitive human are graphed in Figure 6.3b, where the difference limen value can be seen to vary somewhat with stimulus sensation level. Although Weber fractions for both humans and monkeys declined with longer standard stimuli, the overall effect was an increasing difference limen – from 4.7 and 12.0 ms, for humans and Japanese macaques, respectively, with a 25.0 ms standard, to 22.0 and 98.0 ms with a 400.0 ms standard. The temporal decrement task proved to be extremely difficult for any monkey to master, and only one animal was successfully tested. However, this individual, a Japanese macaque, then produced results almost identical to its previous performance in the increment procedure.

Peak-position discrimination

Hopp and his colleagues (in press) have tested the differential sensitivity of Japanese macaques and humans to variations in coo call peak position in the direct manner exemplified by Sinnott's work. Here, the stimuli were synthetic calls that were standardized with respect to duration (360 ms) and frequency (104-Hz upward frequency modulation from a 560-Hz baseline value) and that formed a continuum of peak positions spaced 20–40 ms apart. Subjects listened for target calls in which peak position differed from that of a repeating standard call. Testing was conducted in both directions, beginning in each case with a standard stimulus whose peak position formed an endpoint of the continuum (i.e., peak positions at 40 ms and 300 ms, respectively). As testing progressed, peak positions of the standard stimuli were moved steadily toward the continuum's midpoint. At each standard peak-position location the difference limen was determined, using a series of target stimuli covering a peak-position range of 100 ms (the method of constant stimuli). The results for human and monkey subjects are graphed in Figure 6.4a, with the former again being two to three times more sensitive than the latter.

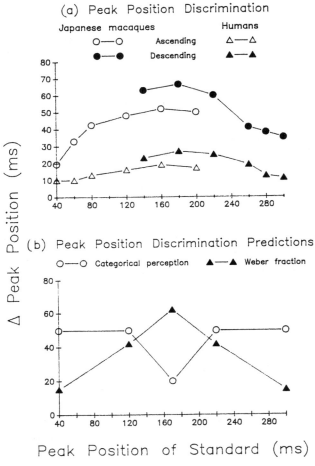

Figure 6.4. (a) Peak-position discrimination difference limens from humans and Japanese macaques tested by Hopp et al. (in press). (b) Peak-position discrimination function predictions based on the categorical perception hypothesis and a hypothetical constant Weber fraction for duration discrimination.

Both functions exhibit an inverted-U shape, indicating greatest resolution of peak-position variation near the endpoints. Intermediate peak positions were relatively difficult to discriminate for both species.

Implications for coo call perception

Frequency modulation detection

An obvious implication of these studies for interpretations of coo call use by Japanese macaques is that acoustic analyses of call use must take into account the auditory sensitivities of these animals. For instance, the Japanese macaques tested by Sinnott and her colleagues (1987a) at 1 kHz showed difference limens ranging from 16 to 35 Hz, varying by individual and the intensity of the standard stimulus. Extrapolating directly from these threshold values obtained under ideal listening conditions to the highly variable conditions of the natural environment is difficult. However, common sense dictates that frequency excursions would have to be substantially greater than the optimal difference threshold value in order to ensure reliable detection under normal conditions. By analogy, human "tone" languages that make use of phonemically distinct word pitches typically allow frequency intervals between these levels that are much greater than the corresponding difference limen (I. Maddieson, personal communication, December 1988). The exaggerated intonation contours typical of adult human speech to preverbal offspring (Fernald, chapter 13 in the present volume) may similarly have their basis in the rather monkeylike frequency resolution capacities characteristic of young infants (Sinnott & Aslin, 1986).

This evidence argues that some frequency peaks measurable in acoustic analysis of coo calls and distinctive to human listeners need not constitute salient perceptual cues for Japanese macaques. In other words, if one observes such a peak and can relate its occurrence to some aspect of an animal's behavior, this observation does not by itself show the peak to be of importance in communication. Coo call overtones exhibit wider frequency excursions than the fundamental frequency and hence might play a role in cases of equivocal fundamental frequency modulation, but May and his colleagues (1988) found that these harmonics are not reliably used by Japanese macaques when performing the peak-position–based labeling task in the laboratory. Furthermore, both Petersen (1978) and May and his coauthors (1988) do report that certain apparently well-formed coo call exemplars that could be classified by the investigators proved to be consistently problematical for the animal subjects.

The frequency decrement results raise analogous questions about the detectability of local minima, or dips. The occurrence of dips in conjunction with a larger frequency peak was used by Green (1975) to distinguish the DEH and DLH coo calls from their smooth-contoured counterparts, as noted earlier. However, given less sensitivity to frequency decrements than increments in Japanese macaques and the small, local nature of these modulations compared to the overall call modulation, it is not clear that dips can function as independent features for acoustic communication. In both cases, the original hypotheses proposed on the basis of field observations may be correct. On the other hand, the psychophysical evidence compellingly suggests that specific tests of the communicative significance of these call attributes are in order.

Temporal resolution and peak position

Analogously, the duration discrimination results suggest that Japanese macaques cannot be expected to resolve temporal features in their calls as precisely as the human observer can. These data also provide a basis for specific predictions concerning how peak position is gauged in coo calls. This judgment may rely on perceptual specializations that extract peak-position information differently from other temporal features of auditory signals. The categorical perception phenomenon described earlier would exemplify this kind of specialization. However, in the absence of categorical perception, or the like, one can expect that basic temporal processing capabilities play the primary role in shaping information extraction. In that regard, Japanese macaques are likely to rely on whichever strategy or combination of strategies provides the best information. For instance, judging peak position in a naturalistic case where only a single call is heard might involve comparing the relative duration of segments preceding and following the peak. Difference limen considerations lead to the prediction that such judgments will be most difficult at intermediate peak positions, where the segments are relatively long and approximately equal. A similar outcome would result if the comparison were being made between the absolute length of one of the segments and a stored cognitive model of coo call features. In the peak-position discrimination task, two calls are compared that are closely spaced in time. Whether peak positions in these stimuli are first recoded as some relative value and then contrasted, or the durations of homologous call segments are compared directly, duration resolution limitations again suggest that the least success will occur at intermediate peak-position locations. Peaks located near either call endpoint necessarily entail the occurrence of a short leading or following segment that is easily discriminated from segments that are slightly longer or shorter.

Thus, a hypothesis based on categorical perception and one based on duration discrimination yield quite different predictions about the form of the peak-position discrimination function. The former predicts that discriminability increases locally at category boundaries. Hence, in the present case, the smallest difference limen should occur at a peak position of 0.67, or possibly between 0.40 and 0.60. Figure 6.4b graphs this function, along with that predicted on the basis of psychophysical considerations. The latter, based on a Weber fraction value of .30 and a total call duration of 360 ms, is clearly more consistent with the data presented in Figure 6.4a than is the categorical perception–based function. Neither the human nor the monkey discrimination function shows any indication of increased resolution at the purported category boundary. Instead, both the general shape of these functions and the relative sensitivity to peak-position variation shown by these two species are consistent with expectations based on the normative characteristics of their respective auditory systems.

Questions about categories in coo calls

An attractive hypothesis that has emerged among speech researchers is that communicatively important continua may embody natural psychoacoustic discontinuities, forming the basis of perceptual categorization (e.g., Macmillan, 1987). Such "regions of natural sensitivity" are not readily apparent in the auditory responses of either Japanese macaques or the other monkey species examined in the studies we have described. The peak-position discrimination function fails to divide the continuum into discrete categories. The evidence of stepwise partitioning of the peak-position continuum provided by the generalization results described earlier is best considered equivocal. However, while the coo call peak-position continuum is not subject to categorical perception by either humans or Japanese macaques, neither is there constant sensitivity across the peak-position range. Instead, the discrimination function shows the apparent converse of categorical perception.

The implications of these findings for coo call categories have been discussed by Hopp and his colleagues (in press). One possibility is that if categorization does occur it may not depend strictly on acoustic cues alone. The absence of a clearly defined perceptual boundary could suggest the absence of a fixed functional boundary. While sounds drawn from the continuum's endpoints are readily classified, interpretation of intermediate sounds may be influenced by the immediate behavioral context. On the other hand, greater sensitivity to small changes in peak locations near an endpoint may indicate that such variation is of communicative importance. For instance, peak position might be iconically related to some aspect of the calling situation. SEH calls, on the one hand, appear to be emitted by individuals that are relatively distant from receivers – young animals separated from their mothers or small subgroups separated from the main troop. SLH calls, on the other hand, are used in situations more likely to involve closer proximity – for example, by estrous females soliciting a potential consort or by a subordinate individual approaching a dominant animal (Green, 1975). Within each of these hypothesized categories, variations in peak position are relatively easy to discriminate and hence might convey graded information. Intermediate peak positions, which are difficult to discriminate, may be used when distance is not an important factor.

If Japanese macaques do partition the peak-position continuum in a discrete manner, the possibility of a third category should be considered. As noted, the laboratory studies involving labeling of coo calls that have been conducted to date have allowed only two possible classifications, leaving the animal subjects with no means of directly indicating nonmembership in either category. Calls falling into a possible intermediate category would necessarily be forced into one of the two available classes (possibly requiring more extensive practice with those specific exemplars) or would be sorted at chance levels. The generalization data are consistent with this possibility.

Conclusions

None of the results we have reviewed shows unequivocally that Japanese macaques do not use coo calls in the manner originally described by Green. Furthermore, the speculations just presented are no more than that. On the other hand, a variety of evidence indicates that substantive issues about categorization of coo calls remain unsettled. Inquiries both in the field and in the conditioning laboratory will be necessary to establish more clearly how perceptually salient peak-position variation maps onto fine-grained aspects of the natural behavior of Japanese macaques and how these animals categorize such variation.

Green reported that playback of recorded coos can result in antiphonal calling by receivers. Relationships between peaks in primary and antiphonal calls could provide one possible index of how the sounds are being sorted. Continued testing in the operant conditioning laboratory should specifically probe the question of categorical use of the calls by making training procedures less dependent on predefined categories: for example, by examining generalization earlier in the training process, or by allowing for a greater number of categories (cf. Owren, 1990). A procedure described by Dooling, Park, Brown, Okanoya, and Soli, (1987), involving multidimensional scaling of reaction times in avian subjects performing in a "same–different" task, could be applied to natural auditory categorization of vocalizations in nonhuman primates as well.

Summary

In examining the vocal repertoires of nonhuman primates, investigators typically perform a taxonomic classification of calls, explicitly seeking to arrive at the functional categories that define call use. However, doing so usually involves an implicit assumption that species-typical perceptual processing does not critically influence category formation. Studies of basic auditory processing in Japanese macaques, on the other hand, suggest that species-typical characteristics may play a significant role in perception, which is not apparent from observation of their natural behavior or acoustic analysis of calls. These animals generally resemble humans in their absolute auditory sensitivity in the low- and middle-frequency ranges. However, they are less sensitive than humans in detecting frequency differences by an order of magnitude and approximately two to three times less precise in resolving small duration differences.

The frequency discrimination characteristics shown by Japanese macaques imply that some of the naturally occurring peaks and dips in coo calls that are clearly detectable by the human investigator do not constitute perceptually salient cues for Japanese macaques. Duration discrimination results indicate that a clear perceptual boundary related to processing of peak information may not exist in coo calls if judgments about temporal position occur in accordance with simple psychophysical considerations. This prediction is supported by discrimination data reflecting minimal detectable thresholds for peak-position differences. In the absence of a clear perceptual boundary, previous evidence pertaining to the number of categories used and placement of functional partitions should be interpreted cautiously. Overall, conditioning-based studies have indicated an important functional role for peak-position variation. However, characterizations of possible categorization involved in the use of these and other nonhuman primate calls should be treated as hypotheses subject to specific empirical testing.

References

Aslin, R., Alberts, J., & Petersen, M. R. (Eds.) (1981). *Development of perception: Psychobiological perspectives: Vol. 1. Auditory, chemosensory and somatosensory systems.* New York: Academic Press.
Beecher, M. D., Petersen, M. R., Zoloth, S. R., Moody, D. B., & Stebbins, W. C. (1979). Perception of conspecific vocalizations by Japanese macaques. *Brain, Behavior and Evolution, 16,* 443–460.
Cheney, D. L., & Seyfarth, R. M. (1982). How vervet monkeys perceive their grunts: Field playback experiments. *Animal Behaviour, 30,* 739–751.
Dooling, R. J., Park, T. J., Brown, S. D., Okanoya, K., & Soli, S. (1987). Perceptual organization of acoustic stimuli by budgerigars *(Melopsittacus undulatus)*: II. Vocal signals. *Journal of Comparative Psychology, 101,* 367–381.
Eaton, G. G. (1976). The social organization of Japanese macaques. *Scientific American, 235,* 96–106.
Ehret, G. (1987). Categorical perception of sound signals: Facts and hypotheses from animal studies. In S. Harnad (Ed.), *Categorical perception* (pp. 301–331). Cambridge: Cambridge University Press.
Gouzoules, S., Gouzoules, H., & Marler, P. (1984). Rhesus monkey *(Macaca mulatta)* screams: Representational signalling in the recruitment of agonistic aid. *Animal Behaviour, 32,* 182–193.
Green, S. (1975). The variation of vocal pattern with social situation in the Japanese monkey *(Macaca fuscata)*: A field study. In L. Rosenblum (Ed.), *Primate behavior* (Vol. 4, pp. 1–102). New York: Academic Press.
Green, S., & Marler, P. (1979). The analysis of animal communication. In P. Marler and J. G. Vandenbergh (Eds.), *Handbook of behavioral neurobiology: Vol. 3: Social behavior and communication* (pp. 73–158). New York: Plenum.
Harnad, S. (1987). *Categorical perception.* Cambridge: Cambridge University Press.
Heffner, H. E., & Heffner, R. S. (1984). Temporal lobe lesions and perception of species-specific vocalizations by macaques. *Science, 226,* 75–76.
Hopp, S. L. (1985). *Differential sensitivity of Japanese monkeys* (Macaca fuscata) *to variation along a synthetic vocal continuum.* Unpublished doctoral dissertation, University of Indiana.
Hopp, S. L., Sinnott, J. M., Owren, M. J., & Petersen, M. R. (In press). Differential sensitivity of Japanese macaques *(Macaca fuscata)* and humans *(Homo sapiens)* to peak position along a Japanese macaque coo call continuum. *Journal of Comparative Psychology.*
Jolly, A. (1985). *The evolution of primate behavior.* New York: Macmillan.
Macmillan, N. A. (1987). A psychophysical approach to processing modes. In S. Harnad (Ed.), *Categorical perception* (pp. 53–85). Cambridge: Cambridge University Press.
Marler, P. (1976). Social organization, communication and graded signals: The chimpanzee and the gorilla. In P. P. G. Bateson & R. A. Hinde (Eds.), *Growing points in ethology* (pp. 239–280). Cambridge: Cambridge University Press.

(1982). Avian and primate communication: The problem of natural categories. *Neuroscience and Biobehavioral Reviews, 6,* 87–94.

Masataka, N. (1983a). Categorical responses to natural and synthesized alarm calls in Goeldi's monkeys (*Callimico goeldi*). *Primates, 24,* 40–51.

(1983b). Psycholinguistic analyses of alarm calls of Japanese monkeys (*Macaca fuscata fuscata*). *American Journal of Primatology, 5,* 111–125.

May, B., Moody, D. B., & Stebbins, W. C. (1988). The significant features of Japanese macaque coo sounds: A psychophysical study. *Animal Behaviour, 36,* 1432–1444.

(1989). Categorical perception of conspecific communication sounds by Japanese macaques, *Macaca fuscata. Journal of the Acoustical Society of America, 85,* 837–847.

Moody, D. B., May, B., Cole, D. M., & Stebbins, W. C. (1968). The role of frequency modulation in the perception of complex stimuli by primates. *Experimental Biology, 45,* 219–232.

Owren, M. J. (1990). Auditory classification of alarm calls by vervet monkeys (*Cercopithecus aethiops*) and humans: 1. Natural calls. *Journal of Comparative Psychology, 104,* 28–40.

Owren, M. J., Hopp, S. L., Sinnott, J. M., & Petersen, M. R. (1988). Absolute auditory thresholds in three Old World monkey species (*Cercopithecus aethiops, C. neglectus, Macaca fuscata*) and humans (*Homo sapiens*). *Journal of Comparative Psychology, 102,* 99–107.

Petersen, M. R. (1978). *The perception of species-specific vocalizations by Old World monkeys.* Unpublished doctoral dissertation, University of Michigan.

(1981). Perception of acoustic communication signals by animals: Developmental perspectives and implications. In R. Aslin, J. Alberts, & M. Petersen (Eds.), *Development of perception: Psychobiological perspectives. Vol. 1: Auditory, chemosensory and somatosensory systems* (pp. 67–109). New York: Academic Press.

(1982). The perception of species-specific vocalizations by primates: A conceptual framework. In C. T. Snowdon, C. H. Brown, & M. R. Petersen (Eds.), *Primate communication* (pp. 171–211). Cambridge: Cambridge University Press.

Petersen, M. R., Beecher, M. D., Zoloth, S. R., Moody, D. B., & Stebbins, W. C. (1978). Neural lateralization of species-specific vocalizations by Japanese monkeys (*Macaca fuscata*), *Science 202,* 324–327.

Petersen, M. R., Zoloth, S. R., Beecher, M. D., Green, S., Marler, P., Moody, D. B., & Stebbins, W. C. (1984). Neural lateralization of vocalizations by Japanese macaques; Communicative significance is more important than acoustic structure. *Behavioral Neuroscience, 98,* 779–790.

Pisoni, D. (1978). Speech perception. In W. K. Estes (Ed.), *Handbook of learning and cognitive processes* (Vol. 6). Hillsdale, N.J.: Erlbaum.

Seyfarth, R. M. (1987). Vocal communication and its relation to language. In B. Smuts, D. L. Cheney, R. M. Seyfarth, R. W. Wrangham, & T. T. Struhsaker (Eds.), *Primate Societies* (pp. 440–451). Chicago: University of Chicago Press.

Seyfarth, R. M., & Cheney, D. L. (1984). The acoustic features of vervet monkey grunts. *Journal of the Acoustical Society of America, 75,* 1623–1628.

Seyfarth, R. M., Cheney, D. L., & Marler, P. (1980a). Vervet monkey alarm calls: Semantic communication in a free-ranging primate. *Animal Behaviour, 28,* 1070–1090.

(1980b). Monkey responses to three different alarm calls: Evidence of predator classification and semantic communication. *Science, 210,* 801–803.

Sinnott, J., & Aslin, R. (1986). Frequency and intensity discrimination in human infants and adults. *Journal of the Acoustical Society of America, 78,* 1986–1992.

Sinnott, J. M., Owren, M. J., & Petersen, M. R. (1987a). Auditory duration discrimination in Old World monkeys (*Macaca, Cercopithecus*). *Journal of the Acoustical Society of America, 82,* 465–470.

(1987b). Auditory frequency discrimination in primates: Species differences (*Cercopithecus, Macaca, Homo*). *Journal of Comparative Psychology, 101,* 126–131.

Sinnott, J. M., Petersen, M. R., & Hopp, S. L. (1985). Frequency and intensity discrimination in humans and monkeys. *Journal of the Acoustical Society of America, 78,* 1977–1985.

Snowdon, C. T. (1982). Linguistic and psycholinguistic approaches to primate communication. In C. T. Snowdon, C. H. Brown, & M. R. Petersen (Eds.), *Primate communication* (pp. 212–238). Cambridge: Cambridge University Press.

Snowdon, C. T., & Pola, Y. V. (1978). Interspecific and intraspecific responses to synthesized pygmy marmoset vocalizations. *Animal Behaviour, 26,* 192–206.

Struhsaker, T. T. (1967). Auditory communication among vervet monkeys (*Cercopithecus aethiops*). In S. A. Altmann (Ed.), *Social communication among primates* (pp. 281–324). Chicago: University of Chicago Press.

Takasaki, H. (1981). Troop size, habitat quality, and home range area in Japanese macaques. *Behavioral Ecology and Sociobiology, 9,* 277–281.

Zoloth, S., & Green, S. (1979). Monkey vocalizations and human speech: Parallels in perception? *Brain, Behavior and Evolution, 16,* 430–442.

Zoloth, S. R., Petersen, M. R., Beecher, M. D., Green, S., Marler, P., Moody, D. B., & Stebbins, W. (1979). Species-specific perceptual processing of vocal sounds by monkeys. *Science, 204,* 870–872.

7. Vocal development in nonhuman primates

DAVID SYMMES AND MAXEEN BIBEN

Background

The number of laboratory and field investigations on vocal development (as opposed to speculations on the subject) has shown a gratifying surge in the last 10 years. This increasing data base has generated several recent review articles that attempt to synthesize the evidence and generate models which may help resolve the ancient "nature versus nurture" dilemma (Newman & Symmes, 1982; Seyfarth, 1987; Snowdon, 1988; Snowdon, French, & Cleveland, 1986). Nowhere do the theoretical biases of primatologists and child development experts diverge more clearly than in dealing with this old problem. The development of language skills in the human infant is viewed as enormously influenced by nurture, and the diligent search for genetic factors is often unrewarded and never supports a model in which nature is dominant.

The development of ape and monkey vocal communication, however, is seen as driven primarily by genetic factors (an "almost casually accepted view," Newman & Symmes, 1982). It may be observed that, once again, constraints on experimental design play an important role in forming such biases; neither nature nor nurture may be manipulated deliberately in human children, for valid ethical reasons, but naturally occurring variation in cultural environment provides a rich source of data on the role of nurture. In animals, both may be manipulated, but controlling rearing conditions, or altering them systematically, is by far the most difficult experiment to carry out. We thus find more studies which exploit natural variation in breeding patterns, hybridization, and similar factors in the nonhuman primate literature.

It is our intent to summarize in a critical manner recent evidence that pertains to vocal development in monkeys and apes. Unfortunately a growing fraction of such evidence is appearing in nonprimary form, free of the constraints of anonymous peer review and short on experimental

123

detail. This problem is by no means confined to the present field, but it does generate an atmosphere in which casually accepted views abound. Three biases are acknowledged by the present authors. One is that the critical experiments regarding the existence of vocal learning in primates have not been done, or done well. (We hope that they may soon be done.) A second is that many lines of evidence may be cited as encouraging this search, although these data are limited, descriptive, indirect, and at times vulnerable to reinterpretation. Finally, we decry the lack of fundamental behavioral data on normal development in primates which would permit a more focused search. We can find little on the content and frequency of early vocal interaction in primate infants, a data base that in principal can be obtained easily and would allow us to make informed guesses about the kinds of deprivation that might expose the role of nurture. We present some new evidence of our own on the squirrel monkey, which begins the study of early vocal interaction in that species.

Recent research in monkey vocalization

Vocalizations that enter or leave the vocal repertoire with maturation

There are many anecdotal accounts of calls made by adult primates which are not heard from infants or, in some cases, juveniles. We cite here only evidence in which spectrographic techniques were included in a comprehensive approach to the vocal repertoire. Probably the best evidence for the appearance of new call types with maturation is found in the work of Gautier on the talapoin monkey (Gautier, 1974). For example, the Type 1 call (noisy), which is well described, is not heard before the age of 1 year. It may function as a mobbing call in this species. Another promising finding is in the cotton-top tamarin (Snowdon, Cleveland, & French, 1983). Three variants of the "long call" are used by adult tamarins, but only one by infants and juveniles. The "normal" and "quiet" long calls do not appear before 2 years of age and are associated with reproductive maturation. Snowdon has offered the speculation that the "combination long call" (the first to appear, and the most variable) has a functional equivalence to subsong in birds, while the normal and quiet long call variants are comparable to full song, with functions of territorial defense and social cohesion (Snowdon et al., 1986). The observation that hormonal changes may facilitate or trigger vocal patterns in primates reminds us of similar phenomena in birds. If a combined effect of appropriate acoustic models and endocrine influence could be demonstrated, then one would indeed have an excellent model of evolutionary convergence.

Parallels between primate vocal behavior and singing in birds have long been proposed (Marler, 1970), but in our view they may have more a formal than functional utility. The bird behavior for which we must seek primate parallels is seasonal, gender-specific, and entirely territorial. Many primates do not defend territories, do vocalize all year, and have ample contributions from both sexes. Snowdon's suggestion that study of monagamous, territorial primates like cotton-top tamarins may exploit a genuine parallel is an intriguing one.

Another example of a new call entering the repertoire comes from the squirrel monkey. In an early report, Winter, Handley, Ploog, and Schott (1973) described a delayed appearance of the "twitter / trill" call, which was not observed until the monkeys were 3 months of age. This finding was especially significant in light of the more general finding that most elements of the repertoire were fully differentiated within a few days of birth. The twitter / trill (now usually named "twitter group"; see Newman, 1985) is a complex, repeating-element call with pronounced frequency modulation (FM). It may be the most demanding call in this species' repertoire in terms of elaboration of neural patterning, and therefore one might expect a slower course of development than in calls of simpler structure. However, the place of this evidence regarding twitters in the present scheme is somewhat unclear; Winter and his colleagues also state that the twitter differentiated out of another (infantile) call, the "location trill," under which reasoning it properly belongs in the next section of this review.

The existence of calls that are used by infants but not by adults is even more frequently reported in the literature. For instance, Gautier (1974) identified a Type 2d call given only by very young infant talapoins, and two calls (Types 3 and 6a) which were rare in adults. The Type 3 call is an example of a separation or isolation call, which is common in infant mammals and in some cases continues into adulthood (for example, in the squirrel monkey).

Many questions remain to be answered about the nature of such temporary vocal forms and their fate in ontogeny. A distinction should be made between call types that truly disappear and those that undergo gradual modification, including the development of variant forms. It is likely that most so-called infant vocalizations belong in the latter category, including examples from vervets and macaques mentioned later in this essay. We are aware of only one reasonably well-documented example of loss from the repertoire of a prominent vocal type during development in New World monkeys. This is the "baby-Piepen call," a type of squirrel monkey isolation call first described by Ploog, Hopf, and Winter (1967). Baby-Piepen are rarely heard after 12 weeks of age (Lieblich, Symmes, Newman, & Shapiro, 1980) but can be elicited by stressful separation from the mother at as late as 24 weeks (Symmes & Biben, 1985). Similar regression to infantile vocal behavior has been noted in juvenile pygmy marmosets when new infant siblings are born (Snowdon, 1989). Calls fitting the description of baby-Piepen, and other typically infantile vocalizations, were obtained from adult males following bilateral tegmental lesions (Newman & MacLean, 1982). This suggests that neural circuitry governing production of the call remains intact but dormant in the adult.

Infantile calls are probably multifunctional. In addition to having a determinative or productive role in vocal development, they may also identify the caller's infantile status. Calls that disappear from the repertoire without modification cannot have the former function but may have the latter.

Vocalizations that demonstrate structural maturation to the adult form

There is a good deal of evidence regarding changes in detailed acoustic structure of certain calls with age, and some of it has been subject to varied interpretation. In pygmy marmosets, the "closed-mouth trill" is the best-studied example from a group of three structurally related but semantically distinct trills. It has been shown to change, over about 40 weeks, from an immature form to an adult form. Duration increases, but average pitch and pitch instability both decline over this period. Snowdon (1988) has argued, on indirect evidence, that these changes are not likely to be dependent on physical maturation but reflect a "flexibility" which cannot be attributed to learning, on present evidence.

In squirrel monkeys, Lieblich and his colleagues (1980) reported thorough parametric studies of the "isolation peep" from birth to 52 weeks of age. Several parameters of the call changed significantly with age, with the greatest change being an increase in call duration. This particular finding was reported earlier by Winter and his colleagues (1973). In the light of more recent evidence that both adult and juvenile squirrel monkeys can alter duration of isolation peeps as a function of separation distance (Masataka & Symmes, 1986), it seems less likely that the reported increases in duration with age were due to physical maturation and more likely that they were an example of acquiring adult contextual rules (see the section entitled "Acquisition of Contextual Rules for Vocalizing and Interpreting Environmental Sounds" later in this chapter).

The major findings of Lieblich and his coresearchers were the presence of individual signature at early ages (later confirmed behaviorally by Symmes and Biben, 1985) and the presence of strong population differences between Roman-arch and Gothic-arch monkeys at early ages (later confirmed behaviorally by Snowdon, Coe, & Hodun, 1985). Both of these findings should probably be interpreted as evidence for the strong role of genetic factors in isolation peep structure. Nonetheless, we cannot rule out a contribution of learning in some details such as curvature and slope that also showed age-related changes. It should be noted that Lieblich and his colleagues looked for evidence that offspring isolation peeps resembled maternal isolation peeps and found very little. However, there is no reason to believe that in this highly social species the most frequently heard isolation peep model was from the mother, since infants could easily imitate aunts or nearby group members.

In vervet monkeys the "grunt" call is used by infants at a very early age but in acoustically immature form. Several years are required for the stabilization of this call to its adult form, which involves at least four variants that are predictably used in specific social contexts (Seyfarth & Cheney, 1986). Several acoustic parameters of grunts change over the period from infancy to adolescence. Somewhat surprisingly (in comparison with the data cited earlier), call duration correlates negatively with age. Dominant frequency declines with age, and the number of repeating units per call also declines.

Further evidence for ontogenetic changes in vocal production is found in a recent study of the various "screams" used by pigtail macaques to recruit allies during agonistic encounters (Gouzoules & Gouzoules, 1989). Screams can be classified, by discriminant analysis, into four contexts, associated with rank of the opponent and severity of the aggression. Screams of 1–2-year-olds are misclassified more often than those of older animals, in part because of errors in production. Some of these changes may be attributed to maturation; for instance, the significantly higher pitch of youngsters' screams may be due to smaller size. However, no such simple explanation is evident for the age-related changes in frequency modulation or bandwidth, suggesting that more complex factors may also be at work.

Simple explanations are also not in order for the "Wrr," a trilled call of vervets (Hauser, 1989). Infant vervets (0–3 months old) produce Wrrs with clearly differentiated pulsatile structure, as do adult vervets (although the contexts are different.) However, at about 3 months, trilled calls disappear entirely from the infant's vocal repertoire, only to reappear in a somewhat altered form at approximately 10 months of age. The resurrected Wrrs are not as clearly pulsed as infant and adult Wrrs, but their contextual usage approximates that of the adult, and both production and usage skills gradually improve over a period of years. The apparent loss, during the 7-month hiatus period, of the motor skill needed to produce distinct pulses demands an explanation. Hauser speculates that this may be due to interference from the acquisition of other calls in the repertoire, similar to the phenomenon of "phonemic regression" in human children who temporarily lose the ability to correctly pronounce some words when they begin to use them in a more complex language milieu.

Vocalizations that are altered by experimental manipulation of rearing conditions

Rational and consistent manipulation of rearing conditions in studies of primate vocal development is quite difficult to achieve. At one extreme is removal of all physical contact with mothers and peers, and minimal human interaction, a procedure which in rhesus macaques, at least, produces profound and enduring emotional disturbances (Harlow, Harlow, & Suomi, 1971; Mitchell, 1968). It has been reported that vocal abnormalities accompany these deficits, even when acoustic contact with normal monkeys is permitted (Newman & Symmes, 1974).

At the other extreme, from the point of view of emotional as opposed to cognitive deprivation, are those studies which have raised apes with enormous attention and stimulation from their human caretakers, including efforts to teach them new forms of communication (review in Ristau & Robbins, 1982). While these studies have had success in training apes to communicate with humans, and even other apes, using tactile or mechanical means, those which addressed the acoustic realm were disappointing. The evidence is simply not convincing that apes can learn new sounds imitatively, altering to some extent their species-typical repertoire. An exception worthy of note is a single report of a pygmy chimpanzee reared in a human environment (Hopkins & Savage-Rumbaugh, 1986). This individual made all the species-typical vocalizations (a conclusion supported by spectrographic evidence) but also developed several functional vocalizations that were not found in pygmy chimpanzees raised in captivity without intense human contact. This finding, and others of a more anecdotal nature (Hayes & Hayes, 1951), raise the possibility that unusual species-atypical sounds may be acquired by apes through learning. Whether the learning is imitative is not clear.

Somewhere in the middle are cases where monkeys or apes were hand raised with some effort to replace species-typical caregiving behaviors with human substitutes but no explicit training to communicate (Boutan, 1913; Gautier, 1966; Winter et al, 1973). These studies (and others no doubt unreported) have suffered from wide differences in the amount and kind of stimulation given the young subjects and have usually not included detailed comparison of the call repertoire at various ages with control information. It is fair to say that such studies have not contributed much to understanding normal vocal development, but they have generally supported a negative conclusion; that is, the hand-reared primate vocalizes normally, provided emotional disturbances are largely avoided.

The most widely cited report in the area of altered acoustic input during development is that of Winter and his colleagues (1973). In this study, four infant squirrel monkeys were raised with their muted mothers alone for 2 weeks, then as a group of four pairs in a single room until age 6 months. One animal was subjected to a deafening procedure at 5 days of age and died at age 4 months. Except for abnormal sounds made by the mother, and sounds made by peers from 14 days onward the young monkeys were isolated from species-typical acoustic input. No details were given regarding the methods of assuring removal of sounds from other monkeys in the area, a critical problem in our experience, since (1) squirrel monkeys have acute hearing, and (2) other studies have shown that even a few minutes of stimulation can compensate for longer deprivation (Thielcke-Poltz & Thielcke, 1960). Nevertheless, the conclusion of this study was that the vocal repertoire appeared normal with respect to acoustic detail and contextual usage, despite rearing without models, and that with the exception of one call type (mentioned earlier) these communication skills were present shortly after birth.

The most effective and convincing route of evidence for the nature–nurture hypothesis is the use of cross-fostering experiments, difficult but by no means impossible in nonhuman primates. Japanese and rhesus macaques are closely related species which readily adopt each other's offspring if the transfer is done with care (Owren & Dieter, 1989). Moreover, their vocal repertoires contain distinctive calls given in similar contexts, including a foraging call which is not given by youngsters until their first birthday. The call is tonal, with prominent harmonic overtones, in both species, but the two differ reliably in the peak frequency achieved by the lowest tonal band.

In a cross-fostering experiment involving one Japanese and two rhesus infants, Masataka and Fujita (1989) recorded foraging calls from both the cross-fostered and normally reared youngsters at 1 year of age. Spectrographic evidence clearly showed that a yearling's foraging calls resembled those of the mother who raised him. Furthermore, playback of foraging calls to adult Japanese and rhesus macaques showed that monkeys preferred the calls of their own species but were unable to tell whether those calls were made by the cross-fostered or the normally reared youngsters. Despite the small sample, these data are a strong argument in support of a role for learning in primate vocal development, all the more so because the prolonged latency of appearance for this call provides ample time for learning to occur. This exciting result should stimulate a renewed search for learning effects on vocal production in other calls and other species.

Acquisition of contextual rules for vocalizing and interpreting environmental sounds

A complex problem in animal communication, and hence in vocal development, concerns the way semantic rules are acquired and employed. Mentalists have long insisted that an internal state superficially similar to human consciousness exists in animals and that processes occurring within that state govern the use and interpretation of vocal signals (the "assessment state" of Green & Marler, 1979). Nativists have found such speculation unnecessary and consider vocal signals to be a form of fixed action pattern, with limited semantic content and obligatory rather than volitional production (Myers, 1976). In our view, the mentalists are showing signs of carrying the field, but the evidence is thin, and the more speculative aspects of their arguments should certainly be approached with due caution.

The source of much of the latest evidence is a continuing study of the vervet monkey of East Africa, which has been brilliantly advanced by Struhsaker, Marler, Seyfarth, Cheney, and others. It is clear that vervets convey in their alarm calls information about the source of danger, and that the calls act as symbolic referents of the predator (Seyfarth & Cheney, 1986). Of great interest in the present context are the further observations that young vervets have not mastered the rules for making alarm calls. They give the alarm when none is needed: that is, when the animal encountered is not dangerous to vervets. This is more likely if the encounter is sudden and at close range. Young vervets also respond inappropriately to the alarm calls of adults that do signal real danger, an error which is corrected in direct relation to an infant's exposure to these calls (Hauser, 1988). The potentially grave consequences of this type of error are usually avoided, however, by the tendency of youngsters to watch adults and do what they do. A different call (the grunt) is used by vervets in intraspecific greeting contexts, and young animals again acquire the ability to use the variant forms in correct contexts some time after mastering the production. All of these examples of delayed acquisition of vocal competence have rather long and complex temporal courses, characterized by different kinds of errors at different ages. The authors conclude that comprehension precedes production, a finding which parallels human speech acquisition, and that at least 2 years are required to achieve full adult skills (Seyfarth & Cheney, 1986). Age-related improvement has also been reported recently for context-appropriate usage of pigtail macaques' agonistic screams (Gouzoules & Gouzoules, 1989).

Are the Seyfarth and Cheney data on alarm call ontogeny evidence for learning? Their own assessment is conservative, noting that reinforcement by adults of appropriate usage by youngsters occurs but may not be necessary. However, if adults did not reinforce correct categorization, predators would probably punish incorrect categorization. Certainly, similar types of categorical mastery by human children would be called learning, although maturation, intelligence, and experience in related discriminations would all play a part.

There is an admirable reluctance to overstep the data in many of the reports so far discussed. Direct tests of the role of vocal models in development are difficult, but progress elsewhere is creating opportunities. For example, a growing number of studies discloses complex rules for vocal communication in primates of both the Old and New World (Biben, Symmes, & Masataka, 1986; Cleveland & Snowdon, 1982; Dittus, 1984; Gouzoules, Gouzoules, & Marler, 1984; Green, 1975; Maurus, Kühlmorgen, Wiesner, Barclay, & Streit, 1985; Robinson, 1984; Symmes & Biben, 1988). These data all point to a system of signals and signal use that is characterized by flexible volitional use (despite individual adaptations) and often employs acoustically similar variants within what was initially thought to be a monolithic call type. We therefore have available a number of behavioral models that lend themselves well to the task of defining the interactions of nature and nurture which underlie vocal development. To date, the models have not been exploited to this end, although exciting possibilities for the use of longitudinal data are now being formulated (Gouzoules & Gouzoules, 1989).

Vocal play and vocalizations associated with play

The determinative role of babbling, or vocal play, in language acquisition in human children (but not in adults learning a second language) has been an incentive to seek parallels in primate vocal development. At first considered a sideline on the road to adult speech, babbling has since been shown to have many points of continuity with early speech (e.g., Oller, Wiemann, Doyle, & Ross, 1975). *Babbling* is by no means an easy term to define. Students of human speech development have found it productive to divide babbling into several categories, each characterized by distinctive vocal content and following a predictable developmental progression: for example, the "canonical babbling" and "variegated babbling" stages described by Oller (1980). Such differentiation has not made it any easier to find examples of similar behavior in the development of monkeys and apes. To date, the only use of the term in the primate literature was as a tentative description of a category of vocal output heard in infant cotton-top tamarins (Snowdon et al., 1986). This included elements of adult vocalizations, some with imperfect structure, given out of context and in unusual juxtapositions. Following the terminology of the human literature, Snowdon used the term "linguistic play" to describe the infants' output, although it is unclear from his description of the context (infant left alone by caregiver) whether the conditions usually associated with play (such as a lack of stress and the meeting of basic needs) obtained. Satisfying the criteria for play may be as important to identifying instances of babbling as is the vocal content of the utterances themselves.

Use of the term "vocal play" to describe any or all of the stages of babbling derives from the observation that human infants appear to enjoy producing these sounds and emit them during periods of contentment with no apparent intention to communicate with the caregiver. In the early stages of babbling, beginning in the 5th month of life, the tactile sensations as well as the noises produced by blowing air, food, or saliva through a constriction in the mouth or pharynx appear to be self-reinforcing and pleasurable to infants (Stark, 1980). Babbling in older children accompanies periods of absorbed play with objects.

While babbling as a form of amusement has not yet been identified in nonhuman primates, it is worth noting that vocal output of an unusually variable nature does accompany social play (but not object play) in a small number of primates. These play vocalizations have recently received intensive study in two species where they are particularly prominent, the squirrel monkey (Biben & Symmes, 1986) and the cotton-top tamarin (Goedeking & Immelmann, 1986).

There are many apparent similarities between vocalizations made during play and vocal play or babbling. Content is one of these. In squirrel monkeys, for instance, vocal output during play includes noisy and tonal elements, some with pronounced FM. These are juxtaposed in various ways to make up four varieties of peep vocalizations which are typically heard only during play. Babbling is abandoned by human children as they develop speech, subsong drops out of the repertoire of maturing birds, and play peeps (and play behavior) drop out of the squirrel monkey repertoire at puberty. Babbling children do not appear to seek, nor do they usually receive, responses based on the content of their utterances. Similarly, no communicative function – that is, no role in affecting the behavior of the play partner – was found for play vocalizations in either monkey species. Rather, the vocal output seemed to be a reflection of the vocalizer's motivation to play or even a source of pleasure in itself. Neither study directly addressed an ontogenetic role for play vocalizations, and, indeed, no good case can be made, because play peeps, unlike babbling, are not a precursor to adult forms. Other types of peeps appear in adult form before or at the same time as play peeps. Therefore play vocalizations, although superficially similar to babbling, are not vocal play. There is therefore not sufficient evidence at this time to determine whether or not the vocal behavior of tamarins cited by Snowdon and his colleagues is vocal play.

Early vocal interactions in the squirrel monkey

An understanding of the processes of vocal development in any species must necessarily begin from a base of knowledge of what is normal output for that species, and the more complete the record the better. We have recently begun an intensive study of vocal development in squirrel monkeys in captive but socially rich conditions, beginning with the first week of life. Of particular interest to us are affiliative calls like the "chuck," which are used in variable, perhaps conversational, ways (Biben et al., 1986; Symmes & Biben, 1988) and that have a slow course of development.

In our preliminary investigations of early vocal behavior, we chose to study isolated mother-infant dyads to simplify the problem of identifying vocalizers. Unfortunately, no one vocalized much in such conditions. Mothers cared for their infants in the usual ways but rarely vocalized to them during the first few months of life. Youngsters, too, made few vocalizations until they began to venture from their mothers' backs in the second or third month (Fig. 7.1). Separated infants made liberal use of isolation peeps and shorter peeps, which seemed to keep the mother abreast of the infant's whereabouts. When the infant was safely returned to the mother's back, silence again reigned.

Only after we repeated the experiments with additional females in the cages did the auditory environment come to life, with frequent exchanges between and among adult females. A typical rate of vocalizing for a group of four adult females (the number studied here) under unstressed quotidien conditions is 172 (± 56, SD) calls per hour (unpublished observations based on 10 hour-long recording sessions). It also was clear that some vocalizations were directed exclusively to infants, as evidenced by proximity, approach, or continued gaze. These calls, which we have termed "caregiver calls," because of their use in several contexts of infant care, were first described by Dumond (1968) and Baldwin (1969). They are tonal calls of relatively low (for squirrel monkeys) fundamental frequency, variable duration, prominent harmonic structure, and variable FM elements concentrated at the ends of calls (Fig. 7.2). Caregiver calls are the major form of address to infants (Biben, Symmes, & Bernhards, 1989), a specificity of usage shared with "motherese," the speech directed by human adults to babies (see Fernald, chapter 13 in the present volume). Another similarity to motherese is the close relationship of pitch contour to context in both (see M. Papoušek, chapter 12 in this volume).

In squirrel monkeys, both mothers and aunts (including nulliparous young females, nonreproductive older females, and mothers who had lost their infants) used caregiver calls. Mothers used relatively short, flat variants of the call while their infants nursed and, with infants old enough to wander, longer variants with terminal frequency leaps to call them back to nurse or for protection. Aunts used more exaggerated variants (greater duration, pitch range, frequency leaps than those of mothers) as part of a general inspection and interest in infants evident from the day of birth. Aunts approached and uttered caregiver calls at close range to awake and even to sleeping infants, while the mother ignored the goings on.

The significance of aunts' caregiver calls became more clear when, in

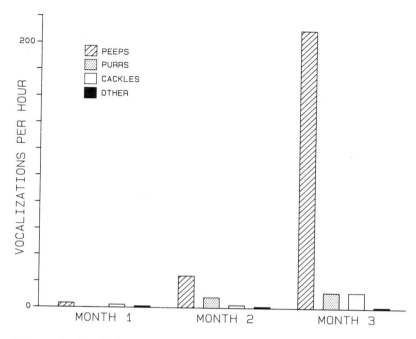

Figure 7.1. Graph depicting rate and type of vocalizing by infant squirrel monkeys in the first 3 months of life, when housed alone with the mother. (Call types from Newman, 1985.)

the first or second week of life, infants began to look toward the calling aunt and to utter vocalizations in return. In a social group with four adult females, infants received an average of 81 calls per hour in their first month of life; more than 90% of these were made by aunts. Infants 1–4 weeks old responded to about 20% of the caregiver calls directed to them, which, combined with "spontaneously" emitted calls, yielded a vocalization rate of 19 infant calls per hour in a social setting, as compared to 7 calls per hour when housed with the mother alone.

Spontaneous calling by infants amounted to only about 15% of their production during the first month, most vocalizing occurring in response to aunts' caregiver calls. The rate of spontaneous calling increased dramatically, to 90% or more, when infants left the mothers' backs. Two- and 3-month-old infants, when off their mothers' backs, received fewer caregiver calls from aunts, but mothers' rate of calling for retrieval and nursing increased. In addition to caregiver calls made in the contexts just mentioned, both aunts and mothers responded to infants' peeps with caregiver calls. Interestingly, mothers rarely addressed

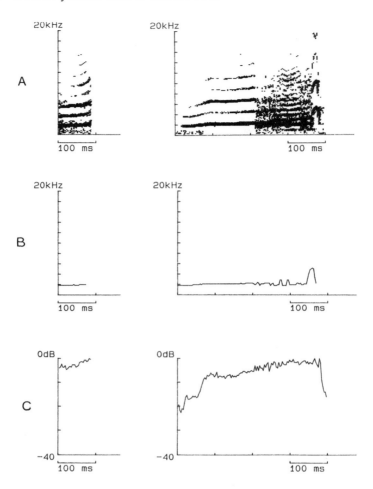

Figure 7.2. (A) Wideband sound spectrograms of caregiver calls recorded from a mother squirrel monkey while nursing her infant *(left)* and from an aunt while inspecting the infant *(right)*; (B) graph of dominant pitch contours for the same calls; (C) graph of amplitude contours for the same calls.

their own infants in the context of inspection. Instead, they acted as aunts, giving caregiver calls to the infants of others.

We are currently analyzing the infantile vocal output from this study, which represents the earliest instances of interactive vocal behavior in this species. The role of aunts in encouraging infant vocal production is an observation which calls into question the restricted traditional view of allomothering as an action performed by a young nulliparous female to gain experience in mothering and points out the importance of the social milieu in stimulating vocal behavior, both adult and infantile.

Future of research in vocal development

It is our view that the subject of vocal development in primates is poised on the edge of a new and highly productive period of research. The weight of direct evidence, although slight in volume and often flawed, is that genetic factors dominate to the exclusion of environmental factors. The weight of indirect evidence is substantial, but inherently insufficient. No amount of description of complex vocal behavior of adult primates, nor careful plotting of its maturation, can substitute for a demonstration of the acoustic models that are critical. We have ample reason to believe that neural substrates have their own timetables in development, and we know that endocrinological changes impinge on these and hence on behavior. It is no doubt valuable to learn more about the limits of heritability of vocal traits through hybridization and selective trait breeding (Newman & Symmes, 1982), but we cannot discover the importance of vocal learning by subtraction. Just as in the remarkable work on song learning in white-crowned sparrows (Marler & Tamura, 1964), we must find the experimental paradigms that permit removal or alteration of the acoustic model in order to create a logically satisfying argument.

Removal of acoustic input in developing primates is quite difficult. Emotional disturbances which accompany isolation rearing confuse, rather than clarify, the place of vocal models. Rearing infants with normal hearing away from critical input is possible but places almost insurmountable demands on laboratory facilities, when one considers the length of time over which the deprivation must be maintained. Deafening infant monkeys is probably an unacceptable approach, both ethically and because the selective surgical destruction of the organ of hearing may be impossible. Attempts to produce squirrel monkeys free of crippling vestibular deficits with demonstrated absence of hearing have failed (Jürgens, personal communication).

Alteration of acoustic input appears to be the method of choice and includes cross-fostering to mothers with differing vocal characteristics, raising infants with their natural mothers (muted or speaking) but in social groups with dialect differences, and artificial alteration of sound input (extreme reverberation, or masking), and repetitive-playback settings. From this range of experimental designs may come the evidence needed to demonstrate that vocal learning occurs in subhuman primates, as it does in birds and humans.

We find it somewhat surprising that some workers in this field appear painfully reluctant to offer explanations of their data which invoke learning. No similar reluctance constrains students of human language acquisition, and we suggest that several of the authors whose work is reviewed here have failed to propose the simplest explanation of their data: that monkeys and apes have a limited capacity for modifying vocal output and a great capacity for refining contextual usage, both of which are dependent on the presence of adequate models and reinforcement. Occam's razor is an indispensable instrument in the ethologist's bag, as long as it does not cut off imaginative experimentation.

References

Baldwin, J. D. (1969). The ontogeny of social behavior of squirrel monkeys (*Saimiri sciureus*) in a seminatural environment. *Folia Primatologica, 11*, 35–79.

Biben, M., & Symmes, D. (1986). Play vocalizations of squirrel monkeys (*Saimiri sciureus*). *Folia Primatologica, 46*, 173–182.

Biben, M., Symmes, D., & Bernhards, D. (1989). Contour variables in vocal communication between squirrel monkey mothers and infants. *Developmental Psychobiology, 22*(6), 617–631.

Biben, M., Symmes, D., & Masataka, N. (1986). Temporal and structural analysis of affiliative vocal exchanges in squirrel monkeys (*Saimiri sciureus*). *Behaviour, 98*, 259–273.

Boutan, L. (1913). Le Pseudo-langage. Observations effectuées sur un anthropoide: Le Gibbon (*Hylobates leucogenys* Ogilby). *Actes de la Société Linnéenne de Bordeaux, 67*, 5–80.

Cleveland, J., & Snowdon, C. T. (1982). The complex vocal repertoire of the adult cotton-top tamarin (*Saguinus oedipus oedipus*). *Zeitschrift für Tierpsychologie, 58*, 231–270.

Dittus, W. (1984). Toque macaque food calls: Semantic communication concerning food distribution in the environment. *Animal Behaviour, 32*, 470–477.

Dumond, F. (1968). The squirrel monkey in a seminatural environment. In L. A. Rosenblum & R. W. Cooper (Eds.), *The squirrel monkey* (pp. 88–145). New York: Academic Press.

Gautier, J. -P. (1966). Mimiques, postures et vocalises chez un jeune singe, *Miopithecus talapoin* captif en milieu humain. *Bulletin de la Société Scientifique de Bretagne, 16*, 67–79.

———(1974). Field and laboratory studies of the vocalizations of talapoin monkeys (*Miopithecus talapoin*). *Behaviour, 51*, 209–273.

Goedeking, P., & Immelmann, K. (1986). Vocal cues in cotton-top tamarin play vocalizations. *Ethology, 73*, 219–224.

Gouzoules, H., & Gouzoules, S. (1989). Design features and developmental modification of pigtail macaque, *Macaca nemestrina*, agonistic screams. *Animal Behaviour, 37*, 383–401.

Gouzoules, S., Gouzoules, H., & Marler, P. (1984). Rhesus monkey (*Macaca mu-*

latta) screams: Representational signalling in the recruitment of agonistic aid. *Animal Behaviour, 32,* 182–193.

Green, S. (1975). Variation of vocal pattern with social situation in the Japanese monkey (*Macaca fuscata*): A field study. In L. A. Rosenblum (Ed.), *Primate behavior* (Vol. 4, pp. 1–102). New York: Academic Press.

Green, S., & Marler, P. (1979). The analysis of animal communication. In P. Marler & J. G. Vandenbergh (Eds.), *Handbook of behavioral neurobiology* (Vol. 3). New York: Plenum.

Harlow, H., Harlow, M., & Suomi, S. (1971). From thought to therapy: Lessons from a primate laboratory. *American Scientist, 59,* 538–549.

Hauser, M. D. (1988). How vervet monkeys learn to recognize starling alarm calls: The role of experience. *Behaviour, 105,* 187–201.

(1989). Ontogenetic changes in the comprehension and production of vervet monkey (*Cercopithecus aethiops*) vocalizations. *Journal of Comparative Psychology, 103*(2), 149–158.

Hayes, K. J., & Hayes, C. (1951). The intellectual development of a home-raised chimpanzee. *Proceedings of the American Philosophical Society, 95,* 105–109.

Hopkins, W. D., & Savage-Rumbaugh, E. S. (1986). Vocal communication in the pygmy chimpanzee (*Pan paniscus*) as a result of differential rearing experiences. *American Journal of Primatology, 10,* 407–408.

Lieblich, A., Symmes, D., Newman, J. D., & Shapiro, M. (1980). Development of the isolation peep in laboratory-bred squirrel monkeys. *Animal Behaviour, 28,* 1–9.

Marler, P. (1970). Birdsong and speech development: Could there be parallels? *American Scientist, 58,* 669–673.

Marler, P., & Tamura, M. (1964). Culturally transmitted patterns of vocal behavior in sparrows. *Science, 146,* 1483–1486.

Masataka, N., & Fujita, N. (1989). Vocal learning of Japanese and rhesus monkeys. *Behaviour, 109*(3–4), 191–199.

Masataka, N., & Symmes, D. (1986). Effect of separation distance on isolation call structure in squirrel monkeys (*Saimiri sciureus*). *American Journal of Primatology, 10,* 271–278.

Maurus, M., Kühlmorgen, B., Wiesner, E., Barclay, D., & Streit, K. (1985). "Dialogues" between squirrel monkeys. *Language and Communication, 5*(3), 185–191.

Mitchell, G. (1968). Persistent behavior pathology in rhesus monkeys following early social isolation. *Folia Primatologica, 8,* 132–147.

Myers, R. E. (1976). Comparative neurology of vocalization and speech: Proof of a dichotomy. In S. Harnad, H. D. Steklis, & J. Lancaster (Eds.), *Origins and evolution of language and speech* (pp. 745–757). New York: New York Academy of Sciences.

Newman, J. D. (1985). Squirrel monkey communication. In L. A. Rosenblum and C. Coe (Eds.), *Handbook of squirrel monkey research* (pp. 99–126). New York: Plenum.

Newman, J. D., & MacLean, P. D. (1982). Effects of tegmental lesions on the isolation call of squirrel monkeys. *Brain Research, 232,* 317–329.

Newman, J. D., & Symmes, D. (1974). Vocal pathology in socially deprived monkeys. *Developmental Psychobiology, 7,* 351–358.

(1982). Inheritance and experience in the acquisition of primate acoustic behavior. In C. T. Snowdon, C. H. Brown, & M. R. Petersen (Eds.), *Primate communication* (pp. 259–278). Cambridge: Cambridge University Press.

Oller, D. K. (1980). The emergence of the sounds of speech in infancy. In G.

Yeni-Komshian, J. Kavanaugh, & C. A. Ferguson (Eds.), *Child phonology*: Vol. 1. *Production* (pp. 93–112). New York: Academic Press.

Oller, D. K., Wiemann, L., Doyle, W., & Ross, C. (1975). Infant babbling and speech. *Journal of Child Language, 3*, 1–11.

Owren, M. J., & Dieter, J. A. (1989). Infant cross-fostering between Japanese (*Macaca fuscata*) and rhesus macaques (*M. mulatta*). *American Journal of Primatology, 18*, 245–250.

Ploog, D., Hopf, S., & Winter, P. (1967). Ontogenese des Verhaltens von Totenkopfaffen (*Saimiri sciureus*). *Psychologische Forschung, 31*, 1–41.

Ristau, C., & Robbins, D. (1982). Language in the great apes: A critical review. In J. Rosenblatt, R. A. Hinde, C. Beer, & M. C. Busnel (Eds.), *Advances in the Study of Behavior* (Vol. 12). New York: Academic Press.

Robinson, J. G. (1984). Syntactic structures in the vocalizations of wedge-capped capuchin monkeys, *Cebus olivaceus*. *Behaviour, 90*, 46–79.

Seyfarth, R. (1987). Vocal communication and its relation to language. In B. Smuts, D. Cheney, R. Seyfarth, R. Wrangham, & T. Struhsaker (Eds.), *Primate societies* (pp. 440–451). Chicago: University of Chicago Press.

Seyfarth, R., & Cheney, D. (1986). Vocal development in vervet monkeys. *Animal Behaviour, 34*, 1640–1658.

Snowdon, C. (1988). Communication as social interaction: Its importance in ontogeny and adult behavior. In D. Todt, P. Goedeking, & D. Symmes (Eds.), *Primate vocal communication* (pp. 108–122). Berlin: Springer.

(1989). Vocal communication in New World monkeys. *Journal of Human Evolution, 18*, 611–633.

Snowdon, C., Cleveland, J., & French, J. (1983). Responses to context and individual specific cues in cotton-top tamarin long calls. *Animal Behaviour, 31*, 92–101.

Snowdon, C., Coe, C., & Hodun, A. (1985). Population recognition of infant isolation peeps in the squirrel monkey. *Animal Behaviour, 33*, 1145–1151.

Snowdon, C., French, J., & Cleveland, J. (1986). Ontogeny of primate vocalizations: Models from bird song and human speech. In D. Taub & F. A. King (Eds.) *Current perspectives in primate social dynamics* (pp. 389–402). New York: Van Nostrand Reinhold.

Stark, R. E. (1980). Stages of speech development in the first year of life. In G. Yeni-Komshian, J. Kavanaugh, & C. A. Ferguson (Eds.), *Child phonology*: Vol. 1. *Production* (pp. 73–92). New York: Academic Press.

Symmes, D., & Biben, M. (1988). Conversational vocal exchanges in squirrel monkeys. In D. Todt, P. Goedeking, & D. Symmes (Eds.), *Primate vocal communication* (pp. 123–132). Berlin: Springer.

(1985). Maternal recognition of individual infant squirrel monkeys from isolation call playbacks. *American Journal of Primatology, 9*, 39–46.

Thielcke-Poltz, H., & Thielcke, G. (1960). Akustisches Lernen verschieden alter schallisolierter Amseln (*Turdus merula* L.) und die Entwicklung erlernter Motive ohne und mit künstlichem Einfluss von Testosteron. *Zeitschrift für Tierpsychologie, 17*, 211–244.

Winter, P., Handley, P., Ploog, D., & Schott, D. (1973). Ontogeny of squirrel monkey calls under normal conditions and under acoustic isolation. *Behaviour, 47*, 230–239.

PART III

Development of nonverbal vocal signals in humans: From cry to speech sounds

Introduction and review

REBECCA E. EILERS

Not long ago, texts on child development described the early stages of vocal development in the prelinguistic infant in terms of random collections of sound types, largely unrelated to the later emergence of conventional human phonologies. When investigators began observing human infant vocalizations with the aid of systematic international phonetic transcription and more recent theoretical innovations such as infraphonology, new insights began to emerge. It was only when new approaches provided more information about the relationship between the infant's accomplishments at various developmental stages and the goal of that development, human speech, that we could begin to understand the significance of infant prespeech vocal activities. Part III reveals how the developing theory of infraphonology has increased our ability to make meaningful comparisons between the vocal behavior of human infants (or adults, for that matter) and that of nonhuman species.

The theory of infraphonology, discussed by Oller and Eilers, developed in part from detailed observations (both acoustic and transcriptional) of infant vocalizations, coupled with a firm belief that infant behavior is goal directed (whether consciously or unconsciously) and that nature seldom wastes time by leading the child to outcomes which cannot be integrated into later and more complex behavior. One of the aims of infraphonology was to account for the development of the segmental phonological system in human speech, and to date infraphonology has provided a rationale for, and definition of, the continuities in this aspect of phonology across the first year of life. Other chapters in part III offer additional perspectives on aspects of human communication that exhibit relatively primitive (precanonical) segmental structures but nevertheless serve as carriers of critical information from infant to caregiver and back.

Lester and Boukydis, in their essay, provide an integrated view of the complex interactions between the biological and the social or biosocial

143

aspects of infant cry. While initially the human infant may have limited signaling options available through cry behavior (perhaps, e.g., simply pain or nonpain), individual mother–infant dyads may develop much more complex cry communications through a "negotiated" history of interactions. The careful methodological work reviewed by Lester and Boukydis illustrates the extent to which human infant cry informs parents about the infant's needs, state, and biological integrity and illustrates some of the biological foundations built into the roots of human interactions. Most accounts of early communicative interactions have excluded cry behavior, on the assumption that it is largely stereotypic and reflexive, but Lester and Boukydis make it clear that the cry is a finely tuned mechanism that serves as the cornerstone for developing social communication.

These authors describe aberrant cry signals and relate them to Jürgens's model of neural control of phonation (chapter 2 of the present volume). In the final chapter of part III, Amorosa considers two groups of children: those with specific language disorders, and those with autism. Amorosa notes that the two disorders result in aberrations in the signaling of affect through vocal communication. She suggests that each arises at a different level of Jürgens's model and that the two disorders differentially affect the ability to express affect vocally.

8. No language but a cry

BARRY M. LESTER AND C. F. ZACHARIAH BOUKYDIS

> But what am I?
> An infant crying in the night:
> An infant crying for the light:
> And with no language but a cry.
>
> Tennyson, *In Memoriam*

Crying is the beginning of human vocal communication and is the primary mode through which the infant's needs and wants are transmitted to the caregiving environment. Early attempts to study cry characteristics included musical notation, line drawings, and wax cylinder recordings, but the systematic scientific study of cry began with the invention of the sound spectrograph. Lynip (1951) showed that types of infant cries could be differentiated based on spectrographic analysis, and it is generally thought that the human newborn is capable of producing two types of cries: a pain cry, and, as Wolff (1969) described, a basic cry that is most frequently heard when the infant is hungry but also at other times. The fact that these cry types could be distinguished generated a fair amount of work on the analysis of infant cry, most of which was carried out in Scandinavia (Truby & Lind, 1965; Wasz-Höckert, Lind, Vuorenkoski, Partanen, & Valanne, 1968). When it was reported that infants with brain disorders had cries that were different from those of normal infants (Karelitz & Fisichelli, 1962; Wolff, 1969), much of the work shifted toward the study of abnormal infants, to determine if cry analysis could be useful in medical diagnosis.

Model of cry production

Crying in the human infant is a complex phenomenon that involves the coordination of respiratory, laryngeal, and supralaryngeal movements.

This work was supported, in part, by NIH grant R01 HD21013 and NIH contract CRMC8512. Thanks are due Cynthia Garcia-Coll for critical review and Mary Ford for secretarial assistance.

145

The neurological integrity of the infant is related to the stability of laryngeal coordination and vocal tract mobility. Hence, the cry provides information about nervous system function. Crying occurs during the expiratory phase of respiration and includes phonation, the production of sound at the larynx. The cry sound is produced when the pressure drop across the glottis causes the adducted vocal folds in the larynx to vibrate. This produces the *fundamental frequency* ($F0$), the frequency of vocal fold vibration and of what we hear as voice pitch. The sound generated at the larynx is then modified by the airways that form the vocal tract to produce the *resonance frequencies*, or *formants*. Although formants are usually thought of in relation to language, resonance frequencies can be described during nonspeech, since acoustic resonances are produced in the vocal tract during the cry.

Figure 8.1 shows the three peripheral sources that determine the cry sound: the subglottal system (including the lungs and the trachea), the larynx, and the supraglottal vocal tract. The subglottal system together with the larynx control features such as the pitch, timing, and intensity of the cry and are closely tied to the autonomic system of arousal (Bastian, 1965). The supraglottal vocal tract produces the formant frequencies that are determined by the contour and cross-sectional area of the upper airway and its motor innervation.

Central nervous system (CNS) control of newborn cry involves the brain stem, midbrain, and limbic system, with later involvement by the cortex. At one level, CNS control is provided by the lower brain stem. The acoustically important muscles of the larynx, pharynx, chest, and upper neck are controlled by the vagal complex (cranial nerves 9–12) and by the phrenic and thoracic nerves. For example, the motor neurons that control glottal closure are found in the nucleus ambiguous. Damage to these cranial nerves affects input to the muscles of the larynx, which control $F0$. Brain stem input also affects the contour and cross-sectional airway of the vocal tract, which determine the formant frequencies.

However, while the brain stem is necessary for the production of the cry, it is not sufficient; higher brain structures seem to be involved. Most of the evidence for the role of higher brain structures in cry production comes from studies in nonhuman primates. Jürgens (Jürgens, 1986; Jürgens & Ploog, 1981) developed a hierarchical model for the control of vocalization that includes animal calls and human nonverbal sounds, but not language.

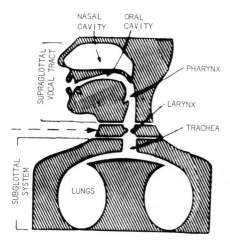

Figure 8.1. Peripheral sources of cry production.

Comparative evidence

The prelinguistic vocal behavior of infants, such as crying, contains the prosodic or qualitative features of speech: characteristics such as intonation patterns, inflection, melody form, and intensity. These are the features that animals use to call and signal each other – in other words, to communicate. The vocal tract of the human newborn, with the larynx in a relatively high position, is in some ways more similar to the vocal tract of a nonhuman primate than it is to that of the adult human. By about 3 months of age, the larynx descends and is repositioned in the pharynx, and this development is partly responsible for changes in the vocal sounds of infants around this age.

The similarities in the vocal apparatus of the newborn human and nonhuman primate have stimulated interest in comparative studies of human infant cries and animal vocalization. The distress call in monkeys is mediated by the limbic system (MacLean, 1973), which includes the hypothalamus, important in the control of emotions, including crying. In fact, every type of vocalization common to macaques can be elicited by stimulating parts of the limbic system (Robinson, 1967). In the squirrel monkey, vocalizations elicitable from the amygdala, hypothalamus, and midline thalamus cannot be distinguished from spontaneously uttered calls (Jürgens & Ploog, 1970). In kittens, direct electrical stimulation of the hypothalamus produces distress calls similar to the spontaneous call of the same animal (Altafullah, Shipley, & Buchwald, 1987).

Hierarchical organization

Based on the work of Jürgens, we can suggest a hierarchical model of the cry control system (Fig. 8.2). Level 1 includes the reticular formation of pons and medulla and is responsible for the coordination of respiratory, laryngeal, and articulatory activity. This is the level of the mechanics of cry production, and it connects with the motor neurons involved in phonation, such as cranial nerve input that controls tension of the intrinsic muscles of the larynx and determines $F0$. This level also connects to the motor neurons in the upper lumbar spinal cord controlling expiratory movements. Level 1 serves as the motor coordination center for the cry; it is not capable of initiating vocalization.

Level 2 includes the periaqueductal gray, or midbrain region, and configures the appropriate response to trigger a specific pattern. This level couples the cry type to the vocal pattern. For example, in the newborn, this would include configuration of the pain or basic (hunger) cry.

The initiation of the cry takes place at Level 3, which includes the limbic system, in particular the hypothalamus. At this level, stimuli are received and integrated based on affective states such as pain or hunger in the newborn. Probably through physiochemical changes, the hypothalamus is activated, and ascending efferent traffic increases the arousal level of the infant. The driving force necessary to produce the cry comes from descending afferent traffic from the hypothalamus, interrupting normal tidal respiration. Subglottal pressure from the lungs initiates movement of the vocal folds, and the glottis is constricted as the larynx is transformed from the respiratory mode to the mode of phonation.

This model implies that the limbic system is necessary for the newborn infant to be able to produce the two types of cries, the pain cry and the basic, or hunger, cry. Lower brain structures are sufficient to produce vocalization. Anencephalic infants can vocalize. However, their vocalizations are abnormal and undifferentiated. They cannot produce the richness or organization of vocal pattern necessary for specific cry types; this appears to require input from the limbic system. It is interesting that the old mammalian brain, which includes the hypothalamic / limbic system, is responsible for self-preservation and for preservation of the species and, according to MacLean (1973), continues to function in humans in the control of emotional feelings that determine behavior.

The fourth level (not included in Fig. 8.2) consists of the motor cortex necessary for the voluntary control of vocalization. In the newborn, the

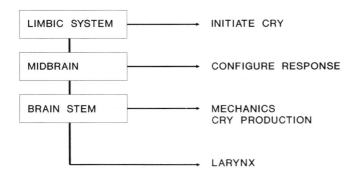

Figure 8.2. Hierarchical model of neonatal cry.

cry is an involuntary response, under limbic / hypothalamic and descending pathway control, even though different cry types can be produced and have signal value for the caretaking environment. Cortical control is probably not involved. As the infant matures, increasing cortical involvement brings voluntary control over vocalization, including cry. Crying can then be used as an instrumental response.

CNS reorganization

This shift from involuntary to voluntary control of the cry probably occurs as a result of the repositioning of the larynx in the vocal tract, mentioned earlier, as well as what has been referred to as a "biobehavioral shift" that also occurs at 2–3 months. Many investigators have pointed to this broad spectrum of change in neurological and behavioral function that encompasses a shift from basic physiological regulation to the beginnings of social regulation occurring at this time (Emde, Gaensbauer, & Harmon, 1976; Papoušek & Papoušek, 1984; Prechtl, 1984). Thought of as a CNS reorganization, the shift includes qualitative transitions in integrative processes such as attention and cognition and in social behaviors such as responsive smiling, eye-to-eye contact, and molding, as the infant becomes a more responsive partner in the dyad. It is also at this point that parents often report that their infants are crying "on purpose," "to get attention," or because they are "bored." These statements reflect the expansion of the cry system to include instrumental responses under voluntary cortical control.

Acoustic analysis

As we learn more about the mechanics of cry production, this informs our work on the measurement and analysis of the cry. While the sound spectrograph was the technology that launched the field, we now know that it has serious shortcomings (Golub & Corwin, 1985), and it is rapidly being replaced by computer-assisted digital signal-processing methods.

Our cry recording and analysis system, developed in collaboration with Physiological Diagnostic Service (P.D.S., Inc., Cambridge, Mass.), was specifically designed for infants. It is fully automated, requiring little human intervention, which is both methodologically preferable and time efficient. The analysis system is based on the acoustic theory of cry production developed by Fant (1960) and Stevens (1964) and was modified for the infant vocal tract by Golub (1980).

The tape-recorded cry is filtered at 5 kHz and digitized at 10 kHz. For each cry unit (defined as a cry utterance of at least 0.5 sec that occurs during the expiratory phase of respiration), the fast Fourier transform is used to compute the log magnitude spectrum for each 25-ms block of the cry unit (Fig. 8.3). Blocks that are inharmonic, containing a high degree of turbulence or dysphonation, are treated separately from harmonic blocks that are mostly phonation.

Three categories of summary variables are computed that reflect determinants of the cry sound. Respiratory influences are indicated by the duration and intensity (energy) of the cry and the ratio of phonation to dysphonation. Laryngeal influences are measured by the fundamental frequency ($F0$), including hyperphonation where $F0$ is greater than 1,000 Hz. Influences of the vocal tract are measured by the formant frequencies ($F1$ and $F2$).

Cry characteristics and biological insult

Since the 1960s, variations in cry characteristics have been documented in a number of medical abnormalities, including cri du chat, Down syndrome, hyperbilirubinemia, encephalitis, meningitis, asphyxia, as well as various forms of brain damage (Lester & Boukydis, Eds., 1985). Cry characteristics have also been associated with factors occurring during gestation that place the infant at risk for later handicap, factors such as premature birth, low birthweight, undernutrition, and poor obstetric

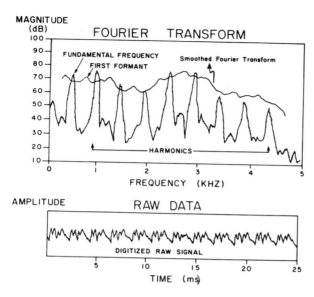

Figure 8.3. Schematic drawing of the computer analysis of a single 25-ms block of the cry. In the lower plot the amplitude of the digitized raw signal is shown for the 25-ms block. The log magnitude Fourier transform of that raw signal is shown in the upper plot, with frequency in cycles per second, or kHz, on the abscissa. Shown also are the fundamental frequency (F0), the harmonics of F0, and the smoothed Fourier transform from which the first formant (F1) is computed.

history (Fig. 8.4). In recent studies of the effect of maternal substance abuse during pregnancy on infants, cry characteristics have been related to the use of cocaine (Lester et al., 1991), alcohol (Nugent, Lester, & Greene, 1990), and marijuana (Lester & Dreher, 1989). In the latter study a dose–response relationship was found between the cry characteristics and the amount of maternal marijuana use during pregnancy. In another study, extreme cry characteristics were found in infants who later died of sudden infant death syndrome (Lester et al., 1989). Studies of cry characteristics in infants at risk have in common the objective of determining if cry analysis can be useful in the early detection of the infant headed for developmental difficulties.

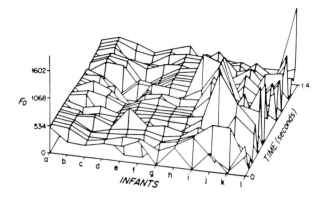

Figure 8.4. Plot of fundamental cry frequency (vertical axis) by 50-ms intervals (depth axis) for infants with the following conditions (from left to right along the horizontal axis): (a–d) healthy, full-term infants; (e–g) healthy preterm infants; (h) difficult-temperament infant; (i) full-term infant with high number of perinatal complications; (j) preterm infant whose outcome was poor at 18 months; (k) infant with meningitis; (l) asphyxiated infant.

Preterm infants

The preterm infant is a prototype of the infant at risk. Although preterm infants are overrepresented among children who later go on to have deviant developmental outcome, the majority of preterm infants develop normally. They are also not a homogeneous group, for additional risk is dependent on the degree of prematurity and the nature and severity of insult and illness.

The data presented in Table 8.1 are from a preliminary longitudinal study (Lester, 1987) in which acoustic cry characteristics were measured at term and at 7 months conceptional age and used to predict developmental outcome at 18 months and 5 years of age in a group of preterm and term infants. By analyzing cry characteristics, we were able to correctly classify infants who scored high or low on the Bayley scales at 18 months and infants who scored high or low on the McCarthy scales, which measure cognitive abilities at 5 years. The cry classification was independent of prematurity, medical complications, and social class. Since this was a small study, a replication is in progress. The graph in Figure 8.5 shows the relationship between the cry and 18-month Bayley scores in a subgroup of infants from the replication study.

Table 8.1. *Classification of 5-year McCarthy General Cognitive Index by neonatal cry measures*

Measure	High cognitive index	Low cognitive index	Fisher's test
High-change fundamental frequency	3	8	
Low-change fundamental frequency	8	2	$p < .007$
High average first formant	3	8	
Low average first formant	8	2	$p < .02$
High average amplitude	9	1	
Low average amplitude	2	9	$p < .007$

Early detection

The literature on cry and biological insult suggests that cry analysis reveals important information about the biological status of the infant, information not provided by other medical data. Cry analysis reflects the functional status of the CNS under stress and holds promise as a noninvasive measure of neurophysiological integrity useful in the early detection of the infant at biological risk.

However, it is unlikely that there will be a one-to-one correspondence between cry characteristics and the infant's medical condition. Cry analysis will more likely provide a benchmark or signal of CNS dysfunction that, when used in conjunction with other information, will lead to differential diagnosis. For example, we would be more concerned about an infant with a grade IV intraventricular hemorrhage and an abnormal cry than about an infant with the same type of hemorrhage and a normal cry. Alternatively, an infant who appears normal on routine pediatric examination but has an abnormal cry may be revealing signs of CNS stress or immaturity that warrant more careful attention. Whether an abnormal cry is a transient sign or an indication of a more serious underlying problem, early detection may lead to medical intervention and psychosocial intervention with the parents to facilitate the infant's rapid recovery and transition into the family.

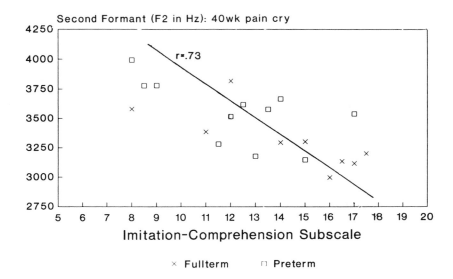

Figure 8.5. Graph comparing neonatal cry with 18-month Bayley scores. Regression line showing correlation between second formant (*F2*) of the cry sound measured during the neonatal period and scores on the imitation–comprehension subscale of the Bayley. Scores measured at 18 months of age in term and preterm infants.

Biosocial model

It is by considering its biosocial aspects that we can understand the dual nature of crying as both a biological indicator and a social signal. Figure 8.6 diagrams a biosocial model for the study of infant cry in which biological effects are due to the cry as an indicator of the neurophysiological integrity of the infant. Social effects describe the communicative and signaling function of the cry, by determining how the cry impacts on the caregiving environment, which in turn predicts the developmental outcome. When we study the cry as a socioemotional signal, we enter a new level of complexity. We now have to consider not only the signal itself but also the receiver, usually the parents, who respond to the cry signal as part of child-rearing efforts.

   From an evolutionary point of view, the cry is regarded as a proximity-eliciting and -maintaining behavior important for survival (Ainsworth, 1973; Bowlby, 1969). As a signal, the cry is not only strong but also has acoustic properties that elicit maximal attention in adults. Humans are particularly responsive to higher-pitched sounds, as the

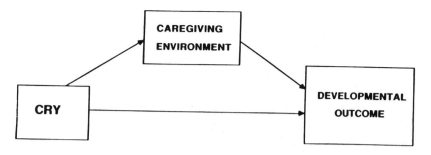

Figure 8.6. Biosocial model of infant cry in which cry characteristics predict developmental outcome directly by measuring the neuropsychological integrity of the infant and indirectly by affecting parenting and the larger caregiving environment.

maximum acoustic response of the ear concerns frequencies above 800 Hz (Davis, 1959). Also, like ambulance sirens, the sound of an infant's cry is dynamic, with variations in rhythmic predictability of pitch and with temporal features such as burst-pause patterns, all of which serve to alert the listener.

It makes sense that from birth infants solicit care from parents and that parents recognize and respond appropriately to the infant's signals. Soon after birth, many mothers recognize the cry of their own infant by its acoustic signaling properties alone (Formby, 1967; Greenberg, Rosenberg, & Lind, 1973; Morsbach & Bunting, 1979; Valanne, Vuorenkoski, Partanen, Lind, & Wasz-Höckert, 1967) and can differentiate among types of cries.

Two approaches to the study of crying and social interaction have been direct observation of parent–infant interaction (Lester, 1984; Bernal, 1972; Pratt, 1981) and laboratory perception paradigms where adults listen to tape recordings of infant cries or watch videotapes of crying babies. Observational strategies have helped to determine important contextual cues, such as time since last feeding (Bernal, 1972) and infant behavioral cues that effect parental response to crying (Bell & Harper, 1977; Lewis & Rosenblum, 1974). The lion's share of studies has used variations of the cry perception paradigm.

Cry perception

Perception of infant crying has been studied by playing tapes of crying infants to adults. The adults' responses to the cries are either monitored physiologically or are recorded on bipolar rating scales. Underlying this work is the assumption that these responses are indicative of how adults behave as caretakers.

Infant and parent characteristics

Adults have been exposed to cries from preterm infants (Frodi, Lamb, Leavitt, & Donovan, 1978; Frodi, Lamb, Leavitt, Donovan, Neff, & Sherry, 1978); Down syndrome infants (Freudenberg, Driscoll, & Stern, 1978); full-term infants with variations in obstetric risk (Zeskind & Lester, 1978); and full-term infants differing in temperament (Boukydis & Burgess, 1982; Lounsbury & Bates, 1982). In general, these studies report differences in perception of the cries as a function of the referent groups compared. Parental factors studied have included parity (Boukydis & Burgess, 1982; Zeskind, 1980; Zeskind & Lester, 1978); gender (Boukydis & Burgess, 1982; Frodi, Lamb, Leavitt & Donovan, 1978; Wiesenfeld, Zander-Malatesta, & DeLoach, 1981); maternal learned helplessness (Donovan & Leavitt, 1985); and cultural background (Zeskind, 1983).

Acoustic characteristics

It is only recently that work has been done which relates measured cry acoustic to adult perception of cry. There are several acoustic parameters that seem to be related to more negative perceptions of the cry. These include higher average fundamental frequency (Adachi, Murai, Okada, & Nihei, 1985; Boukydis & Burgess, 1982; Lester, Garcia-Coll, & Valcarcel, 1989; Porter, Miller, & Marshall, 1986; Zeskind & Lester, 1978; Zeskind & Marshall, 1988; Zeskind, Sale, Maio, Huntington, & Weiseman, 1985); more variability in the fundamental frequency (Lester et al. 1989; Zeskind & Marshall, 1988); higher formant frequencies (ibid.); less voiced phonation (a ratio indicative of the amount of phonation in the cry); and greater frequency and longer duration of pauses between cry bursts (Lounsbury & Bates, 1982).

Medical risk

Rating scales for cry characteristics were developed to determine how adults perceived the cries of infants whose medical history suggested that they were high- or low-risk infants (Zeskind & Lester, 1978), since the acoustic features of such infants' cries had been described. Adults, regardless of child-care experience, rated the high-risk infant cries as more "urgent," "grating," "sick," "arousing," "piercing," "discomforting," "aversive," and "distressing" than those of low-risk infants. The cries of the high-risk infants were perceived on two separate dimensions – one that recognized the unpleasant quality of the cry, and another that indicated the sick and urgent nature of the cry. The second dimension was not observed in the ratings of the low-risk cries, suggesting that information communicated in the cry differs as a function of medical risk.

In recent work (Boukydis & Lester, 1987), we compared the relative influence of medical risk and cry acoustics on parents' cry perception in response to cries from healthy preterm, sick preterm, and healthy full-term infants. Acoustic characteristics representing respiratory, laryngeal, and vocal tract activity (e.g., duration, $F0$ and $F1$) were strongly related to parent ratings on the cry perception scales. More importantly, when we used multiple regression analysis to look at the relative contribution of medical risk status compared with cry acoustics as predictors of parent's perception ratings, we found in all cases that cry acoustics, not risk status per se, explained more of the variance in parents' perceptions of the cry characteristics. In other words, how parents perceive the cry has more to do with the sound of their infant's cry than how at-risk their infant is judged to be. Infant behavioral cues rather than medical status may determine parenting behavior.

Temperament

The concept of "difficult temperament," particularly in early infancy, is virtually defined by crying, irritability, or fussiness. Lounsbury and Bates (1982) studied 4 to 6 month-old full-term infants identified as being of "easy," "average," or "difficult" temperament, based on maternal responses to the Infant Characteristics Questionnaire (Bates, Bennett-Freeland, & Lounsbury, 1979) and observations by trained observers. Spectrographic analyses of the cries of these infants recorded at home prior to a feeding indicated that the cries of those considered of difficult, as opposed to average or easy temperament, showed a higher peak fundamental frequency and more frequent and longer pauses between cry bursts. Older mothers rated the "difficult" infant cries higher on the dimensions of "anger / irritation" and "spoiled" and judged the infants as crying for more psychological / emotional reasons ("fright," "frustration," "wanting attention") than easy temperament infants, who were seen as crying out of routine physical discomfort (hunger, wet diapers).

Boukydis and Burgess (1982) used the cry stimuli from the study just described and found that the "difficult" infant cries elicited the highest levels of arousal in parents, as measured by skin potential. On the cry characteristics scale, the cries of these infants were rated as more "grating," "arousing," "piercing," "aversive," and "discomforting" than the cries of infants with average or easy temperament. Parents listening to the cries of "difficult" infants reported more irritation and were more likely to think the infants were spoiled.

Table 8.2 presents some results from our ongoing longitudinal study of preterm infants in which we found a correlation between our data on acoustic cry characteristics and on maternal cry perception and maternal ratings of infant temperament on the Infant Characteristics Questionnaire. The acoustic cry analysis and cry perception ratings were done when the preterm infants returned to the hospital for examination at their expected date of delivery (40 weeks of gestational age). Most of them had been discharged several weeks earlier. The Infant Characteristics Questionnaire was administered to the mothers when the infants were 9 months of age (corrected for prematurity).

The fact that acoustic characteristics of the cry at term predict maternal ratings of temperament 9 months later suggests that mothers are reacting to behaviors inherent in the infant. This would support the original construct of temperament, in which a strong constitutional basis was assumed. The significant relationships with the cry perception scales could simply mean that the mothers were accurate in reading their infants' cues. Alternatively, cry perception could reflect a change in the mothers' understanding and feelings about the infants which could affect their behavior toward the infants. In this light, cry perception may be useful in the study of the transactional aspects of early parenting (Seifer & Sameroff, 1986).

Social support

In a study of crying and the caregiving environment, we analyzed the cries of term and preterm infants at term age and, one month later, measured parents' requests for social support, using the NETHELP interview (Boukydis, Lester, & Hoffman, 1988). Acoustic characteristics of the cries were related to the number of health services parents contacted in the first month, total number of visits and calls to health care professionals,

Table 8.2. *Correlations between cry features, cry perception, and Infant Characteristics Questionnaire ratings in preterm infants*

	Fussy / difficult 9-month	Unadaptable 9-month
Cry features		
Phonation (%)	−.43	−.45
Hyperphonation (%)	.40	
Variability (F0)	.60	
Variability (F1)	−.39	
Duration	.45	
Maternal cry perception		
Urgent	.45	
Grating	.45	
Arousing	.45	
Piercing	.36	
Discomforting	.56	
Aversive	.48	
Distressing	.58	

contacts with relatives and friends, network size, and to the parents' overall difficulty in adjusting to becoming a parent.

The cry features that were found to be related to requests for social support were those that we know, from the cry perception literature, parents find to be aversive. Therefore, cries which had a higher and more variable F0 and F1, and cries that were less voiced and had more turbulence, were rated as negative (e.g., "aversive") in the cry perception study. Parents find these cries more demanding and more difficult to interpret, and the meaning of the infant's cues is hard to read. As a result, parents whose infants' cries have these characteristics find it more difficult to adjust to parenthood and seek more outside help from both the formal (health care professionals) and informal (family / friends) systems of support around them.

Methodological issues

One problem in the cry perception paradigm used in some studies is the selection of cries with extreme acoustical properties, cries that constitute supernormal stimuli. These cries may elicit extreme, and unrepresentative, responses from listeners.

In other studies, no information is provided about the acoustics in the cry sample, making it difficult to tell how representative the cry was and what acoustics were influential. Labeling a crying baby as "premature" can induce greater autonomic arousal and negative ratings among parents (Frodi et al., 1978b). However, when the cry of a premature baby was dubbed onto a videotape of a crying term baby in this study, the preterm cry elicited greater arousal and negative ratings than when the normal full-term cry was used; presumably, the acoustical properties of the preterm cry were important.

Another problem has to do with identification of cry stimuli. Parents respond differently if the cry that they hear is from their own infant (Wiesenfeld et al., 1981) and vary their responses depending on whether they know the crying infant is their own child (Boukydis, Lester, Peucker, & Wolk, 1988). The responses of those who are unrelated to a crying infant may not predict the responses of the parents to their own child's cry.

Factors other than acoustics and contextual cues relate to parents' response to their infant's cry. Perception studies which take into account parental personality factors such as learned helplessness (Donovan & Leavitt, 1985), cultural background (Zeskind, 1983), and history of abuse (Frodi, 1985) indicate differences in the cry's impact on the caregiving environment.

Many of the studies reviewed are analog studies, using standardized cries recorded on audio- or videotape, studies designed to elaborate on some of the factors thought to be connected with infant crying and with cry perception. Naturalistic observation of parent–infant interaction in the past has tended to employ broad categories to record cry bouts. These categories have not been reflective of the acoustic and temporal information in the cry. In using the information generated from analog studies, it would be important to incorporate strategies to record cries or record more detailed information about cry characteristics when doing direct observations of parent–infant interaction and the impact of crying on the caregiving environment. The notion that cry perception is a mediator of parenting behavior implies that studies need to determine the relationship among cry acoustics, parent perception, and parenting behavior.

Studies which have used cry acoustics have differed in methods of acoustic analysis and have typically averaged characteristics, such as $F0$, across a lengthy cry sample. This strategy ignores different temporal acoustic parameters, such as rapid rise or fall in pitch, which may be salient to communication and which may influence perception. It is known that the different segments (early, middle, later) of a cry sample have an influence on perception (Zeskind, Sale, Maio, Huntington, & Weiseman, 1985), and it is assumed that there are different temporal acoustic parameters between the segments that effect perception ratings. Todt suggested the value of studying multiple changes in cry characteristics, including measures of variability (1988). Cry samples were played to adults who were asked to respond by turning their head when they thought a crying infant should be cared for and nursed (checking response), or by lifting their hand when they felt the crying was unpleasant (distress response). The predictability of the checking response was enhanced when cry parameters occurred simultaneously; distress responses were more likely when there was an increase in frequency range and noise.

Parenting problems

Deficit model

The recurrent finding that certain infant cries are perceived as aversive invites speculation as to how these cries affect the quality of the infant–caregiver relationship. Murray (1979) suggested that prolonged exposure to the cry elicits strong emotions that tip the parent's motivation from altruistic to egoistic, so that alleviating the parent's distress takes priority over concern for the infant. In other words, the cry "turns off" the parent. Frodi theorized that crying can be linked to child abuse or nonnurturing parenting behavior by assuming that through crying the child comes to be perceived by the parent as an aversive, aggression-eliciting stimulus (Frodi, 1985). Frodi's work, showing negative ratings and increased autonomic arousal to the cry of a preterm infant (labeled or real) (Frodi et al., 1978b; Frodi, Lamb, & Willie, 1981) and to normal infant cries by abusive mothers (Frodi & Lamb, 1980) is used to support this argument.

In a study of teenage mothers (Lester, Garcia-Coll, & Valcarcel, 1989), we found that most of these mothers do not accurately perceive their infant's cry. In the older control mothers in this study, the cry perception ratings were positively correlated with the acoustic characteristics of their own infant's cry. Higher-pitched and more variable cries were perceived as more negative. Teenage mothers showed the opposite reaction: The higher-pitched and more variable cries of their infants were rated as more positive. These teenage mothers seem to misperceive their infant's behavior; they may not respond appropriately to their infant's signals. This may be a deficit in what Papoušek and Papoušek (1987) describe as the "intuitive" parenting skills of these mothers that could jeopardize the developing parent–infant relationship.

Adaptive model

It is also possible that the "aversive" cry may function as an adaptive signal by communicating the infant's jeopardized condition to the caregiving environment (Lester & Zeskind, 1978). The biological tendency for survival would favor positive caregiver responses when "something wrong" is perceived in the infant. This is not to deny feelings of anger or other negative emotions that parents might experience related to the cry but to emphasize that only in rare circumstances are these feelings acted out directly on the infant. We know that most high-risk infants recover and develop normally (Sameroff & Chandler, 1975) and that parenting failures, especially child abuse, are rare events. One may then wonder if the warning quality of the cry serves an adaptive function and promotes infant welfare.

The finding (Zeskind & Lester, 1978) that high-risk infant cries were perceived along the dual dimensions "sick and urgent" and "aversive," whereas low-risk infant cries were perceived only as "aversive," and that caregivers more often chose contact / comfort responses such as picking up and cuddling for high-risk than low-risk infant cries (Zeskind, 1980) is evidence that the infant at risk communicates a unique message; an early warning system communicates that the infant needs special caregiving.

Using structural equation modeling, we found that extreme cry characteristics (such as higher and more variable pitch) predicted positive caregiving responses, which in turn predicted higher mental scores (Lester, 1984). The cry was a signal to the caregiving environment that the infant was in jeopardy and resulted in positive parenting. While it is recognized that in an unusually stressed and nonsupportive environment an "aversive" cry may violate the limit of caregiver control behavior and result in suboptimal parenting, in most cases the sick / urgent quality of the cry will elicit caregiving behavior that facilitates infant development.

Colic

Colic is a model for the study of the interplay between biological and social aspects of the cry. Colic is most often equated with excessive crying. The colicky infant has been described as "one who, otherwise healthy and well fed, had paroxysms of irritability, fussing or crying lasting for a total of more than three hours a day and occurring on more than three days in any one week and . . . paroxysms continued to reoccur for more than three weeks" (Wessel, Cobb, & Jackson, 1954). Using this broad definition, colic occurs in 8%–40% of the infant population.

However, in addition to descriptions of the intensity, frequency, and duration of the crying, a second set of characteristics has also been used to describe an apparent pain / symptom complex in the colicky infant. During these paroxysms (which appear as sudden attacks or fits), but not at other times, affected infants are hypertonic or neurolabile. The cry itself is often high pitched, reaching a screaming level, and the sound of the cry (coupled with facial grimacing) indicates that the infant is in severe pain. Associated with the onset of crying there is increased motor activity, flexion of the elbows, clenching of the fists, and generalized hypertonicity of musculature. The knees are either drawn up or stiff and extended; the abdominal wall is tense; and the abdomen may become distended. Eyes may be tightly closed or opened wide; the back is arched; the face is red; the feet are cold; and brief periods of breath holding have been observed. Bowel sounds are increased, and there is considerable gas. The infant is difficult if not impossible to console and may resist or struggle with attempts to sooth. Between spells, these infants have a normal cry and are not hypertonic.

Infants who are awarded the label "colicky" can be divided into two groups: infants with excessive crying and infants with "true" colic. Excessive crying, defined on the basis of intensity, frequency, and duration of the crying, occurs in up to 30% of the infant population. These infants are on the upper end of the continuum of normal crying; they fall above the 75th percentile of the distribution reported by Brazelton (1962). This is crying within normal limits, albeit at the extreme end of normal.

What we call "true" colic occurs in about 8% of the population. These are infants who, in addition to meeting the criteria for excessive crying, show the clinical signs just mentioned: a paroxysmal, high-pitched pain cry, with the infant inconsolable and hypertonic. The graph in Figure 8.7 represents the acoustic analysis of the cry of a 3-month-old infant

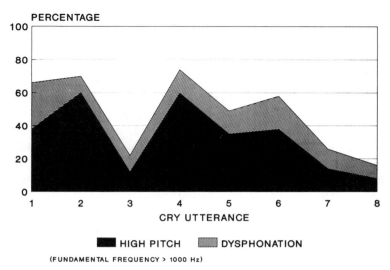

Figure 8.7. Infant with colic cry characteristics. A single 30-sec episode of the cry of a 4-month-old infant with colic. For each of the eight utterances that were measured in this cry, the proportion of the sound with high pitch and dysphonation or turbulence are shown.

who showed this clinical picture of colic. The cry shows periods of very high $F0$ and extreme variability in $F0$ as well as considerable turbulence. The colic episode was triggered by minimal stimulation during a behavioral assessment.

In our view, underlying colic is an imbalance of the autonomic nervous system, resulting from immaturity of the CNS. The imbalance is in the dynamic interplay between the sympathetic nervous system and the parasympathetic nervous system. In response to stimulation, sympathetic activity is greatly exaggerated whereas parasympathetic activity is greatly reduced, resulting in a dominance of sympathetic over parasympathetic activity. These infants show an extreme aversive reaction to stimulation that other infants do not experience as so aversive. The heightened-sympathetic / low-parasympathetic response to stimulation or sympathetic dominance triggers the sudden-onset, high-pitched pain cry and hypertonia. The inhibition normally provided by the parasympathetic nervous system is diminished. As a result, the infant lacks self-regulatory capacities for soothing and is unable to benefit from caretaker attempts at soothing: The crying becomes inconsolable.

The neurophysiological pathways involved in producing the colic symptoms are mediated by vagal input. As noted earlier, input from the vagal complex determines the acoustic characteristics of the cry. CNS input to the stomach is also provided by the vagus nerve; when vagal input is reduced, sympathetic activity is increased and tachygastria occurs. In infants with colic, stimulation triggers sympathetic dominance that produces changes in the acoustic characteristics of the cry, spasms in the gastrointestinal tract, generalized muscle hypertonia, and poor soothability. The underlying autonomic imbalance is due to immaturity of the CNS, perhaps related to the biobehavioral shift, thought to occur around 2–3 months, mentioned earlier.

The view that colic is biologically based enables us to better understand the role of parenting; parental characteristics will also determine how parents behave toward their colicky infant. The parents' behavior will in turn affect the behavior of the infant, which may exacerbate the crying as well as affect the developing parent–infant relationship. What is triggered by crying as a biologically based condition may develop into crying as mediated by social-emotional factors in the parents. In other words, while colic may be self-limiting in some respects, it is not necessarily limited to "self." As a relationship problem, colic may have consequences for the infant's development after the crying stops.

A reexamination of cry types

This discussion of colic serves to highlight the main theme of this chapter, the complex interaction between the biological and the social or biosocial aspects of infant cry. In this light it may be useful to reexamine some original constructs in the field, the notion of cry types, and to think about their developmental significance.

There has been considerable interest in the question of whether cry types can be identified. This includes work on the classification of emotional expression, on the continuity of development of infant sounds from crying to babbling to language, and comparative studies on the evolutionary significance of call structures. This topic is also of current interest in the field of neonatology with respect to the evaluation of pain in the neonate. The fact that cries due to pain can be distinguished from nonpain cries has led to the use of the cry response as a measure of pain and as evidence that human newborns experience pain. This in turn has been used as a physiological rationale for the use of analgesia and anesthesia during medical procedures in neonates.

We know little about the developmental course of the infant's ability to show the pain cry versus the nonpain cry. Figure 8.8 shows the re-

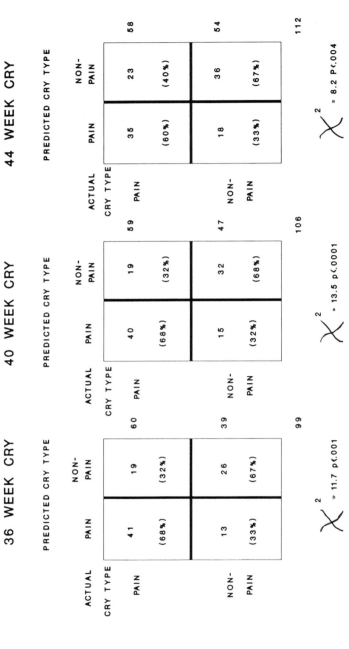

Figure 8.8. Classification of cry types in preterm infants. Results of discriminant function analysis used to classify cries as pain versus nonpain based on acoustic characteristics in preterm infants at 36, 40, and 44 weeks conceptional age. The chi-square test shows that at all three ages a significant number of infant cries were correctly classified as pain or nonpain based on their acoustic characteristics.

sults of a discriminant function analysis in which pain and nonpain cries were recorded from preterm infants at 36, 40, and 44 weeks conceptional age. The discriminant function was based on the acoustic characteristics from our cry analysis system and shows that the cries were significantly classified into their appropriate type. That preterm infants can produce these cry types before their expected date of delivery has clinical implications for the management of pain in the preterm infant not only with respect to medical procedures but also to the handling of such infants in the special care nursery. It also shows that the preterm infant is capable of signaling differential messages to the parents. Parents of infants in the special care nursery often comment that hearing a robust cry is a sign to them of that their baby is recovering and doing well.

Graded versus discrete signals

From an evolutionary point of view, the signal value of the cry has been of interest as a releaser of parental behavior that carries specific messages. Biologically significant sounds are described as discrete or graded, and there is debate over which category the cry fits. Discrete signals operate in an on–off manner, have little variation in intensity or duration, and convey fixed messages. Graded signals are more variable and change with the motivational state of the signaler. They do not convey specific messages and their acoustic structure is difficult to describe. The meaning of graded signals depends to some extent on the physical properties of the acoustic signal but also on contextual cues.

The application of this distinction to the cry of the human infant is not straightforward. It may seem tempting to argue that the human cry starts off as a discrete signal with two types (pain and nonpain) and then shifts to a graded signal. This shift may be due to changes in the position of the larynx and a shift in the hierarchical control of crying from limbic to cortical involvement. However, the notion of a graded signal may be too simplistic to describe the vocal communication system that infants and parents negotiate in the course of reciprocal signaling and caregiving interactions. The presence of a feedback system in the development of social interaction, with continued dynamic readjustments of the infant–parent relationship, calls into question the notion of species-specific call patterns.

Transactional process

We suggest that infants and parents develop specific cry-signaling communication systems that can be acoustically described. The 6-month-old who is bored uses a cry vocalization to signal this information to the mother, and she often knows exactly what the baby means. She knows both because of the acoustic properties of the signal and because she uses contextual cues (the baby has been awake for only an hour and has already been fed). However, the signal system for this infant–mother dyad is the product of a 6-month negotiation process between them. The acoustic structure of this "bored" cry may be unique as compared with other cries from this infant, but the acoustic structure of the bored cry may not be unique across infants; that is where the graded signal concept may break down. All infants may use different cries to signal changing motivational states, but whether or not these signals are species-specific or develop solely on an individual dyadic basis is not clear.

Developmental process

The pain cry does seem to be unique in the newborn and older infant, and it makes sense to describe the newborn cry as discrete, with two types: pain and nonpain. In the process of "getting to know" their neonate, parents make an initial judgment of the cry as pain or nonpain and, if nonpain, use contextual cues to make the next caregiving response. Hunger is usually the first interpretation. Feeding the infant is also an opportunity for social interaction, so that what starts out as ministering to physical needs engages face-to-face interaction.

As the infant develops, spends more time awake and in alert states, and becomes more interested in social interaction, nonpain cries become differentiated and signal different needs. This process is a mutual one, requiring input from both the infant and the mother. The infant contributes both a biological (evolutionary) component and a learned component. The biological component is what has been referred to as periods of unexplained fussiness that occur as part of changes in temperament associated with the biobehavioral shift in the first few months. These periods of crying "for no reason" serve to promote social interaction and facilitate the infant's transition to becoming a more active social partner.

The learned component from the infant has to do with how the physical characteristics of the cry are modified for this dyad. It is the fine tuning of the acoustic system, based on a history of responses from the mother, that enables the infant to produce a cry signal that the mother readily labels as "bored." When the mother picks up her crying infant, she is doubly rewarded: The crying stops, and a mutually satisfying interaction can occur. The infant learns that his cry works: Mom comes to play and provides stimulation that the baby needs. Mom learns that her infant needs more than changing and feeding and can signal those needs. She derives more pleasure from her infant as a social partner and learns something about herself: that she is a successful, competent mother who can read her infant's signals and respond to her infant's needs. This reinforces her intuitive parenting (Papoušek & Papoušek, 1987) and strengthens her self-esteem.

Signaling capacities of the partners

When we describe the acoustic characteristics of cry types, the emphasis is more on the uniformity than on the variability of the acoustic features. However, there is wide variation in acoustic characteristics among infants, even within cry type. There also appears to be more variability in human infant cries than in the calls that have been reported in nonhuman primates. Human infants show substantial individual differences in their ability to signal the environment or in what has been referred to as the "clarity" of their cues. Likewise, mothers vary in their ability to read their infant's signals and cues. Thus, the process of working out a cry signal system will depend upon these individual differences in both infant and mother; how they understand and signal each other, and how each modifies the other's behavior through reciprocal interactions. This does not rule out the possibility that, individual variation notwithstanding, human infants do exhibit species-specific, graded cry signals. However, the application of these evolutionary principles will need to take into account the complexity of the cry signal system, including the larger social context in which this system develops in human mother–infant dyads.

Final comment

We have seen the cry as part of a mutual regulatory system between infant and parent. Appreciation of the social context includes cultural variation. In less industrialized cultures, where infants are in closer proximity to the mother, perhaps being carried by her during the day and sleeping with her at night, the significance of crying is different for both mother and infant. The infant can use proximal signals, body movements, to which the mother responds before the infant needs to become aroused enough to produce a cry. Because the early communication system is based more on proximal than distal signals, the cry may function more as a true distress signal, and infants may not develop the same repertoire of cries as they do in cultures that require more distal signaling and ascribe more complex meaning to the cry. Our need to study and interpret cry types may be a consequence of the way we teach our infants to communicate with us and the cultural value we place on vocal signals.

References

Adachi, T., Murai, N., Okada, H., & Nihei, Y. (1985). Acoustic properties of infant cries and maternal perception. *Toboku Psychologica Folia, 44*(1–4), 51–58.

Ainsworth, M. D. S. (1973). The development of infant–mother attachment. In B. M. Caldwell & H. N. Ricciuti (Eds.), *Review of child development research* (Vol. 3, pp. 1–94). Chicago: University of Chicago Press.

Altafullah, I., Shipley, C., & Buchwald, J. S. (In press). Voiced calls evoked by hypothalamic stimulation in the cat. *Experimental Brain Research.*

Bastian, J. (1965). Primate signalling systems and human language. In I. Devore (Ed.), *Primate behavior: Field studies of monkeys and apes* (pp. 585–606). New York: Holt, Rinehart & Winston.

Bates, S., Bennett-Freeland, C. A., & Lounsbury, M. L. (1979). Measurement in infant difficultness. *Child Development, 50,* 794–803.

Bell, R. Q., & Harper, L. V. (1977). *Child effects on adults.* Hillsdale, N.J.: Erlbaum.

Bernal, J. (1972). Crying during the first 10 days of life and maternal responses. *Developmental Medicine and Child Neurology, 14,* 362–372.

Boukydis, C. F. Z., & Burgess, R. (1982). Adult physiological response to infant cries: Effects of temperament of infant, parental status, and gender. *Child Development, 53,* 1291–1298.

Boukydis, C. F. Z., & Lester, B. M. (1987). Cry acoustics and cry perception in parents of term and preterm infants. Paper presented to the Society for Research in Child Development, Baltimore. April.

Boukydis, C. F. Z., Lester, B. M., & Hoffman, J. (1988). Parenting and social support networks in families of term and preterm infants. In C. F. Z. Boukydis (Ed.), *Research on support for parents and infants in the postnatal period.* Norwood, N.J.: Ablex.

Boukydis, C. F. Z., Lester, B., Peucker, M., & Wolk, S. (1988). Cry perception and parental perception of cry and temperament in preterm and term infants. Paper presented to the International Conference on Infant Studies, Washington, D.C. April.

Bowlby, J. (1969). *Attachment and loss: Vol. 1. Attachment.* New York: Basic Books.

Brazelton, T. (1962). Crying in infancy. *Pediatrics, 29,* 579–588.

Davis, H. (1959). Excitation of auditory receptors. In J. Field (Ed.), *Handbook of physiology: Vol. 1. Section 1, Neurophysiology.* Baltimore: Williams & Wilkins.

Donovan, W. L., & Leavitt, L. A. (1985). Physiology and behavior: Parents' response to the infant cry. In B. M. Lester & C. F. Z. Boukydis (Eds.), *Infant crying: Theoretical and research perspectives* (pp. 263–277). New York: Plenum.

Emde, R. N., Gaensbauer, T. J., & Harmon, R. J. (1976). Emotional expression in infancy: A biobehavioral study. *Psychological Issues, 10,* Monograph No. 37.

Fant, G. (1960). *Acoustic theory of speech production.* The Hague: Mouton.

Formby, D. (1967). Maternal recognition of infant's cry. *Developmental Medicine and Child Neurology, 9,* 293–298.

Freudenberg, R., Driscoll, J., & Stern, G. (1978). Reactions of adult humans to cries of normal and abnormal infants. *Infant Behavior and Development, 1,* 224–227.

Frodi, A. (1985). When empathy fails: Aversive infant crying and child abuse. In B. M. Lester & C. F. Z. Boukydis (Eds.), *Infant crying: Theoretical and research perspectives* (pp. 263–277). New York: Plenum.

Frodi, A., & Lamb, M. C. (1980). Child abusers' responses to infant smiles and cries. *Child Development, 51,* 238–241.

Frodi, A. M., Lamb, M., Leavitt, L., & Donovan, W. (1978a). Fathers' and mothers' responses to infant smiles and cries. *Infant Behavior and Development, 1,* 187–198.

Frodi, A. M., Lamb, M., Leavitt, L., Donovan, W., Neff, C., & Sherry, D. (1978b). Fathers' and mothers' responses to the appearance and cries of premature and normal infants. *Developmental Psychology, 14,* 490–498.

Frodi, A., Lamb, M. C., & Willie, R. (1981). Mother's responses to the cries of normal and premature infants as a function of the birth status of their child. *Journal of Research in Personality, 15,* 122–133.

Golub, H. L. (1980). *A physioacoustic model of infant cry production.* Unpublished doctoral dissertation, Massachusetts Institute of Technology.

Golub, H. L., & Corwin, M. J. (1985). A physioacoustic model of the infant cry. In B. M. Lester & C. F. Z. Boukydis (Eds.), *Infant crying: Theoretical and research perspectives* (pp. 59–82). New York: Plenum.

Greenberg, H., Rosenberg, I., & Lind, J. (1973). First mothers rooming in with their newborns: Its impact upon the mother. *American Journal of Orthopsychiatry, 43,* 783–788.

Jürgens, U. (1986). The squirrel monkey as an experimental model in the study of cerebral organization of emotional vocal utterances. *European Archives of Psychiatry and Neurological Sciences, 236,* 40–43.

Jürgens, U., & Ploog, D. (1970). Cerebral representation of vocalization in the squirrel monkey. *Experimental Brain Research, 10,* 532–554.

(1981). On the neural control of mammalian vocalization. *Trends in Neurosciences, 4,* 135–137.

Karelitz, S., & Fisichelli, V. R. (1962). The cry thresholds of normal infants and those with brain damage. *Journal of Pediatrics, 61,* 679.

Lester, B. M. (1984). A Biosocial model of infant crying. In L. Lippsitt & C. Rovee-Collier (Eds.), *Advances in Infancy Research* (Vol. 3, pp. 167–212). Norwood, N.J.: Ablex.

(1987). Prediction of developmental outcome from acoustic cry analysis in term and preterm infants. *Pediatrics, 80,* 529–534.

Lester, B. M., & Boukydis, C. F. Z. (Eds.) (1985). *Infant crying: Theoretical and research perspectives.* New York: Plenum.

Lester, B. M., Corwin, M., & Golub, H. (1989). Early detection of the infant at risk through cry analysis. In J. Newman (Ed.), *The physiological control of mammalian vocalization* (pp. 99–118). New York: Ablex.

Lester, B. M., Corwin, M. J., Sepkoski, C., Seifer, R., Peucker, M., McLaughlin, S., & Golub, H. L. (1991). Neurobehavioral syndromes in cocaine-exposed newborn infants. *Child Development, 62,* 694–705.

Lester, B. M., & Dreher, M. (1989). Effects of marijuana use during pregnancy on newborn cry. *Child Development, 60,* 765–771.

Lester, B. M., Garcia-Coll, C. T., & Valcarcel, M. (1989). Perception of infant cries in adolescent and older mothers. *Journal of Youth and Adolescents, 18,* 231–243.

Lester, B. M., & Zeskind, P. S. (1978). Brazelton scale and physical size correlates of neonatal cry features. *Infant Behavior and Development, 1,* 393–402.

Lewis, M., & Rosenblum, L. A. (1974). *The effects of the infant on its caregiver.* New York: Wiley.

Lounsbury, M. L., & Bates, J. E. (1982). The cries of infants of differing levels of perceived temperamental difficultness: Acoustic properties and effects of listeners. *Child Development, 53,* 677–686.

Lynip, A. (1951). The use of magnetic devices in the collection and analysis of the preverbal utterances of an infant. *Genetic Psychology Monographs, 44,* 221–262.

MacLean, P. (1973). *A triune concept of the brain and behavior.* Toronto: University of Toronto Press.

Morsbach, G., & Bunting, C. (1979). Maternal recognition of their neonates' cries. *Developmental Medicine and Child Neurology, 21,* 178–185.

Murray, A. D. (1979). Infant crying as an elicitor of parental behavior: An examination of two models. *Psychological Bulletin, 86,* 191–215.

Nugent, J. K., Lester, B. M., & Greene, S. (1990). Maternal alcohol consumption during pregnancy and acoustic cry analysis. Paper presented to the Seventh International Conference on Infant Studies, Montreal.

Papoušek, H., & Papoušek, M. (1984). Qualitative transitions during the first trimester of human postpartum life. In H. F. R. Prechtl (Ed.), *Continuity of neural functions from prenatal to postnatal life* (pp. 220–244). London: Spastics International.

   (1987). Intuitive parenting: A dialectic counterpart to the infant's integrative competence. In J. D. Osofsky (Ed.), *Handbook of infant development,* 2nd ed. (pp. 669–720). New York: Wiley.

Porter, F. G., Miller, R. H., & Marshall, R. E. (1986). Neonatal pain cries: Effects of circumcision on acoustic features and perceived urgency. *Child Development, 57,* 790–802.

Pratt, C. (1981). Crying in normal infants. In W. I. Fraser & R. Grieve (Eds.), *Communicating with normal and retarded children.* Bristol, U.K.: Wright.

Prechtl, H. F. R. (1984). Continuity and change in early neural development. In H. F. R. Prechtl (Ed.), *Continuity of neural functions from prenatal to postnatal life* (pp. 1–15). London: Spastics International.

Robinson, B. (1967). Vocalization evoked from the fore-brain in *Macaca mulatta.* *Psychology and Behavior, 2,* 345–354.

Sameroff, A. J., & Chandler, M. J. (1975). Reproductive risk and the continuum of caretaking casualty. In F. D. Horowitz, M. Hetherington, S. Scarr-Salapetek, & G. Siegel (Eds.), *Review of Child Development Research* (Vol. 7, pp. 187–244). Chicago: University of Chicago Press.

Seifer, R., & Sameroff, A. J. (1986). The concept, measurement, and interpretation of temperament in young children. *Advances in Developmental and Behavioral Pediatrics, 7,* 1–43.

Stevens, K. N. (1964). Acoustical aspects of speech production. In W. O. Fenn & H. Rahn (Eds.), *Handbook of physiology: A critical comprehensive presentation of physiological knowledge and concepts* (Vol. 1). Washington, D.C.: American Physiological Society.

Todt, D. (1988). Serial calling as a mediator of interaction processes: Crying in primates. In D. Todt, P. Goedeking, & D. Symmes (Eds.), *Primate vocal communication* (pp. 88–107). Berlin: Springer.

Truby, H., & Lind, J. (1965). Cry sounds of the newborn infant. *Acta Paediatrica Scandinavica, 163,* 7–59.

Valanne, E. H., Vuorenkoski, V., Partanen, T. J., Lind, J., & Wasz-Höckert, O. (1967). The ability of human mothers to identify the hunger cry signals of their own newborn infants during the lying-in period. *Experientia, 23,* 768–769.

Wasz-Höckert, O., Lind, J., Vuorenkoski, B., Partanen, T., & Valanne, E. (1968). The infant cry: A spectrographic and auditory analysis. *Clinics in Developmental Medicine* (Report No. 29). London: Spastics International.

Wessel, M. A., Cobb, J. C., Jackson, E. S. (1954). Paroxysmal fussing in infancy: Sometimes called "colic." *Pediatrics, 14,* 421–424.

Wiesenfeld, A., Zander-Malatesta, C., & DeLoach, L. (1981). Differential parental responses to familiar and unfamiliar infant distress signals. *Infant Behavior and Development, 4(3),* 305–320.

Wolff, P. (1969). The natural history of crying and other vocalizations in early infancy. In B. Fox (Ed.), *Determinants of infant behavior* (Vol. 4, pp. 81–109). London: Methuen.

Zeskind, P. S. (1980). Adult responses to cries of low and high risk infants. *Infant Behavior and Development, 3,* 167–177.

   (1983). Production and spectral analysis of neonatal crying and its relation to other biobehavioral systems in the infant at-risk. In T. Field & A. Sostek (Eds.), *Infant born at-risk: Physiological, perceptual, and cognitive processes.* New York: Grune & Stratton.

Zeskind, P. S., & Lester, B. M. (1978). Acoustic features and auditory perceptions of the cries of newborns with prenatal and perinatal complications. *Child Development, 49,* 580–589.

Zeskind, P. S., & Marshall, T. R. (1988). The relation between variations in pitch and maternal perceptions of infant crying. *Child Development, 59,* 193–196.

Zeskind, P. S., Sale, J., Maio, M. L., Huntington, L., & Weiseman, J. R. (1985). Adult perceptions of pain and hunger cries: A synchrony of arousal. *Child Development, 56,* 549–554.

9. Development of vocal signaling in human infants: Toward a methodology for cross-species vocalization comparisons

D. KIMBROUGH OLLER AND REBECCA E. EILERS

Cross-species comparisons of sounds

Alphabetic / phonetic descriptions

How are the communicative sounds of nonhumans similar to or different from sounds utilized in human languages? The first inclination of one who wishes to make the comparison implied in this question may be to use human phonology as a point of reference. By this method, one might ask which of the many phonetic units of the International Phonetic Alphabet are produced by particular nonhuman creatures. When one describes the crowing of a game rooster as "cock-a-doodle-doo" or the call of another well-known bird as "kill-deer," one engages in application of human alphabets to nonhuman systems of vocalization. Such a method offers little insight, because the rooster does not actually say "cock-a-doodle-doo," and the killdeer never pronounces its name. The description assumes fallacious commonalities between the human and nonhuman vocalizations and ignores obvious differences.

In order to place the interspecies comparison of vocal sounds in perspective, it is useful to begin by considering general characteristics of vocal systems and how they are utilized; having established a perspective, a firmer foundation will have been prepared for the cross-species comparison of sound characteristics. Hockett's (1960) "design features" of the communicative systems of human languages include "discreteness" and "duality of patterning." The alphabetic system is a reflection of these fundamental features of design, and nonhuman vocal systems often either lack the features entirely or possess them to such a limited

This work was supported by NIH/NIDCD grant 5-RO1-DC00484-03 to D. Kimbrough Oller.

extent that an attempt to characterize the nonhuman system alphabeti-
cally would be fraught with confusion and false assumptions.

According to Hockett, the human system possesses discreteness in
that the alphabet-level (segmental phonetic) units have categorical values: A change in the acoustic characteristics of one sound segment (say
the *b* in *bin*) is taken as irrelevant from the standpoint of transmission
value (meaning) unless it results in a shift to a new meaning category
(say *pin*). Human languages routinely include lexicons of thousands of
words constructed from such discrete alphabetic / phonetic units. Nonhuman vocal systems often include an inventory of discrete calls or call
types (e.g., one for threat, one for affinity, one for alarm), but the categorical lexicon is, according to current knowledge of nonhuman systems, usually small in number by comparison with human languages
(Green et al., 1977).

The power of the human system in creating an extensive lexicon is
dependent upon the duality of patterning referred to by Hockett. Duality results from the fact that the individual alphabetic units of the phonetic / phonemic system of humans are independent of meaning and,
further, are recombinable and reorderable for the construction of meaning units. Thus the words *act*, *cat*, and *tac(k)* are all composed of the
same phonemic units, but they are lexically entirely distinct. None of
the three words is more similar in meaning to either of the others as a
result of its common usage of phonemic elements than it is to any word
composed of wholly different units, say *horse* or *lunch*. The lack of predictability of meaning (or signaling value) based upon the particular signaling units used to represent the meaning illustrates a duality that has
thus far been difficult if not impossible to demonstrate in nonhumans.

It is important to emphasize the "recombinability / reorderability"
characteristic implied by duality. If they are recombinable, a small number of phonemic units can be utilized to create an enormous lexicon by
stringing the units uniquely. Nonhuman systems that have been studied with regard to potential recombinability appear to show either no
restructurings or changes that are far more limited than can occur in
human speech (Hailman, Ficken, & Ficken, 1985, 1987). A system that
has no recombinability is restricted to a "lexical" inventory size that can
be no greater than the number of discrete units in the system.

The human system does not, of course, utilize discrete units exclusively. It also employs continuous parameters wherein small changes in
acoustic value result in corresponding small changes in transmission value;
for example, as one raises one's voice gradually, one may sound increas-

ingly angry or upset. Such continuous variations correspond to "paralinguistic" signaling and do not play a role in differentiating lexical items.
The human vocal system maintains a fundamental distinction between
certain dimensions that are manipulated continuously to paralinguistic
effect and the segmental phonetic features that are interpreted categorically to lexical effect.

Nonhuman systems appear in some cases to rely heavily for communicative value on signal dimensions that are varied continuously. Green's
(1975a) description of Japanese monkeys' vocal systems shows clear utilization of continuous variations for communicative purposes. The potential for substantial subtlety of communication is manifest in the continuous variations seen in the monkey calls. Whether human or
nonhuman systems possess greater subtlety of paralinguistic transmission within the context of any particular emotional dimension (such as
anger or fear) that might be expressed within a continuous vocal parameter is uncertain. Other nonhuman systems that show continuous gradations of vocal parameters with meaning effects have been reported for
the rhesus monkey by Rowell and Hinde (1962), the chimpanzee by Marler
(1969), the macaque by Green (1975b), and the squirrel monkey by Schott
(1975).

In the context of Hockett's model, it is possible to see why a direct
alphabet-level comparison of human and nonhuman systems is absurd.
By avoiding the alphabetic trap it is possible to conduct a sensible discussion of certain of the similarities and differences between the systems. Human systems possess recombinability to an extraordinary extent; other natural systems of animal communication, as far as currently
available methods and data permit us to judge, usually do not possess
it at all. Human systems utilize discreteness widely, while nonhuman
systems usually do so to a more limited extent, and perhaps in different
ways. Only in cases where both discreteness and reorderability are used
freely can an alphabetic description have merit.

Acoustic descriptions

Having rejected the alphabetic description of nonhuman sounds because an alphabetic system utilizes discreteness to such a great extent
and because the system is clearly designed to allow duality of patterning, one might return to pose the original question: How are nonhuman
sounds similar to or different from the sounds of human language?
Hockett's model provides a framework for discussing only how the sounds

"function" similarly and differently while leaving aside the question of the relationship between human and nonhuman sounds per se.

Suppose one chooses a purely acoustic method of description as the basis of a comparison between the vocal sounds of humans and non-humans. Using this approach, one could, for example, consider the duration of sounds, measure spectral patterns, and determine pitch contours. Having made measurements, data upon which comparison could be based would be available, but one would be left with a critical question: How do we know whether or not the particular sounds analyzed are representative? A brute-force method of simply comparing a large number of randomly selected sounds from both species would be cumbersome and uninsightful. An intelligent comparison requires that the essence of the sound systems of the two species be juxtaposed. A simpleminded acoustic description cannot extract that essence.

A new level of description

What is needed is a guiding model to specify what is crucial, what is truly representative, about the acoustic patterns of each sound system. Put another way, we need to ascertain the system of rules of acoustic patterning that determine whether or not a sound pertains to a given system. Having specified the scheme of rules – let us call it an *infrasound scheme* – we should have a basis for observing the vocal sounds of any creature and judging their similarity to and difference from the sounds of another vocal system. It is important to recognize that an infrasound scheme would not merely be an elaboration of acoustic description but a new level of description, utilizing acoustic parameters to define the discrete concrete units of a given communicative system.

To our knowledge, the first attempt to specify such an infrasound scheme has been pursued in our laboratories, in an effort to address a slightly different issue (Oller, 1978, 1986). Sounds of human infants, especially at very early stages, differ substantially from those of mature human languages. In order to account for the growth of the infant's sound-producing capability, it is necessary to address the extent to which infant sounds at each stage bear a resemblance to the mature system. An alphabetic system of description proves as useless to that task as it does to the task of comparing human and nonhuman sounds. Likewise, the purely acoustic approach lacks the guiding principles necessary to indicate the essence of the mature system to which the infant sounds must be related.

The key to the illumination of the process of human infant sound development has been the creation of a theoretical framework that can
provide an account of the relationship between the vocalizations of infants and the speech of mature language users. The framework constitutes an infrasound scheme and specifies criteria that sounds must meet
in order to qualify as pertaining to spoken human language. Since the
criteria are general in nature, the framework offers important advantages over other possible ways of describing vocalizations.

The goals of the present essay are to (1) outline the human infrasound
scheme (we have called it *infraphonology*, or *metaphonology*); (2) indicate
the manner in which the scheme can help us discover stages of vocal
development of the first year of life in humans; (3) review results of
empirical research that indicate the power of the infraphonological system in revealing previously misunderstood patterns of infant development; and (4) provide suggestions about how infrasound schemes for
nonhuman animals could be developed, affording an appropriate basis
for a rich comparison of the sounds used for communication in various
species.

Infraphonology

Infraphonology specifies the rules by which sounds can be judged as
pertaining, or not pertaining, to a *potential* human language. The concrete phonetic elements of natural languages include segmental (alphabetic) units (consonants and vowels) and suprasegmental units (intonation contours, stress or accent units, and tones). Languages differ
substantially in their systems of concrete units; in fact, in each of the
realms just mentioned, individual languages have special properties –
differing numbers of and qualities of vowels and consonants, differing
usage of intonation, stress, and tones. In order to recognize the common
ground of all languages, one must regard, not the concrete units, but
the general characteristics that are shared by different languages.

A useful starting point in seeking shared properties is an overview of
the rhythmic organization of languages, for in this domain languages
have much in common. The minimal rhythmic unit of all human languages is the syllable. Syllables are strung together to form higher-level
rhythmic units – feet, phrases, utterances, and broader discourse units.
The time course of syllables is remarkably similar from language to language, apparently due to general human timing tendencies (Delattre,
1965; Turner, 1985). Both in perception and production of rhythmic se-

quences, humans perform minimal rhythmic acts, such as finger tapping, hand writing, or repetitive syllable production, within similar time frames, judging, for example, from results reported in Kelso, Tuller, and Harris (1983); Semjen, Garcia-Colera, and Requin (1984); and Turner (1985). Inherent cyclicities of rhythmic speech production result in a tendency for syllables to have durations of from 100 to 500 ms in most circumstances.

Our first attempt at detailing an aspect of infraphonology focused on the syllable, the Minimal Rhythmic Unit (MRU) of natural human languages. Because there is tremendous variability from language to language in allowable syllable types, it was necessary to target the essential properties of prototypical MRUs. The notion "canonical syllable" is intended to include the vast majority of commonly occurring syllables in natural languages and to exclude nonsyllables and those syllables that are language-specific (nonuniversal).

A *canonical syllable* consists of a "nucleus" of energy (a vowel) and at least one "margin" (a consonant), which together fit within the syllabic time frame (100–500 ms). The amplitude of the nucleus must be greater than that of the margin by some minimal amount (we have tentatively suggested the value 10 dB). The nucleus must be the product of what linguists call "normal phonation," a method of vocalization that can be specified physiologically but that for present purposes can be defined simply as the kind of vocalization one uses when producing a common vowel (say "ah" or "ee") in citation form (e.g., speaking, not singing, crying, or growling). Whispering, falsetto voice, creaky voice, and a variety of other phonation types (which in some instances are used in speech) are not allowable in canonical syllables. There are two reasons for excluding other phonation types: (1) All languages employ normal phonation as their fundamental syllable-nucleus source, whereas other phonation types are used sparingly if at all in most languages; (2) it enormously simplifies our description if we concentrate on the fundamental shared features of phonetic systems.

In addition to having a normal periodic phonation source, a canonical nucleus must be the product of a vocal tract that is relatively open and not positioned at rest, a pattern that exploits the human vocal tract's potential as a resonating tube. We refer to this pattern as "full resonance" or "full vocalicness." A closed or at-rest tract yields a spectral frequency pattern of "quasi vocalicness" or "quasi resonance," where the vast majority of energies are at low frequencies (for adult males, below 1,000 Hz). The spectral result of producing a canonical vowel is one in which energies deviate from the pattern associated with a vocal tract at rest. The vowel [a] is produced by a vocal tract that is wide open (low jaw, low tongue position). The vowel [i], also an acceptable vowel for canonical syllables, is less open but still yields a spectral tilt with significant high-frequency energies. A prolonged nasal consonant, on the other hand, produces far more limited high-frequency energies and is thus disallowed as a canonical syllable nucleus. Some languages (American English is one) utilize nasal "consonants" as syllable nuclei (note American pronunciation of *button*, where the final syllable has no vowel), but again such nuclei are not used often, and many languages disallow syllabic consonants altogether. Since full vocalicness implies high amplitude, one consequence of the rule that canonical syllable nuclei must have full vocalicness is maximization of the amplitude distinction between the nucleus and the margins. Presumably, one reason why languages rarely use quasi-vocalic nuclei is that it is important not to obscure the distinction.

A canonical syllable is required to possess at least one margin (or consonant), because marginless syllables are relatively rare. The margin(s) must relate to the nucleus through (a) spectral (formant) transition(s) of limited duration. We have tentatively set the range at 25–120 ms, values consistent with data from adult English speakers (Gay, 1978), since shorter transitions are virtually impossible to produce and since longer transitions are perceived as slurred or otherwise aberrant. Indeed, judging from segment and syllable duration data, it can be deduced that languages all over the world use syllables that include transitions within this duration range (Delattre, 1965; Lehiste, 1970; Turner, 1985).

Our intention in attempting to quantify constraints on canonical syllables is merely to establish a starting point in the specification of standards against which other vocalization systems can be compared. The specific values noted can be revised to accord with empirical evaluations of speech without fundamentally altering the applicability of the approach. For example, if we change the transition duration requirement to 25–130 ms, we naturally include a number of "syllables" that would otherwise be excluded from the notion "canonical syllable." It may ultimately be best to specify the constraints probabilistically, indicating that as the duration of the transition increases beyond some point, the result is increasingly unacceptable as a potential syllable.

The canonical syllable criteria indicated here are, of course, merely a beginning in the generation of an infrasound scheme for human languages. Additional issues must be treated in the future. A list of future topics might include the following. (1) We need to outline the constraints on larger rhythmic units (feet, phrases, utterances, discourse units) and on their time courses, boundary-marking devices, and prominence indicators (accents). (We have made a first attempt in Oller and Lynch, in press.) (2) Paralinguistic expression rules need to be treated, specifying what role such features as repetition, pitch, and intensity play in the continuous adjustment of emotional content. (3) The discreteness issue, as implied by Hockett's model, needs to be specified with respect to how syllables are analyzed into contrastive units (phonemes, phonological features); how these units vary from language to language; and the number of contrastive units within individual linguistic systems. Finally (4), the duality / recombinability issue, another topic of Hockett's model, needs to be detailed in terms of the roles of repetition, sequences of different discrete units, and lexical / syntactic generation through recombination of unique orders of minimal units and lexical items. All of these topics will result in constraints on human phonologies that can be utilized in interesting ways in the comparison with human infant sounds and vocalizations of other animals.

Stages of human infant vocal development

Having specified some of the key characteristics of MRUs in human languages, it is possible to make sense out of the wide variety of sounds produced by human infants in the first year of life. It is important to note that the goal of the following description is not to account for all the biological functions that may be associated with human infant sounds, but rather to account for the relationship between such sounds and speech. The sounds focused on may have additional functions, and the relationship of the sounds to speech may be entirely unintentional and opaque to the infant. It remains of interest for us to note the relationship with speech, because in so doing we provide an account of the emerging capacity to produce sounds that could constitute speech, independent of whether the infant knows it or not.

The first step in the process of making sense out of infant sounds is distinguishing sounds that do or do not bear the potential of arbitrary meaning. In general, this distinction corresponds to what have been called "voluntary" and "involuntary" sounds. The production of these two categories of sound appears, in mammals, to be managed by different brain mechanisms (Jürgens & Ploog, 1981; Jürgens, chapter 2 of the present volume). When an infant cries in pain, the sound is understood naturally by all normal humans. The sound has a natural, biologically fixed meaning or signaling value. The value is not arbitrary, in several senses: It is constant across cultures; it is not redefinable in the same way that words can be reassigned different meanings by convention; and it is not learned. Other "vegetative" sounds, such as coughs, sneezes, involuntary grunts, and sighs, are similarly nonarbitrary and biologically fixed. To say that the sounds are involuntary is not to say that they cannot be produced on purpose. It is merely to indicate that there are circumstances under which their production is involuntary.

Considering words, however, it can be seen that in general they are not produced involuntarily and that there is no inherent relationship between their sounds and meanings. As Hockett (1960) points out, *whale* is a small word that represents a large creature, while *microorganism* is a large word that represents a small creature. But perhaps even more importantly, the relationship is culture-specific and definable by convention. Thus it is possible (and in fact normal) to redefine words or make up new words, a process that occurs routinely in, for example, scientific inquiry.

The human infant produces many involuntary sounds, and they bear the same relationship to speech in infancy that they bear in adulthood. On the other hand, a wide variety of sounds produced in infancy are not like involuntary sounds of adults. They are substantially different from the sounds of speech and also clearly are not in the same category as involuntary sounds. They include squeals, growls, raspberries, ingressive–egressive sequences, and many others. Partly because such sounds are produced in patterns that suggest the infant has control of their production, it is clear that they are voluntary and nonarbitrary. The question here is not Why do these sounds occur? but rather How do they indicate an emerging capacity for speech? The infraphonological framework affords a natural basis for answering the question.

Infants appear to go through four stages of development, each corresponding to the unfolding of a key capacity to manipulate vocalization in ways that are infraphonologically necessary (Oller, 1980; for parallels, see Koopmans-van Beinum & van der Stelt, 1986; Roug, Landberg, & Lundberg, 1989; Stark, 1980; Zlatin, 1975). In Stage 1 (the *phonation stage*), infants 0–2 months of age produce quasi-vocalic sounds in normal phonation, the kind of phonation that will be utilized in speech for canonical syllables. These sounds have no transparent biological function but are produced repetitively, and perhaps intentionally. Of course, other sounds (mostly involuntary) also occur during the phonation stage, but they almost always lack normal phonation and could not form the basis of an arbitrary sound–meaning system because they have fixed values.

In Stage 2 (the *primitive articulation stage*), most infants go through a period (age 1–4 months) of producing sequences of quasi-vocalic sounds and protoconsonantal margins articulated at the back of the throat. The articulations may or may not include friction noise or phonation during the closures. The key fact of the primitive articulation stage is that the infant manifests an ability to produce normal phonation and to articulate simultaneously. Infraphonology leads us to recognize in this event the emergence of a primitive distinction between nucleus and margin.

In Stage 3 (the *expansion stage*, age 3–8 months), a variety of new sound types is brought under control. Fully vocalic sounds (the precursors of vowels) are produced repetitively. Squeals and growls are utilized in patterns that suggest the infant is exploring the ability to manipulate pitch, a parameter that plays a critical role in infraphonology, both at the level of MRU and at that of larger rhythmic units. In addition, pitch plays a key role in early interactions of parents and infants (see the chapters in this volume by Fernald; Papoušek; and Papoušek & Bornstein). Similarly, voluntary yells and whispers suggest exploration of the amplitude parameter. Raspberries show further exploration of the ability to produce articulated sounds, enlisting the lips and tongue to the task. Finally, in "marginal babbling" infants produce sequences of fully resonant nuclei and margins in a pattern that, except for its timing, meets all the requirements of canonical syllabicity. In marginal babbling the formant transitions duration are generally too long, often exceeding 200 ms.

The *canonical stage* (age 5–10 months, in most infants) is the culmination of processes that result in the production of well-formed syllables. When infants say [dada] and [baba], they articulate sequences that in many cases are words in natural languages. During the canonical stage, numerous infant sounds indeed can count as instances of real words, even though the infant may not know that any meaning is associated with the sounds. The key advance of the canonical stage over the expansion stage is that timing of margin and nucleus has been brought under control to the point that the infant abides by the constraints of the infraphonological model.

It is important to note that in the absence of a guiding model, the vocalizations of infants could seem bewildering in complexity and random in content – in fact, Jakobson's (1941) account of infant vocalizations referred to "randomness," "wild sounds," and occurrence of "all the sounds of all the world's languages." These characterizations are thoroughly incorrect, but it is understandable that they were made in the absence of a model to guide the interpretation of infant sounds.

Other patterns of infant sounds in the light of infraphonology

Relationship with early child speech. Another myth that resulted from early discussions of infant vocalizations (also attributable largely to Jakobson) is that there is no relationship between infant vocalizations and the speech of the young child. In fact, once an infraphonological framework is available it is possible to see a distinct relationship. In the first place, there is a clear progression from the phonation stage to the canonical stage in ability to produce the kind of vocalizations that are used by young children when they begin to talk. Second, there is a distinct predictability of the particular sounds and syllable types used in canonical babbling and early meaningful speech. A series of empirical studies (de Boysson-Bardies, Sagart, & Durand, 1984; Oller, Wieman, Doyle, & Ross, 1976; Vihman, 1986) has shown that the sound inventories of early child speech and babbling are remarkably alike. The clarity of these demonstrations depends upon the infraphonological distinction between canonical and precanonical vocalization.

Differences in babbling of deaf and hearing infants. A traditional belief about the development of infant sounds is that the same types of sounds are produced by deaf and hearing infants. This belief proves to be mistaken in the light of infraphonologically oriented investigations of vocal development (Oller & Eilers, 1988; Stoel-Gammon & Otomo, 1986). In fact, deaf infants do not appear to enter the canonical stage during the first 10 months of life, while hearing infants do so, with rare exceptions (see Stark, Ansel, & Bond, 1989). The traditional false belief about deaf babbling appears to be the result of a lack of framework to highlight significant events in infant sound development. No investigator armed with an infraphonological descriptive system would fail to note that deaf infants do not enter the canonical stage on time. On the other hand, previous studies of deaf babbling focused on alphabetic descriptions (e.g., Mavilya, 1969) or very general and linguistically unspecified categories (e.g., Lenneberg, Rebelsky, & Nichols, 1965). Such studies viewed infant vocalizations through glasses that obscured the distinction between canonical and precanonical sounds.

Criteria for comparison of human and nonhuman infrasound schemes

It is clear that there is much to be gained by using an infraphonological approach to the description of infant vocalization. In order to compare human and nonhuman vocal systems sensibly, an infrasound scheme approach also seems in order. Because different nonhuman systems are so widely varied, a generally applicable method will have to consider design features at a level similar to that suggested by Hockett and to provide elaboration of details regarding the implementation of features in concrete systems. In what follows, we offer a preliminary sketch of procedures for comparing human and nonhuman vocal signaling systems.

Constraints on formation of minimal rhythmic units. A profitable first step in establishing an infrasound scheme for any vocal communicative system would be the isolation of discrete units in time, focusing on MRUs. In order to facilitate comparison of MRUs across systems, the normal range of durations and also the time course of transitions from MRU to MRU (if units can be strung) should be specified. The method by which units occurring within the designated time frames are recognized need to be indicated: For example, if MRUs are marked by peaks of amplitude and / or pitch within vocalized sequences, it is important to specify the required amplitudes and / or pitches in terms of magnitude, rise time, or whatever characteristics serve a defining role. Spectral frequency patterns may also play a defining role in MRUs. If there is a functional distinction between nucleus and margin, it needs to be defined acoustically: For example, if a nucleus is uniformly higher in amplitude than its margins by some minimum amount, the relationship should be specified. If the relationship of margin and nucleus is not constant across all vocalization categories then the context-sensitive nature of the relationship must also be specified. Furthermore, if margin and nucleus are distinguished, transition requirements need to be specified temporally and spectrally. The range of possible unit types (both margins and nuclei) need to be delimited with abstract acoustic characterization. Many of the essential properties of this approach appear to have been implemented in descriptions of the "conversational" vocalizations of squirrel monkeys by Newman, Smith, and Talmage-Riggs (1983) and by Symmes and Biben (1988), who find acoustic elements with at least a primitive nucleus ("mast") and margin ("flag") distinction.

Having once designated rules of formation for MRUs for a particular nonhuman vocal system, a comparison with human sounds at the level of the infrasound scheme should be enlightening. Relative time frames for occurrence of MRUs and comparative abstract acoustic properties can be directly assessed. The presence or absence of a margin–nucleus distinction may be particularly important, because of the role the distinction plays in the system of contrastive units found in human languages.

Combinability of MRUs. Having considered the definition of MRUs in a vocal system, the utilization of units in strings needs to be addressed. There are several ways MRUs can be combined, perhaps the simplest being repetition. If repetitive usage of discrete units occurs, constraints on length or on which units can be repeated need to be determined; furthermore, if the tendency to use repetition varies by vocalization category, that needs to be indicated quantitatively. More complex sequences of units can include alternation among discrete units or other orderings. In the lexically most powerful systems, full recombinability will occur (as in the human system), and very flexible recombinations of units will produce lexical items with signaling values that are unrelated to the sequences chosen. In the human system, recombinability operates at additional levels, due to the fact that lexical items can be recombined in strings according to a syntax that specifies the strings and accompanying structures related to sentence meaning. For any infrasound scheme, it will be of major interest to determine whether or not any reordering of units results in systematic alteration of signaling values. It is speculated that cetaceans may show recombinability with meaning change, but research methods to illustrate the suspected capability have been difficult to develop (Bastian, 1967; Lang & Smith, 1965).

Range of contrastive units within community and within species

In a vocal communicative system where only a few signal values are transmitted, there would appear to be no need for a large range of contrastive value-bearing sound types. The sounds used can function as individual gestalts, each having a unique sound that need not be analyzed beyond the recognition of distinctiveness from the other sounds of the system. MRUs may constitute gestalt signals individually. Understanding the human vocal system requires analysis of MRUs into nuclei and margins, and further into contrastive phonemic units at the level of nucleus and margin independently. It seems likely that the evolutionary reason for this breakdown of the MRUs is economy; by utilizing a system of contrasts within MRUs, information transmission can be accelerated, and, similarly, lexical storage and retrieval can be made more efficient.

The human system commonly includes 30–40 contrastive phonemic units. In assessing the number of contrastive units in nonhuman systems for comparative purposes, it is important to consider not only the size of the inventory but also its organization. The kind of contrastive units that occur need to be specified acoustically, and the nature of the contrasts should be detailed. (For example, are they categorical or "discrete," to use Hockett's terminology?) Furthermore, one should seek to determine whether the nonhuman system includes analysis of MRUs into an additional level of subunit segments.

The human system also provides a model of a further complexity in range of contrastive units due to the utilization of at least two levels of unit categorization. The phonemic or alphabetic level has been noted previously: For example, in English, / p / is distinct from / m / and from / b /. However, there is an additional level of functional distinction embedded within the phonemic level. For instance, / p / is distinct from / b / in the phonemic feature of voicing, a feature that also characterizes the distinction between / t / and / d / or / k / and / g /. The featural distinctions have productive consequences within human phonological systems (playing a role, for example, in sound change over generations, perceivability of individual words, and lexical categorization / memory and retrieval). The number of contrastive features within a human phonological system is always substantially less than the number of phonemic units, which suggests that the organization by feature may have some advantage of economy (such as in storage or retrieval). The question of whether nonhuman systems make use of a featural system embedded within a segmental system is of major interest. Since the advantage of the featural system, like the phonemic system, seems to be one of economy in management of the lexicon, it would appear that such a system would occur only in circumstances where a large lexicon is involved.

While individual languages utilize 30–40 segmental units (and perhaps half that many features), it is important to recognize that the class of phonemic units from which natural human languages can draw is much larger – at least in the hundreds. At any point in time a particular language utilizes only a small subset of the possible units, but, across just a few (say 15–20) generations (and thus without major influence from biological evolution), change in the phonetic characteristics of the units occurs, without exception.

In describing the range of contrastive units in vocalizations of other species, it is important to consider both the number of units that is functional within a community and the number that is functional across all members of the species in question. In so doing, one obtains a measure of the role of cultural transmission and learning in the vocal system of the species.

Paracommunicative parameters. In various species, it appears that the expression of degree of emotion may be manifest in continuous variation of specific parameters. In the human system, loudness and pitch vary in a continuous fashion with emotional tension. Similar variations occur in other primates (see citations in the section on alphabetic / phonetic description). How these parameters relate across species is a subject of great potential interest. While the human system clearly outstrips other primate systems in its system of discrete signals, it may be that at the level of paracommunicative parameters we share much with other primates.

Acoustic description of how parameters are varied continuously needs to be specified for comparative purposes. Are the relative roles of amplitude and pitch similar in human and nonhuman systems? Is the range of variation similar? Does repetition play a role in the intensity of vocal communication, and, if so, how?

Structure of larger rhythmic units (LRUs). MRUs of the human system of vocalization are not only strung together, they are structured in several larger unit types. The procedures by which LRUs are defined are complex, and while there are universal approaches to marking structures such as phrases and sentences, there are also language-specific characteristics. For example, utterance / sentence boundaries in English can be marked by pauses, by augmented duration of final syllables, and by pitch and amplitude drops (at least in declarative utterances). Other languages use similar, but not identical, methods. For example, Spanish does not appear to use syllable duration to the same extent that English does to mark boundaries.

There are at least four relevant levels of LRU structure: the metric foot, the phonological phrase, the line, and the discourse unit (e.g., paragraph). All these unit levels involve complex rules of acoustic expression. The reason human systems include such complexity is that higher-level rhythmic units provide expression for combinations of lexical items in syntactic groupings. If a nonhuman system is to manifest any similarity of LRUs (or even the existence of LRUs), it would seem logical to expect that the nonhuman system would have a syntax of some note. The complexity of many bird calls (consider that of the mockingbird, for example) is thus suggestive of syntactic organization, and Hailman and his colleagues (1987) have found some degree of syntactic organization in the song of the black-capped chickadee.

For cross-species comparisons, it is important to determine whether nonhuman systems utilize LRUs, and, if so, how these LRUs are structured acoustically. The role of amplitude and pitch in groupings of MRUs into larger units can be compared across human and nonhuman systems.

Conclusions

Attempts to compare vocal systems across species are doomed to confusion if they use human segmental / alphabetic units as the sole categories of comparison. Alphabetic systems are the reflection of a complex method by which large lexicons can be developed. If a nonhuman system lacks a large lexicon, it is scarcely sensible to expect it to have developed an alphabetic system. Similarly, if nonhuman systems do not have complex segmental systems, they could hardly be expected to have developed systems with subsegmental features. Finally, if there is no syntactic system, it is hard to see what motivation there might be for the creation of a system of LRUs. Consequently, as one approaches the comparison of human and nonhuman vocal systems, it is prudent to consider at the beginning at what level comparisons should be made.

Clearly, design-feature comparisons, in the style of Hockett, are always possible and potentially quite informative. Furthermore, in an infrasound scheme it is possible in all cases to describe the MRUs of nonhuman systems and thus to lay the groundwork for a sensible comparison of the sound characteristics of human and nonhuman vocal communication. While the development of infraphonology for human vocal communication is still in an early stage, the future would seem to hold major opportunities for fruitful cross-species comparisons.

References

Bastian, J. (1967). The transmission of arbitrary environmental information between bottlenose dolphins. In R. G. Busnel (Ed.), *Animal sonar systems, biol-*

ogy and bionics (pp. 803–873). Jouy-en-Josas: Laboratoires des Physiologie Acoustiques.

De Boysson-Bardies, B., Sagart, L., & Durand, C. (1984). Discernible differences in the babbling of infants according to target language. *Journal of Child Language, 11,* 1–15.

Delattre, P. (1965). *Comparing the phonetic features of English, French, German, and Spanish.* Philadelphia: Chilton.

Gay, T. (1978). Effects of speaking rate on vowel formant movements. *Journal of the Acoustical Society of America, 63,* 223–230.

Green, S. (1975a). Variation of vocal pattern with social situation in the Japanese monkey (*Macaca fuscata*): A field study. In L. A. Rosenblum (Ed.), *Primate behavior* (Vol. 4, pp. 1–102). New York: Academic Press.

(1975b). Dialects in Japanese monkeys: Vocal learning and cultural transmission of locale-specific vocal behavior. *Zeitschrift für Tierpsychologie, 38,* 304–314.

Green, S. M., Darwin, C. J., Evans, E. F., Fant, G. C. M., Fourcin, A. J., Fujimura, O., Fujisaki, H., Liberman, A. M., Markl, H. S., Marler, P. R., Miller, J. D., Milner, B. A., Nottebohm, F., Pisoni, D. B., Ploog, D., Scheich, H., Stevens, K. N., Studdert-Kennedy, M. G., & Tallal, P. A. (1977). Comparative aspects of vocal signals including speech group report. In T. H. Bullock (Ed.), *Dahlem workshop on recognition of complex acoustic signals. Life Sciences Research Report, 5,* 209–236.

Hailman, J. P., Ficken, M. S., & Ficken, R. W. (1985). The "chick-a-dee" calls of *Parus atricapillus*: A recombinant system of animal communication compared with written English. *Semiotica, 56,* 191–224.

(1987). Constraints on the structure of combinatorial "chick-a-dee" calls. *Ethology, 75,* 62–80.

Hockett, C. F. (1960). The origin of speech. *Scientific American, 203,* 88–96.

Jakobson, R. (1941). *Kindersprache, Aphasie, und allgemeine Lautgesetze.* Uppsala: Almqvist & Wiksell.

Jürgens, U., & Ploog, D. (1981). On the neural control of mammalian vocalization. *Trends in NeuroSciences, 4,* 135–137.

Kelso, J. A. S., Tuller, B., & Harris, K. S. (1983). A dynamic pattern perspective on the control and coordination of movement. In P. F. MacNeilage (Ed.), *The production of speech* (pp. 137–173). New York: Springer.

Koopmans-van Beinum, F. J., & van der Stelt, J. M. (1986). Early stages in the development of speech movements. In B. Lindblom & R. Zetterstrom (Eds.), *Precursors of early speech* (pp. 37–50). New York: Stockton.

Lang, T. G., & Smith, H. A. P. (1965). Communication between dolphins in separate tanks by way of an electronic acoustic link. *Science, 150,* 1839–1844.

Lehiste, I. (1970). *Suprasegmentals.* Cambridge, Mass.: MIT Press.

Lenneberg, E. H., Rebelsky, G. F., & Nichols, I. A. (1965). The vocalizations of infants born to deaf and hearing parents. *Human Development, 8,* 23–37.

Marler, P. (1969). Vocalizations of wild chimpanzees: An introduction. *Recent Advances in Primatology, 1,* 94–100.

Mavilya, M. (1969). Spontaneous vocalizations and babbling in hearing impaired infants. Unpublished doctoral dissertation, Columbia University (University Microfilms No. 70-12879).

Newman, J. D., Smith, H. J., & Talmage-Riggs, G. (1983). Structural variability in primate vocalizations and its functional significance: An analysis of squirrel monkey chuck calls. *Folia Primatologica, 40,* 114–124.

Oller, D. K. (1978). Infant vocalization and the development of speech. *Allied Health and Behavioral Sciences, 1,* 523–549.

(1980). The emergence of the sounds of speech in infancy. In G. Yeni-Komshian, J. Kavanagh, & C. Ferguson (Eds.), *Child phonology: Vol. 1. Production* (pp. 93–112). New York: Academic Press.

(1986). Metaphonology and infant vocalizations. In B. Lindblom & R. Zetterström (Eds.), *Precursors of early speech* (pp. 21–36). New York: Stockton.

Oller, D. K., & Eilers, R. E. (1988). The role of audition in infant babbling. *Child Development, 59,* 441–449.

Oller, D. K., & Lynch, M. P. (in press). Infant vocalizations and innovations in infraphonology: Toward a broader theory of development and disorders. In C. Ferguson, L. Menn, & C. Stoel-Gammon (Eds.), *Phonological development.* Parkton, Md.: York Press.

Oller, D. K., Wieman, L. A., Doyle, W. J., & Ross, C. (1976). Infant babbling and speech. *Journal of Child Language, 3,* 1–11.

Roug, L., Landberg, I., & Lundberg, L. J. (1989). Phonetic development in early infancy: A study of 4 Swedish children during the first 18 months of life. *Journal of Child Language, 16,* 19–40.

Rowell, T. E., & Hinde, R. A. (1962). Vocal communication by the rhesus monkey (*Macaca mulatta*). *Proceedings of the Zoological Society of London, 138,* 179–194.

Schott, D. (1975). Quantitative analysis of the vocal repertoire of squirrel monkeys (*Saimiri sciureus*). *Zeitschrift für Tierpsychologie, 38,* 225–250.

Semjen, A., Garcia-Colera, A., & Requin, J. (1984). On controlling force and time in rhythmic movement sequences: The effect of stress location. In J. Gibbon & L. Allen (Eds.), *Timing and time perception. Annals of the New York Academy of Sciences, 423,* 168–182.

Stark, R. E. (1980). Stages of speech development in the first year of life. In G. Yeni-Komshian, J. Kavanagh, & C. Ferguson (Eds.), *Child phonology Vol. 1. Production* (pp. 73–90). New York: Academic Press.

Stark, R. E., Ansel, B. M., & Bond, J. (1989). Are prelinguistic abilities predictive of learning disability? A follow-up study. In R. L. Masland & M. Masland (Eds.), *Preschool prevention of reading failure* (pp. 3–18). Parkton, Md.: York Press.

Stoel-Gammon, C., & Otomo, K. (1986). Babbling development of hearing-impaired and normally hearing subjects. *Journal of Speech and Hearing Disorders, 51,* 33–41.

Symmes, D., & Biben, M. (1988). Conversational vocal exchanges in squirrel monkeys. In D. Todt, P. Goedeking, & D. Symmes (Eds.), *Primate vocal communication* (pp. 123–132). Berlin: Springer.

Turner, F. (1985). *Natural classicism.* New York: Paragon.

Vihman, M. M. (1986). Individual differences in babbling and early speech: Predicting to age three. In B. Lindblom & R. Zetterström (Eds.), *Precursors of early speech* (pp. 95–112). New York: Stockton.

Zlatin, M. (1975). *Explorative mapping of the vocal tract and primitive syllabification in infancy: The first six months.* Paper presented to the American Speech and Hearing Association, Washington, D.C.

10. Disorders of vocal signaling in children

HEDWIG AMOROSA

Vocal signaling includes both verbal and nonverbal oral communication. Several types of deficit can lead to disorders of vocal signaling. Two of them will be discussed in this essay: a lack of sufficient control over the fine motor systems necessary to produce an utterance, and a failure to match the acoustic output with the communicative intent and with the situational context in which the utterance is produced.

All types of vocal signals, whether nonverbal emotional signals, expressions of emotion during verbal utterances, or intonation expressing the more formal aspects of language, depend on the ability of the speaker to control the intensity, spectral energy distribution, fundamental frequency, and time structure of an utterance sufficiently well to effect the necessary changes in acoustic output (Trojan, 1975). For example, vocal intensity gives an indication of the kind of reaction an utterance invites (ibid.). But an intensity change can also play a formal role, for example, as a marker for stress or as an indication that an utterance is about to end. Vocal intensity is controlled by subglottal air pressure, which in turn is controlled by the speech breathing system (Tanaka & Gould, 1983).

Fundamental frequency and time structure are used in a similar manner in the nonverbal expression of emotion and in verbal communication. Changes in fundamental frequency depend on the interaction of the tonus of the vocal folds with subglottal pressure, that is, it is controlled by an interaction of the phonatory system and the speech breathing system. The time structure of an utterance is influenced both by the pauses and by the interaction of the articulatory movements with the actions of the vocal folds. Thus there are three systems – the speech breathing system, the phonatory system, and the articulatory system – that must be controlled not only in isolation but also together to produce the intended acoustic output.

In addition to control of motor output, there must also be an ability to match the vocal signal with the communicative intent, the emotional state, the nonverbal message, and the linguistic requirements (Ploog, 1987). A mismatch between the verbal and nonverbal messages of an utterance or between the nonverbal message and the situational context can be confusing to the listener.

When we look at problems in vocal signaling in children, we have to keep in mind that the underlying disorder may not always be the same. Some children have a deficit in motor control of the individual systems needed to produce a given signal or coordination among the systems, whereas others can reproduce a pattern quite readily but do not seem to know which intonational pattern is appropriate to the content of a particular utterance and the context in which it is uttered.

In the following, two groups of children are discussed who have disorders of vocal signaling that have quite different effects on the listener. The first group includes children with specific developmental disorders of speech and language (ICD-9, 315.3); the second children with early infantile autism (ICD-9, 299.0) (Remschmidt & Schmidt, 1986). Since for neither group are there any systematic studies of nonverbal emotional signals such as laughing, crying, or moaning or any studies on the expression of specific emotions in verbal utterances, the discussion is based on analyses of intonation patterns in spontaneous speech and sentence repetition, that is, neutral speech.

Specific developmental disorders of speech and language

Among children with disordered speech and language development, there are some whose speech and / or language impairment cannot be explained adequately by a low nonverbal IQ, a hearing loss, or a neurological or psychiatric disorder. These children are usually slow in uttering their first words and remain unintelligible for a long time. They have problems using grammatical markers and correct word order well into their school years. Some of the children also have impaired receptive language. Many of them learn to read and spell quite slowly and only with special help.

Studies of children with specific developmental speech and language disorders have shown that these children frequently have problems in fine motor coordination involving all three of the systems needed to produce verbal utterances: the speech breathing, phonatory, and articulatory systems. These problems are evident in analyses of the intensity, fundamental frequency, and time structure of utterances.

Intensity

The speech breathing system controls the intensity of utterances by regulating the subglottal air pressure. Sufficient pressure must be maintained for the duration of an utterance, a type of control learned only slowly during language acquisition. Insufficient control of the speech breathing system can result in extreme variability in intensity within an utterance.

In 1988 I reported my study of 24 children between the ages of 4, 6, and 8 years who fulfilled the ICD-9 criteria for specific developmental disorders of speech and language and whose spontaneous speech with their teachers and / or caregivers was unintelligible. Age-matched children without a history of speech and language problems served as the control group.

In repetitions of the syllable / ta /, the variability of intensity from syllable to syllable was significantly greater in the children with unintelligible speech than in the control group.

In addition to the acoustic analysis of syllables, tape recordings of at least 30-min duration that contained spontaneous speech and repetitions of series of simple syllables and sentences by the children were rated by two speech therapists. The distribution of dots in Figure 10.1 shows that frequent pauses and irregular pauses for breathing as well as unusual changes in volume were significantly more common in the children with disorders of speech and language development than in the control group. Thus the children with speech / language disorders had difficulty controlling the intensity of their utterances – a sign of insufficient fine motor control of the speech breathing system.

Fundamental frequency

In vocal signaling the tension of the vocal folds in interaction with the subglottal air pressure is mainly responsible for the fundamental frequency level. Fine regulation of this system must be acquired during language acquisition if the changes that are necessary for intelligible speech are to be effected. Changes in vocal fold tension or insufficient adjustment to changes in subglottal air pressure result in audible voice phenomena (Fig. 10.2).

With von Benda, Dames, and Schäfersküpper, I reported in 1986 that

	1	2	3	4	5	6	7	8	9	10	11	12	13	14	15	16	17	18	19	20	21	22	23	24
Increased no. of pauses	●		●	●	●		●	●		●					●		●	●	●	●			●	●
Irregular pauses		●	●	●		●		●	●			●	●				●			●	●	●	●	
Speaking during inhalation		●	●		●		●												●				●	
Unusual changes in volume		●	●		●	●					●	●	●	●	●	●					●		●	●

	1	2	3	4	5	6	7	8	9	10	11	12	13	14	15	16	17	18	19	20	21	22	23	24
Increased no. of pauses	●	●	●					●				●		●										
Irregular pauses																								
Speaking during inhalation				●					●			●												
Unusual changes in volume																								

Figure 10.1. Abnormalities observed in speech breathing. A dot indicates the presence of a given abnormality. *(Top)* Findings for 24 children with unintelligible speech; *(bottom)* findings for 24 children with normal speech and language development. (Children are listed by increasing age.)

our subjects with unintelligible speech showed more abnormal vocal phenomena than the children in the age-matched control group. These abnormal phenomena persisted over an 18-month period (Amorosa, von Benda, & Wagner, 1990). This indicates that the unintelligible children had more problems coordinating the tonus of the vocal folds with the subglottal air pressure than would be expected in children of their age.

Time structure

The third important aspect of vocal signaling is the time structure of the utterance. Here articulatory parameters play the clearest role, but both the phonatory and speech breathing systems also contribute. Irregular pauses for breathing, resulting from insufficient control over the subglottal air pressure or late onset of vocal fold vibration, can change the time structure of an utterance. Children with specific developmental speech and language disorders are often diagnosed as "clutterers" because of the variability in their speech rate.

Several authors (Amorosa, 1988; Dames, 1986; Dames & Lautenbacher, 1989; von Benda, 1984) have shown that when repeating an utterance several times, these children speak more slowly and with a much more irregular tempo than age-matched control children. This is true for repetition both of simple syllables and of meaningful sentences. The graph in Figure 10.3 shows the variability of 10 repetitions of the five-syllable utterance "Ipi saw ipi," spoken by three groups of 10 children each.

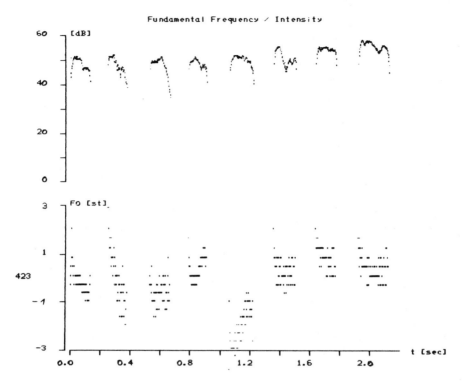

Figure 10.2. An example of an intersyllabic pitch break during the "contin-uous" repetition of the syllable / ka / spoken by a 5-year-old boy with un-intelligible speech.

Insufficient control over the time structure is in part a result of insuffi-cient fine motor control of all three systems involved in vocal output (Amorosa, 1988). The children with specific disorders of speech and lan-guage development had problems controlling each of the factors con-tributing to intonation: intensity, fundamental frequency, and time structure.

Effects on communication

How do these deficits influence the children's ability to use intonation in communication? Several authors have commented that children with specific speech and language disorders have normal intonation and that some of them even use intonation to compensate for a lack of verbal skills (De Hirsch, 1967; Menyuk, 1978; Myklebust, 1954). Von Benda (1984) asked trained listeners to judge the intonation of children with speech

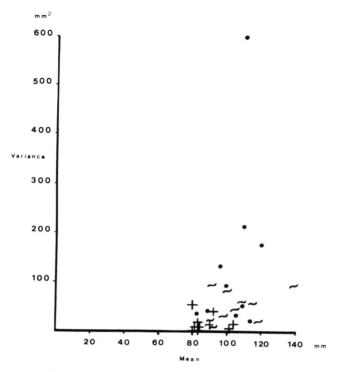

Figure 10.3. Scatter graph showing the mean length of 10 repetitions of the utterance "Ipi saw ipi" and the variance by subject, measured from spectrograms in mm. Children with normal speech and language development: + = 10–12 years old (N = 10); ~ = 5–6 years old (N = 10). Children with specific developmental disorders of speech and language: • = 10–12 years old (N = 10).

and language disorders from short samples of tape-recorded spontaneous speech. Even though the listeners scored deficits on individual parameters (e.g., problems with time structure or low variability in fundamental frequency), none of them found the intonation as such to be abnormal.

Moreover, intensity and fundamental frequency contours show that even though there are differences in the details between the children with and without speech / language deficits, the general contours are similar. The differences seem to be such that the listener can attribute them to motor control problems.

As mentioned before, there are no systematic studies on nonverbal problems. Clinical judgments do not indicate any abnormalities in laughing, crying, or sighing, although, if the assessments are based on tape recordings, the children are often judged to be much younger than they actually are.

Early infantile autism

Children with early infantile autism usually show abnormalities in their development from early on. Besides stereotypies, compulsive behavior, and marked deficits in social behavior, autistic children have abnormal language development. Only about half such children speak at all. Those who do show grammatical deficits similar to the deficits seen in children with developmental speech and language disorders, but their main disturbance is clearly in the communicative use of language. Usually these children are considered to have an "odd," "monotonous," or "robot-like" intonation.

Intensity

Studies of autistic children's utterances show no sudden intersyllabic intensity changes such as are found in children with disorders of speech and language development. But the intensity varies more widely in autistic children than in children without autism, whether or not the latter have speech and language deficits. Voice fading at the end of an utterance is often observed (Fig. 10.4), but there is no indication that this is due to insufficient control of the speech breathing system (von Benda, 1984).

Fundamental frequency

The range of the fundamental frequency within an utterance is greater in autistic children than in normal children matched for age and IQ score (von Benda, 1984; von Benda & Amorosa, 1987). There are no abnormalities of vocal fold vibration, the signals being regular during voiced parts of utterances. Voice phenomena such as pitch breaks, observed in the children with abnormal speech and language development, are usually not seen in autistic individuals. Most autistic children are able to sing melodies correctly, which shows their ability to control pitch, whereas this is impossible for the majority of the language-impaired children.

Time structure

The time structure of utterances produced by autistic children differs from that in language-impaired and normal children. The duration of

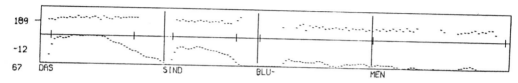

Figure 10.4. Contours of fundamental frequency and intensity for the utterance "Das sind Blumen" (These are flowers), spoken by a 17-year-old
autistic adolescent. The intensity contour shows voice fading. *(Top)* Pitch
contour, with mean F0 given in Hz on the left. *(Bottom)* Intensity contour,
with maximum value per utterance given in dB (negative value on the
left). The number in the lower lefthand corner indicates the speaking rate,
in ms per cm, from the original computer printout.

utterances varies, but this is not because of an overall irregularity of
timing, as in the language-disordered children; rather, it is due to sudden speech rushes that are not explainable by the sound structure of the
words rushed, by articulatory problems, or by semantic content (von
Benda, 1984).

From the experimental evidence available so far, it appears that autistic children, if they develop language at all, have no fine motor problems
affecting control of intensity, fundamental frequency, and time structure. This is supported by clinical observations: When imitating a model
or in echolalic speech, autistic children are able to repeat utterances with
appropriate intonation, but when producing spontaneous utterances they
do not use intonation appropriate for the content or situation.

Von Benda (1984) showed that the time structure and the contours of
fundamental frequency and intensity of utterances spoken by autistic
children are different from those in normal children matched for age and
IQ score. In the autistic children, the maxima and minima of fundamental frequency and intensity occur in different syllables, and they are not
correlated with each other or with an increase or decrease in speaking
rate. Each child seems to have its own, idiosyncratic pattern for the three
parameters, a pattern that it repeats over and over, independent of the
particular words used in the utterance and the semantic content. In contrast, the patterns of normal children are quite similar to each other (Figs.
10.5 and 10.6).

Effects on communication

Because of the unexpected, and at times contradictory, messages in the
intonational patterns of autistic children, it is difficult for the listener to

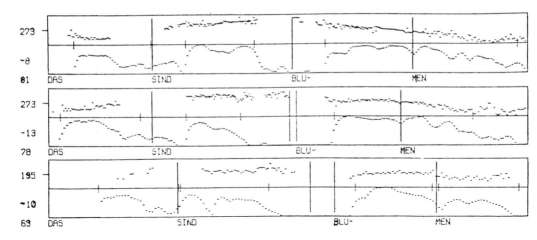

Figure 10.5. Contours of fundamental frequency and intensity for three children with normal speech / language development for the same utterance as in Figure 10.4.

decide where phrase boundaries are, which syllables carry stress, and whether a statement or a question is intended. In von Benda's study (1984), even trained phoneticians made global-impressionistic statements similar to those found in the literature on autism, when judging the intonation of autistic children's utterances from tape recordings. Most of these statements had negative connotations, whereas the statements about children with speech and language disorders were neutral.

A study by Ricks and Wing (1975) showed that even preverbal autistic children have idiosyncratic vocal signaling. Parents of autistic children can interpret the vocal signals of their own autistic child according to specific situations likely to elicit specific emotions, but they are unable to interpret the utterances of other autistic children, whereas parents of normally developing preverbal infants can often recognize the specific situation that led to a given vocal signal in both their own and other infants. This can be seen as an indication that even though autistic children are able to express various emotions, they can do so only in their own idiosyncratic way.

Conclusion

These two disorders of vocal signaling in children are quite different. Children with specific disorders of speech and language development

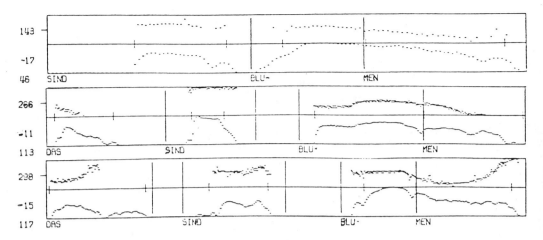

Figure 10.6. Contours of fundamental frequency and intensity for three autistic children for the same utterance as in Figure 10.4 and 10.5.

have problems of fine motor control in the three systems important for oral communication: the speech breathing, phonatory, and articulatory systems. These problems can be demonstrated in recordings of spontaneous and elicited speech through acoustic analysis and through judgments by trained listeners. No systematic studies have been made of emotional vocalizations (e.g., laughing, moaning, or crying) or on the emotional intonation of verbal utterances in this group of children. Even though clinical observations indicate that there are no obvious abnormalities here, systematic studies including acoustic analysis might show deviations similar to those found in the intonation contours of spontaneous speech samples and due to the same problems of fine motor coordination.

The differences in the contours of intensity and fundamental frequency and in the time structure, compared with the speech of normal children, are large enough to be noted by trained listeners, but they never lead to a global judgment of "odd" or "strange" intonation. Clinical observations also show that these anomalies are never unusual enough to make it difficult to infer the emotional state of the child.

In terms of the three subsystems of neural control of vocal utterances described by Jürgens (1986, and chapter 2 of the present volume), the dysfunction is most likely to be in the third subsystem. This subsystem consists of the motor cortex with its connected structures, namely, the cerebellum, ventrolateral thalamus, somatosensory cortex, putamen, and pyramidal tract. In which structure the dysfunction is located and whether this is the same structure in all children is unclear, however, and more studies are needed.

In terms of Marler, Evans, and Hauser's analysis of the development of signaling behavior (chapter 4 of the present volume), the breakdown in the system occurs early in the development of production skills. But since the deviations are not so great that the listener is liable to misinterpret the vocal signal, they usually do not interfere with the early interactive routines between child and caregiver and hence allow the further development of vocal exchanges.

Children with early infantile autism clearly have a different disorder. These children have adequate control over the three fine motor systems necessary for vocal output, as they show in their perfect imitations of model sentences – for example, in echolalic speech – but they do not use the intonational patterns of normal children in their spontaneous utterances. This leads to negative reactions in others and to the judgment that the intonation in autistic children is "odd," "bizarre," "robot-like," or even "nonhuman." Moreover, these children do not use the expected intonational patterns in their nonverbal emotional vocalizations, as the study of Ricks and Wing (1975) showed.

Bormann-Kischkel (1990) and Hobson, Ouston, and Lee (1988) showed that autistic children, adolescents, and adults can match photographs of nonemotional events to relevant sounds on a tape recording but that when they are asked to match photographs of faces showing emotion to emotionally expressive voices they perform much more poorly than control subjects matched for age, sex, and IQ score.

The findings summarized thus far indicate that it is not only the intonation of spontaneous utterances that is abnormal in autistic individuals but also the ability to match perceived differences in intonational pattern with facial expressions of emotions. This is backed by clinical observations that autistic children do not seem to recognize the emotional state of a partner from nonverbal signs and that it is difficult for a caregiver to recognize the emotional state of an autistic person unless he or she is quite familiar with that individual.

In terms of the three subsystems of neural control of vocal utterances described by Jürgens (chapter 2 of the present volume), in autistic individuals the disorder may be in the second subsystem (the periaqueductal gray, the anterior cingulate cortex, and the subcortical limbic structures), which is necessary for the connection between emotional states and the motor expression of these states. Possibly the perception of species-specific intonational patterns is not connected to emotional states in the same way in autistic children as in normal individuals. If so, then the autistic children cannot benefit from intonational patterns used frequently by mothers in their dialogues with infants to influence the state of the baby, promote turn taking, and prepare the baby for communicative and later verbal interactions (see chapter 12 by M. Papoušek and chapter 13 by Fernald in the present volume).

Systematic studies of the types of emotional vocalizations in children with and without abnormalities, combined with studies of the children's ability to perceive and interpret vocal signals, are necessary to better understand the abnormalities of vocal signaling in children and their relationship to disorders of neural control.

References

Amorosa, H. (1988). Die Untersuchung kindlicher Sprechbewegungsstörungen mit Hilfe der akustischen Analyse. Unpublished postdoctoral dissertation, University of Munich.

Amorosa, H., von Benda, U., Dames, M., & Schäfersküpper, P. (1986). Deficits in fine motor coordination in children with unintelligible speech. *European Archives of Psychiatry and Neurological Sciences, 236*, 26–30.

Amorosa, H., von Benda, U., & Wagner, E. (1990). Voice problems in children with unintelligible speech as indicators of deficits in fine motor coordination. *Folia Phoniatrica, 42*, 64–70.

Bormann-Kischkel, C. (1990). *Erkennen autistische Kinder Personen und Emotionen?* Regensburg: Roderer.

Dames, K. (1986). Einfluß der Syntax auf die Zeitstruktur der Nachsprechleistungen sprachentwicklungsgestörter und sprachunauffälliger Kinder. In G. Kegel, T. Arnhold, K. Dahlmeier, G. Schmid, & B. Tischer (Eds.), *Sprechwissenschaft und Psycholinguistik: Beiträge aus Forschung und Praxis* (pp. 144–216). Opladen: Westdeutscher Verlag.

Dames, K., & Lautenbacher, S. (1989). Die Zeitstruktur von Nachsprechleistungen bei sprachentwicklungsgestörten und sprachunauffälligen Kindern. In G. Kegel, T. Arnhold, K. Dahlmeier, G. Schmid, & B. Tischer (Eds.) *Sprechwissenschaft und Psycholinguistik: Beiträge aus Forschung und Praxis* (Vol. 3, pp. 269–285). Opladen: Westdeutscher Verlag.

De Hirsch, K. (1967). Differential diagnosis between aphasic and schizophrenic language in children. *Journal of Speech and Hearing Disorders, 32*, 3–10.

Hobson, R. P., Ouston, J., & Lee, A. (1988). Emotion recognition in autism: Coordinating faces and voices. *Psychological Medicine, 18*, 911–924.

Jürgens, U. (1986). The squirrel monkey as an experimental model in the study of cerebral organization of emotional vocal utterances. *European Archives of Psychiatry and Neurological Sciences, 236*, 40–43.

Menyuk, P. (1978). Linguistic problems in children with developmental dysphasia. In M. O. Wyke (Ed.), *Developmental dysphasia* (pp. 135–158). London: Academic Press.

Myklebust, H. R. (1954). *Auditory disorders in children.* New York: Grune & Stratton.

Ploog, D. (1987). Unser Gehirn – das Organ der Seele und der Kommunikation. *Fundamenta Psychiatrica, 2,* 53–71.

Remschmidt, H., & Schmidt, M. (Eds.) (1986). *Multiaxiales Klassifikationsschema für psychiatrische Erkrankungen im Kindes–und Jugendalter nach Rutter, Shaffer und Sturge.* Bern: Huber.

Ricks, D. M., & Wing, L. (1975). Language, communication, and the use of symbols in normal and autistic children. *Journal of Autism and Childhood Schizophrenia, 5,* 191–221.

Tanaka, S., & Gould, W. J. (1983). Relationships between vocal intensity and noninvasively obtained aerodynamic parameters in normal subjects. *Journal of the Acoustical Society of America, 73,* 1316–1321.

Trojan, F. (1975). *Biophonetik.* Mannheim: Bibliographisches Institut.

Von Benda, U. (1984). Untersuchungen zur Intonation autistischer, sprachent-wicklungsgestörter und sprachunauffälliger Kinder. In H. Günther (Ed.), *Forschungsberichte des Instituts für Phonetik und Sprachliche Kommunikation der Universität München, 20,* 1–232.

Von Benda, U. & Amorosa, H. (1987). Intonation as a potential diagnostic tool in developmental disorders of speech communication. In *Proceedings of the Eleventh International Congress of Phonetic Sciences, Tallinn, Estonia, U.S.S.R.* (Vol. 5, pp. 160–163). Tallinn: Academy of Sciences of the Estonian S.S.R.

Development of nonverbal vocal signals in humans: Interactive support in preverbal dialogues

Introduction and review

REBECCA E. EILERS

It is the theme of finely tuned interactions that characterizes the essays in part IV. Hanuš Papoušek and Bornstein spell out a theory of didactic caregiving as a prominent feature of intuitive parenting skills. These skills are seen as facilitating the infant's communicative development, and strong empirical evidence is brought to bear which establishes a relationship between didactic parental intervention and later measures of language development. The essay is especially exciting because it brings together the work of two laboratories that have had somewhat different focuses over the years.

Mechthild Papoušek concentrates first on the infant side of the parent–infant dyad. She finds that voiced units in the infant's precanonical repertoire signal to the mother critical information about the infant's state and interactional readiness. These vocalizations elicit "motherese," which contains the melodic contours that are also the focus in Fernald's cross-cultural studies. Motherese, in turn, by promoting optimal arousal and turn-taking interactions, specifically supports the infant's ability to continue the interactions. M. Papoušek describes the subtlety of this mutual regulation in intricate and fascinating detail. From the well-orchestrated interactions, the infant learns that his or her vocalizations have differential consequences and (perhaps) that the consequences are predictable; in return, the mother receives positive feedback about the effectiveness of what the Papoušeks describe as "intuitive parenting" skills.

Fernald's theme may be stated (with apologies to MacLuhan) as "the medium [the parent's intonation contour] is the message," at least in the beginning. Fernald contends that infants are predisposed to make sense out of human speech through attention to consistent patterns of intonation that are probably universal components of speech to infants. Mothers (and other caregivers) use special signaling techniques when conversing with infants, and these techniques lead to acoustic proper-

207

ties that have special significance for babies. Fernald proposes a four-stage model, which uses the perceptual prominence and intrinsic affective qualities of a small set of speech contours as a starting point. The model compellingly builds toward the ultimate contribution of intonation contours to the establishment of arbitrary sound–meaning correspondences in mature language.

All in all, these essays present a complex view of the interactionally based communicative competence of the human organism. Inspired by cross-cultural and cross-species comparisons, they are replete with both longitudinal and cross-sectional data embedded within rich theoretical constructs. As such, they present the most elaborated view of early vocal development available.

11. Didactic interactions: Intuitive parental support of vocal and verbal development in human infants

HANUŠ PAPOUŠEK AND MARC H. BORNSTEIN

Several years ago, quite independently and from different perspectives, our two laboratories began to investigate a central but neglected aspect of parent–infant interaction, namely, didactic caregiving. We vary somewhat in our definitions of didactics, emphasize different components, and use complementary methodological strategies to examine didactics empirically; however, our approaches and our interests are converging and mutually reinforcing.

In this essay, we first briefly spell out a theory of didactic caregiving as it is embedded in intuitive parenting. In the succeeding two sections, we review representative findings from our respective laboratories concerned with the microanalysis of parental verbal didactics and infant vocal development, and with the macroanalysis of parental didactics and the development over time of infants' and children's verbal and communicative competencies. In the penultimate section, we make some comparative observations about didactics in human, as opposed to nonhuman, species. These studies and observations lead, in the conclusion, to a synthesis of theory, methodology, and results concerning didactic interactions.

Toward a theory of intuitive parenting and didactics

Interpreters of early human development used to refer to the infant's need for adequate nutrition, hygienic care, emotional bonding, and protection from danger. They gave much less consideration to the child's need to acquire knowledge, understand things and events in the world, and communicate with other conspecifics. To witness infants solving difficult learning tasks and cognitive problems with no other environmental reward than the intrinsic pleasure of success, as we have done in earlier studies (H. Papoušek, 1977; Papoušek & Papoušek, 1979a), gave evidence of the necessity to pay more attention in research to the circumstances under which these neglected needs of infants might be satisfied.

A closer look at the infant's ordinary environment revealed few favorable physical circumstances but plenty of social interactions (Papoušek & Papoušek, 1984). Social interchanges, particularly vocal ones, appeared to be potential chances for environmental contributions to the growth of infant integrative capacities and communicative capacities. Our initial studies of infant conditioning indicated the very early existence of learning capacities and constraints and documented that learning capacities quickly improve during the first months of life, as a result of both physical maturation and practice (H. Papoušek, 1967).

Analyses of early social interaction reveal a close relationship between preverbal communication and infant integrative development (Papoušek & Papoušek, 1981, 1982). Interactional dialogues include innumerable episodes in which caregivers make themselves predictable, controllable, and contingent, initiate instrumental learning, and affectively reward successful learning. Communicative development and acquisition of speech represent the main targets of most naturalistic lessons. At the same time, caregivers' vocal displays represent the main channel for offering infants lessons for practicing cognitive operations and for learning in general. In these terms, early preverbal communication appears to play a dual role in behavioral development: On the one hand, it satiates the infant's need for communication; on the other, it allows the infant to profit from the caregiver's experience.

From this perspective, the parent–infant dyad represents a didactic system par excellence, with polar differences between the partners in terms of degrees of communicative competence and amounts of integrated life experiences. The reason that the system long escaped scientific attention seems to rest on one particular circumstance: Parents are unaware of their didactic competence for teaching infants. They carry out didactic interventions unknowingly, and they cannot consciously report them in interviews or questionnaires.

In humans, communication is one of the most significant means of biological adaptation that has been selected for during evolution. In its many forms, including written words and modern mathematical symbols or electronic codes, communication has allowed an enormous accumulation of knowledge across ages, distances, and even across borders between species. It has codetermined the development of human culture and cultural institutions toward forms that foster still greater improvement of communication. However, it has also improved the biological adaptation of humans, increasing survival rates, population growth, resistance to epidemics, utilization of hostile environments, and compensation for biological constraints in locomotion (Papoušek, Papoušek, Suomi, & Rahn, 1991).

The biological relevance of preverbal communication allows us to make several predictions. First, preverbal communication may be based on biogenetically mediated regulatory programs. Second, such programs may have been selected with a certain surplus and may have included not only the evolution of predispositions in the infant but also the co-evolution of supportive predispositions in the caregiving environment. Third, biogenetically mediated behavioral tendencies often escape conscious notice and rational control; conversely, they are less demanding energically and quicker to carry out, so that they may function more reliably in long and fast sequences of actions (Papoušek et al., 1991).

Evidence on these predicted aspects of communication also indicate their innateness in humans, however difficult this may be to prove directly. The universality of such behavioral tendencies across sex, age, and culture, their nonconscious character, and their early appearance during individual development have been suggested as indirect evidence of a prevailing biogenetic determination in the infant's predisposition for communicative development and in the parent's for guidance (Papoušek & Papoušek, in press-a).

Our hypotheses attribute additional dimensions to early human communication. Infants, often considered altricial on account of their slow development in locomotion, appear precocious with respect to communicative development. In fact, delayed locomotion appears to be adaptive, because it facilitates intimate dyadic interchanges for as long as it takes to acquire the first words. During that time, parents – or other caregivers in general – engage in a large number of interchanges that have clearly didactic overtones. Parents finely adjust their interventions to individual infants with respect to the momentary state of infant alertness, attention, affective mood, and limit of tolerance. They support newly emerging skills, in particular, and direct their development toward the forms best adapted for future use. Therefore, we suggest that there is a primary, biologically determined model of didactics subsumed by intuitive parental behaviors and that it mainly concerns means of preverbal communication – facial, vocal, and gestural – that pave the way for speech (Papoušek & Papoušek, 1978, 1979a). The evolutionary determinants of speech pointed out by Lieberman (1984) – a vocal tract allowing fine differentiation of speech sounds, and nervous structures capable of processing and producing fast strings of signals as well as abstract symbolic representations – seem to include an additional species-specific system of environmental support to infant speech acquisition as well (Papoušek & Papoušek, 1987a).

This new conceptual approach to preverbal communication calls for new research methods. Stimulus–response designs are not suitable for the analysis of dialogic interchanges, for several reasons: Communicative signals represent both responsive and stimulating behaviors simultaneously. Infants are not only responsive recipients of parental stimulation but also elicitors and activators of parental behaviors, and both partners function as complex, highly dynamic, self-regulating systems. Nevertheless, stimulus–response designs may still be used to elucidate the effect of individual communicative components, in verification. Methods using preselected items facilitate clinical or cross-cultural studies but reduce the probability of detecting unpretended behavioral patterns, in contrast to the unbiased observational methods under naturalistic conditions typical of ethological research. The discovery of novel behavioral patterns may call for the analysis of their functional significance in a short-term microanalytic study and also in a suitable combination of naturalistic home observations with experimental laboratory verifications. Conversely, evaluation of their predictive significance for later development in the child may require the use of long-term, macroanalytic methods. Audiovisual recording makes these approaches feasible; such recordings help to replace speculative interpretations with verifiable ones, and they permit identical observations by several specialists from various disciplines (Papoušek & Papoušek, 1987b).

The thesis of the universality of parenting predispositions does not contradict the significance of individual variability during social interaction. Neither does it lower the innate character of the role of learning in expressing predispositions during early interactions. Fundamental infant capacities for integrating experience, combined with supportive tendencies in the social environment, seem to be universal and innate. Yet the combinations, structural and sequential alternatives, overt expressions of those predispositions, and their interdependence in dyadic interactions are variable among individuals and, in combination with unique voiceprints, allow infants and caregivers to identify each other.

Microanalytic studies of parental didactics and infant vocal development

We turn now to the subject of the relations between parental noncon-scious didactic activities and infant communicative development. Mi-croanalytic studies have revealed the first fundamental communicative skills learned during development, as well as their counterparts in in-tuitive parental didactics. The findings concern the interrelationship be-tween communicative, emotional, and cognitive capacities. They point, in one direction, to nonverbal precursors of human communication in other animals and, in the other, indicate unique human predispositions. The findings raise new questions concerning the functional interrela-tionships, which call for further research as topics of immediate rele-vance not only to developmentalists but also to psychiatrists and thera-pists.

Since the first successful attempts to investigate fundamental forms of learning in infants, as well as more complex integrative capacities, such as the detection of and behavioral adjustment to rules in environmental events, including simple numerical concepts (H. Papoušek, 1967; Pa-poušek & Bernstein, 1969), a vast number of studies has revealed sur-prising integrative competencies in infants (for a review, see Harris, 1983). Close to the beginning of postpartum life, human infants express inten-tionality and internal representation of the external world in ways which used to be assumed to function first on the base of language. Infants, as do adults, attend selectively to invariant features, detecting them in complex configurations, conceptualizing them, and extrapolating them beyond the momentary situational context up to the level of symbolic signs.

Thus, newborn infants can profit from intrauterine exposure to the maternal voice and identify it after birth (DeCasper & Fifer, 1980). The capacity to segregate coherent auditory streams from other elements in the auditory background and to group them perceptually according to gestalt laws has been demonstrated in infants as young as 6 weeks (De-many, 1982; Fassbender, 1989). Five-month-old infants are able to match vocal sounds with corresponding pictures of faces articulating those sounds (Kuhl & Meltzoff, 1982).

In comparison with speech, nonverbal communication provides only a limited number of patterns; nevertheless, humans utilize it for far more variable and adaptive forms of communication than do other mammals or birds. Moreover, humans utilize it in rather unique ways to facilitate steps toward speech acquisition in progeny. No matter how well the infant's early integrative capacities function, studies of infant learning suggest that their efficiency is still limited and subject to further improvement, most probably ascribable to maturation as well as practice (H. Papoušek, 1967, 1977).

Developmental constraints are particularly clear in the infant's production of vocal sounds. (The development of this capacity is discussed in detail in the chapters by Oller and Eilers, and by M. Papoušek, in the present volume.) The immature vocal tract, with insufficient supralaryngeal cavities, allows no fine modulation of fundamental voicing. Moreover, the neural regulation of breathing is not yet capable of prolonging expiration for the purpose of modifying vocal signals other than the cry. However, this initial incapacity to modulate vowels and to segment expiration to form chains of consecutive syllables may give the social environment a chance to influence the developmental process in infant communication and guide it toward communicative integration within the culture.

The effects of culture become evident soon after birth in the perceptual competence of infants. Infants differentiate speech sounds from other sounds (Eimas, Siqueland, Juszyk, & Vigorito, 1971) and perceive categorical differences in voicing, not only on the basis of innate universal predispositions but also on the basis of early experience in a given cultural environment (Lasky, Syrdal-Lasky, & Klein, 1975; Streeter, 1976; Werker & Tees, 1984).

One important avenue of environmental influence on early vocal communication can be found in mutual vocal matching between caregivers and infants. Vocal matching reflects the infant's capacity for vocal imitation and the parent's tendency to imitate infant sounds from the first postpartum interactions, thus providing a modeling / imitative frame that offers frequent displays of imitable models and much corrective feedback to infant vocal practice (Kaye, 1982; Papoušek & Papoušek, 1989). Vocal matching plays a significant role in human preverbal communication and seems to be specific to humans. Parents encourage infant imitation, engage infants in playful applications of vocal matching, and affectively reward successful matching. Empathetic matching in vocal and facial expressions of emotional feelings provides infants with feedback which may function as a "biological echo" or a "biological mirror" and influence the development of the self-concept (Papoušek & Papoušek, 1989).

The significance of early vocal imitation has engendered increasing interest among linguists in relation to establishing automated neuro-motor circuits (Lieberman, 1984) and links among perceived articulatory movements, auditory perceptions, and corresponding motor controls (Studdert-Kennedy, 1983). This interest has also been nourished by evidence about neonatal imitation of manual and facial gestures (Field, Woodson, Greenberg, & Cohen, 1983; Meltzoff & Moore, 1983), infant intermodal integration of speech sounds (Kuhl & Meltzoff, 1982; Spelke, 1979; Studdert-Kennedy, 1983), and the primacy of parental imitation (Papoušek & Papoušek, 1987b).

With a certain leap in skills, parents display models for imitation in those patterns that have newly appeared in the infant's repertoire and require practice. Thus, the timing of models corresponds to the order in which elementary prerequisites for speech develop: It starts with the prolongation and melodic contouring of fundamental vowel-like voicing, continues with playful instigation of consonants and segmentation of expiration, and leads to the use of canonical syllables and first words. We found evidence of this sequence in a long-term study of 17 German mother–infant dyads (Papoušek & Papoušek, 1989).

Parents, siblings, and other caregivers appear in the light of these new findings as natural, nonconscious, yet excellent teachers: They establish optimal conditions for teaching interventions, devote their main efforts to the most important means of adaptation, gradually order and adjust teaching tasks to infant constraints, motivate infants effectively, teach playfully, and reward progress with vivid emotional engagement. They do so unknowingly, and the unintentional, intuitive character of their interventions guarantees that these caregivers can cope with the fast flow of interactional episodes without becoming worn down due to excessive rational decisions (Papoušek & Papoušek, 1987b).

Preverbal vocal signals, facial expressions, and other bodily gestures used to be interpreted as mere graded, noncategorical expressions of infant affect. In our view their significance seems to be broader. Our own studies on infant learning (H. Papoušek, 1969, 1977) give evidence of an intimate relation between emotional / behavioral states preceding the application of experimental stimulation. On the other hand, the course of integrative processes influences consecutive states and elicits vocal and facial expressions interpretable as signs of distress or pleasure resulting from infant coping with experimental tasks. Since infants can hardly be expected to hide their internal feelings intentionally, overt expressions of affect in problematic and learning situations can serve caregivers as feedback about infant coping and as guideposts to facilitate didactic overtures.

Caregivers' facial expressions also serve as a means of referential guidance for infants in novel and problematic situations. Not knowing what to do, infants may check the caregiver's face, which unintentionally expresses encouragement or discouragement (Klinnert, 1984).

Analyses of the facial movements of infants reveal other functions relevant to preverbal communication (Papoušek & Papoušek, in press-b). For instance, a half-open mouth and upper lip raised so as to display a smile and the upper teeth have been identified as a "play face" (van Hooff, 1972), signaling to the social environment that the individual's concurrent behaviors are meant as joyful rather than serious acts. Parents tend to use this signal when they try to demonstrate potential unpleasant consequences of inappropriate infant behaviors. Infants and children show a play face while exploring the potential consequences of behaviors which caregivers reject or prohibit. The biological roots of the play face are particularly well documented in comparative research, and human beings share this form of signaling with other primates.

Another example of the role of facial movements is various oral instructions which caregivers unknowingly display to infants in feeding situations or to provoke vocalization (Papoušek & Papoušek, 1987b). During hand or spoon feeding, caregivers unwittingly demonstrate lip and tongue movements suitable to the reception of food. The biogenetic origin of these "instructions" may be seen in their universality across sex, age, and cultures and in their emergence in infants around the age of 10 months (Papoušek & Papoušek, 1979b).

Facial models for the proper production of speech sounds constitute particularly frequent examples of intuitive instruction and are used time and time again during parent–infant dialogues. It is therefore not surprising that several behavioral strategies have coevolved in intuitive parenting to direct the infant's visual attention to the parent's face. According to our observations (Papoušek & Papoušek, 1987b), parents position their faces in the middle of the infant's visual field, use various vocal and nonvocal gestures to capture the infant's visual attention, and reward the infant's achievements with striking "greeting responses" (high-raised eyebrows, slight retroflexion of the head, half-open mouth), often followed with vocal greetings and invitations to vocal interchange.

Obviously, the earliest vocal interchanges are embedded in complex behavioral patterns and involve complex predispositions on the part of both infant and parent. These are ascribable to coevolution of a species-specific environmental support to the infant acquisition of speech. Patterns of support also change with the infant's progress. For instance, face-to-face interactions are particularly important during the first postpartum months but decrease, in favor of interventions in which parents confront infants with other people and with objects in the immediate environment, as soon as the infant starts reaching, pointing, sitting, or crawling.

A complete understanding of the biological origins of intuitive parenting awaits comparative investigations in nonhuman primates and other animals. Infancy research has richly profited from cooperation between researchers in the human and primate areas, as exemplified in studies by Chevalier-Skolnikoff (1982), Vauclair and Bard (1983), and those in part II of the present volume.

Inasmuch as intuitive parental interventions are often elicited by behavioral cues from the infant, they function as contingent responses, and infants may learn how to control them through instrumental learning. That a vocal or facial signal may influence parental behaviors is undoubtedly crucial to the infant's future mastery of speech. It concerns the role of communicative signals in eliciting answers from the social environment, in the sense of Bühler's concept and of Scherer's reminder (in chapter 3 of the present volume).

These appealing aspects of vocal signals have attracted less attention in comparative research and in experimental analyses of communication than have expressions of feelings or representations of situational contexts. However, our long-term observations on German mother–infant dyads studied microanalytically give evidence that during the first year of life infants acquire the capacity of using their feelings as intentional communicative signals (Papoušek, Papoušek, & Koester, 1986). This developmental process manifested itself in a transition from tonic to phasic features, in either fussy or pleasurable vocal and facial expressions. Tonic features, in the form of unintentional autonomic responses with slowly increasing or decreasing intensities and relatively long durations of either emotional expressions or shifts from one emotional state to the other, were the only type of emotional expressions in 2- and 4-month-olds. However, during the second half of the year, displays of joy or cry increasingly appeared, in fast phasic forms of short signals with sudden onsets and stops and eventually with fast shifts from joy to cry, and vice versa – that is, in forms that are typically reserved for communicative signals.

Two psychobiological aspects of preverbal communication deserve attention: (1) Intuitive parenting interventions offer the infant many opportunities to master vocal control and elementary communicative skills and thus mainly involve procedural learning. In contrast to data-based, declarative learning, procedural learning is more resistant to amnesia and therefore represents the more meaningful type of learning during the first year of life (Papoušek & Papoušek, 1984). (2) Parent–infant vocal interchanges convincingly exemplify a match between twofold behavioral programs, selected for during coevolution: development of infantile predispositions for speech acquisition in preverbal infants, in didactic harmony with parental predispositions for facilitating the acquisition of speech in infants and for affective enrichment of infant motivation for that achievement (Papoušek & Papoušek, 1987b, in press-a).

Preverbal communication plays a twofold instigative role in human development. It meets the infant's need to be near and to communicate with another individual, and it represents an important avenue for didactic interventions from the social environment, allowing caregivers to share their experiences, to guide the development of infant predispositions toward an optimal social integration, and to support infant cognitive growth in general (Papoušek & Papoušek, in press-a). Consequently, deficient preverbal communication may unfavorably affect not only communicative development as such but the infant's mental development in general. The next part of our essay addresses this consequence.

Macroanalytic, longitudinal studies of parental didactics and infant verbal development

What concurrent and predictive validity has didactic caregiving for children's mental development, and according to what mechanisms of action does it function?

We standardized the general conduct of observations of mothers and infants so as to permit comparability across several samples: Dyads were observed at home in naturalistic interactions at optimal times for infants, and mothers were asked to follow their usual routines and, as far as possible, to disregard the observer's presence. To evaluate the generalizability of findings, some studies were replicated in a different culture, specifically among Japanese.

First we observed activities of primiparous mothers and infants at 2 and at 5 months of age. In an analysis of mother and infant exchanges, we found, significantly, that specific mother and infant activities corresponded: For example, mothers who engaged their infants more often socially had infants who did more social orienting (but not didactic – that is, environmental – orienting); conversely, more maternal didactic encouragement was associated with greater infant environmental (rather than social) orienting. Significantly, mothers' activities did not positively covary at either age, nor did those of their infants. Further, some maternal activities were stable during this period, some developmentally increased, and some developmentally decreased; infants' activities were unstable, but most increased over time. In addition, mothers and infants influenced one another over time in specific ways. For example, mothers who tended more often to orient their infants didactically at 2 months not only had 2-month-olds who oriented more to the environment but they had 5-month-olds who explored properties, objects, and events in the environment more, even when stability in the infant and concurrent maternal stimulation at 5 months were both controlled (Bornstein & Tamis-LeMonda, 1990).

In a second, concurrent study, we examined the relationship between mothers' didactic caregiving and language production, language comprehension, play competence, and attention span in their 13-month-old toddlers. We found that flexible language production and flexible language comprehension covaried and that play competence covaried with flexible language comprehension and with attention span. By contrast, neither language production nor language comprehension related positively to attention span. Maternal didactic stimulation related significantly to toddler language comprehension and to play but not to language production or to attention span. Structural equation modeling showed that the common variance underlying language comprehension and play competence differed from the variance underlying play competence and attention span and that maternal didactics related significantly to the "play / language" factor in toddlers but not to the "play / attention" factor (Tamis-LeMonda & Bornstein, 1990).

We have also examined the potential longer-term effects of didactic caregiving in infancy in several different longitudinal studies. In one, we assessed mothers' active and responsive didactic caregiving and infants' habituation at 5 months for their predictive relevance to toddlers' language comprehension, language production, and pretense play at 13 months. (Mothers' didactics were also assessed at 13 months.) We again used structural equation modeling to examine the unique contributions of maternal stimulation of each kind and infant habituation to toddlers' cognitive abilities. Active didactic caregiving at 5 months predicted toddlers' language competence, and both active and responsive caregiving predicted a latent variable of language and play, each when the other was partialed. This finding held after the influence of habituation in the infants at 5 months was partialed and after the influence of maternal didactics at 13 months was also partialed. Links between early parental didactics and later verbal development and representational ability in children are apparently direct, not simply mediated by child capacity or by continuing maternal didactic caregiving. Infants whose mothers engaged more often in didactic caregiving, active or responsive, had more flexible or decontextualized language comprehension and exhibited more advanced symbolic representational abilities as toddlers (Bornstein & Tamis-LeMonda, 1989; Tamis-LeMonda & Bornstein, 1989).

In a second longitudinal study, we explored individual differences and developmental changes in mother and toddler nonsymbolic and symbolic play across the second year of life. To do so, we developed a single coding system to assess play sophistication in both mothers and toddlers. Characteristics of mother and toddler play were regularly associated at the two ages, and over time mother and toddler play sophistication changed in similar ways. For example, between 13 and 20 months, mothers and toddlers both moved toward more sophisticated levels of pretense play, and changes in one partner's play were regularly associated with changes in the other partner's play. Moreover, significant changes in mothers' and toddlers' play persisted after covarying partner influences were taken into account. Our findings indicated that individual differences and age-related changes in toddler second-year play were mediated by mother play, although they were also partly motivated by processes independent of mother (Tamis-LeMonda & Bornstein, 1991).

We have also found evidence of a long-term outcome of early didactics in a third longitudinal study. Mother–child dyads were seen at three points in development. At 4 months and at 1 year, we evaluated mothers' didactics. At 1 year, we assessed productive vocabulary size in the toddlers, and at 4 years we assessed children's verbal intelligence by the Wechsler Preschool and Primary Scale of Intelligence. Four-month-olds whose mothers engaged in didactics more possessed larger productive vocabularies at 1 year of age, and they scored higher on a standardized test of verbal intelligence at 4 years. Babies were also observed in a habituation assessment in the laboratory. Path modeling helped to determine the relative contributions of maternal didactics at 4 months versus 12 months on the child's outcome at 4 years. Maternal didactics at 4 months contributed more strongly to the child's test performance at 4 years than did the same maternal didactics at 12 months. Maternal didactics also predicted child verbal intelligence, over and above the significant predictive power of habituation measured earlier in infancy (Bornstein, 1985).

Our data concur with those of others: Several researchers have uncovered a relationship between the mothers' didactic forms of behavior and the development of children's skills. The evidence is perhaps strongest for infancy and toddlerhood. For example, maternal stimulation in the first year predicts play competence at 1 year (Belsky, Goode, & Most, 1980), habituation efficiency at 1 year (Riksen-Walraven, 1978), cognitive competence at $1\frac{1}{2}$ year (Clarke-Stewart, 1973), cognitive / language competence at 2 years (Olson, Bates, & Bayles, 1984), language performance at 3 years (Bee et al., 1982), and school performance at 6 years (Coates & Lewis, 1984). Significantly, too, like Kazuo Miyake, we determined that maternal didactic caregiving activities possess predictive relevance for the child's developing intellectual competence in non-Western culture. Specifically, we found that Japanese mothers who more often engaged their 5-month-olds didactically, actively or responsively, had children who scored higher on the Japanese version of the Peabody Picture Vocabulary Test when they reached $2\frac{1}{2}$ years of age (Bornstein, Miyake, Azuma, Tamis-LeMonda & Toda, 1990).

Caregiving alone does not determine the course or outcome of individual development. Caregiving modes wax and wane in effectiveness, modulated by the developmental status of the child and by individual differences among children. A type of interaction may have telling consequences at an early developmental period or at a later one, at an early but not at a later one, or at a later one but not at an early one. The motor, mental, and social status of the child undoubtedly help to determine whether, and modify how, different caregiving experiences affect development. Moreover, if didactic caregiving exerts its effect on infants early in development, those effects could persist from that point, or they could persist only in aggregation – that is, in their consistency through time (Bornstein, 1989).

Additionally, infant competencies might differentially affect caregivers in ways that subsequently redound to the infants *qua* children. An example of such complex interactive effects emerged when we investigated the role of didactic activities in 1-year-olds' developing verbal competencies. In this study, mothers and infants participated in two home visits, one designed to assess interaction and the other independently to assess infant language competency. When relations between mother and baby were evaluated, it was discovered that maternal object-centered didactics in the home were significantly associated with infant language skills. However, our understanding of these relations was greatly enhanced through the application of hierarchical regression techniques designed to uncover simultaneous and conditional effects of different maternal activities on infant skills. Regression analyses confirmed that maternal didactics were a positive factor in infants' developing competencies. However, the potential influence of this activity appeared to be conditionally related to other maternal activities, as well as to the active or receptive role of the child in the interaction. For example, 1-year-olds whose mothers exerted a high degree of control over didactic exchanges profited most in their language if their mothers also frequently engaged in social activities. Where infants were more controlling of didactic exchanges with their mothers, however – that is, where infants initiated and maintained object-centered activities more than their mothers – maternal social input was negligibly, and sometimes negatively, associated with infant language skill (Vibbert & Bornstein, 1989).

A comparative perspective

We now turn to set some of our findings in a larger comparative and evolutionary perspective. In primates, particularly in apes, the complexity of neural structures approaches the complexity of the human brain and presumably allows chimpanzees, in particular, detailed differentiation of facial and manual gestures as well as the capacity to learn how to use such gestures as signs for communication with human caregivers (Gardner & Gardner, 1969). However, chimpanzees lack a vocal tract comparable to that of humans, and hence they cannot learn to speak. Children surpass chimpanzees in communicative capacity at approximately 3 years of age and can be viewed as precocious in communication, although in most other respects (as previously noted) human children have usually been considered altricial, on account of their relatively slow locomotor development.

Vocal imitation and vocal play have been considered to be important to speech learning and to speech evolution (Lieberman, 1984; Studdert-Kennedy, 1983). The vocal play, or babbling, of human infants may be paralleled by the constant stream of highly variable vocalizations in cotton-top tamarins and marmosets separated from their parents (Snowdon, 1982). Outside humans, vocal imitation has been reported in only a few species of songbirds and marine mammals. Primate studies have not yet been successful in demonstrating vocal learning, perhaps because too few primate species and too few vocalization types have been studied (Newman & Symmes, 1982).

Pointing out similarities and dissimilarities in communicative processes, comparative research helps to uncover the specificity of behavioral tendencies subserving human communication either in general or in a closer relation to parental care of infant progeny. We have reported one intriguing example in the regulation of eye-to-eye contact on infant attention in mirror situations (Papoušek & Papoušek, 1974). Eye-to-eye contact also draws the infant's attention to the caregiver's face, where a complex display of muscle activities (particularly in the perioral and periorbital areas) offers finely differentiated examples of the production of both vocal and nonvocal communicative signals – expressions of internal states and emotional feelings, as well as indicators of the course of thought processes (Fridlund, Ekman, & Oster, 1982). Thus, it seems to be adaptively relevant for the infant to learn to pay close attention to the caregiver's face. Correspondingly, it may be especially relevant for parents to support and reinforce this kind of infant learning.

Adult parents seek a vertically parallel, face-to-face posture in relation to the infant and use various forms of stimulation in order to increase the probability of mutual visual contact. This parental tendency is rather unique in the animal world. Not even infrahuman primate parents have been reported to try to catch the infant's eye, although nonhuman primates may carefully observe newborns and infants and sporadically be in eye-to-eye contact with them (Ehardt & Blount, 1984). Humans, of course, have good reason to draw their infant's attention to their faces, since facial behaviors mediate many relevant messages, including instructions for the proper production of speech sounds and for feeding.

Conclusions

Didactics as a scholarly discipline deals with methods of conveying knowledge. It was first professionally and scientifically developed during the Enlightenment. Comenius, author of the seminal work *Opera didactica omnia* (1657), wrote a primer for "maternal schools," the predecessors of today's nursery schools. In *Schola materni gremii* (1628), Comenius expressed unusually progressive beliefs: "(1) that educational care for children should be started during infancy and be based upon parental care; and (2) that education for children in both preschool and school should be carried out playfully." Obviously, Comenius's advice was based on rich empirical experience in educational activity and on the intuitive insights of a loving parent. Comenius was a religious dualist, a believer in the existence of the immortal soul who stressed the mutual interrelations between the mind's needs and bodily health and growth.

A close look at the human infant's niche in nature reveals a limited set of learning situations that result from interactions with the physical, inanimate environment (Newson, 1979; Papoušek & Papoušek, 1984). By contrast, a wealth of interesting stimulation is provided by the infant's social environment. Social stimulation of the infant by caregivers is rich, multimodal, and reciprocal. Microanalytic and longitudinal macroanalytic analyses reveal several kinds of episodes interpretable as supporting infants' integrative capacities during dyadic interactions. This stimulation so matches the infant's integrative competencies that it invokes the impression of didactic intervention.

Theories of human evolution have tended to pay far more attention to aggressive than to prosocial behaviors, yet evidence of parental support for the acquisition of speech and language during development calls for a general reconsideration of the role of prosocial behaviors in human evolution. Care for dependent progeny and prosocial behavior in general have recently aroused increased interest among theoreticians of human evolution (Lovejoy, 1981).

Theories concerning the evolution of speech have not yet seriously examined the scripts by which parents help their infants to acquire first language. Nevertheless, parents seem universally – albeit unknowingly – to follow similar patterns in guiding infants from the initial stages of insufficient respiratory control to the advanced stages of using meaningful words in complex ways (Papoušek & Papoušek, 1981). Our approach focuses attention on parents' contribution to their infants' integrative and communicative capacities. We have suggested that parents may provide much of this support unkowingly in the form of intuitive, relatively universal behaviors which we have labeled "didactic," and we have described the behavioral repertoire of parental didactics based on our present level of knowledge and discussed its significance for some key integrative processes in infants.

For a long time, parental participation in infant vocal and verbal development was viewed as consisting of consciously performed and culturally determined behaviors. However, our earliest observations indicated to us that parental behaviors also comprise elements of psychobiological preadaptedness. We saw these elements in universality (across age, sex, and culture), in early functioning during development, and in the absence of conscious awareness, as when we interviewed parents after our observations to find out to what degree they were aware of their performance and the meaning of the behaviors they displayed during the interactions and when we tested the degree to which parents are able to control their behaviors.

The human infant may be precocious in developing integrative prerequisites of speech; however, these prerequisites – at least in their elementary forms – are not species-specific human capacities. Chimpanzees, for instance, reach a sufficient level of abstraction and symbolization to acquire a sign language, although they lack the anatomical and physiological qualities of the vocal tract which allow the production and rich modification of voice. Conversely, some birds possess the necessary vocal tract tools but lack the complexity of thought and culture typical of higher primates. Thus, human beings seem to possess an advantageous combination of capabilities that, in general, are present separately in various animal species. With respect to present knowledge about early parent–infant communication, we question the assumption that the evolution of integrative capacities and vocal tract alone explains the evolution of speech. We suggest that early didactic support of infants' communicative development in general, and perhaps vocal play in particular, should also be considered and systematically examined as key determinants of vocal and verbal development.

Focusing on parent–infant interactions, we must acknowledge two consequent hypotheses: (1) Parent–infant interactions are didactic on account of polar differences between the two in the amount of integrated life experience; (2) parent–infant interactions are special, since there is a polar difference in communicative capacities between the adult having advanced speech and the infant lacking any speech.

Why, then, have didactics previously escaped the scrutiny of the research microscope? There may be two chief reasons. First, didactics have typically been viewed as a product of human culture involving solely verbal communication. Therefore, they have probably not been considered in interactions where speech is absent in at least one partner. In some precursory form, however, didactic tendencies may have contributed to the emergence of culture. Surprisingly, even Bruner (1971), who admitted various precursors of human competencies in the animal world, considered instruction, as such, to be strictly a species-typical characteristic of human culture (p. 118). Conversely, Liedtke (1976), after serving a wealth of comparative material on the presence of both the educational tendencies in animal parents and the need to learn in the young, concluded that the idea of a biological evolution of didactics cannot be rejected. Second, neglect of didactic aspects in human parent–infant interactions may have resulted from a dearth of knowledge about infants' integrative competencies before they were exposed by systematic research.

References

Bee, H. L., Barnard, K. E., Eyres, S. K., Gray, C. A., Hammond, M. A., Spietz, A. L., Snyder, C., & Clark, B. (1982). Prediction of IQ and language skill from perinatal status, child performance, family characteristics, and mother–infant interaction. *Child Development, 53*, 1134–1156.

Belsky, J., Goode, M. K., & Most, R. K. (1980). Maternal stimulation and infant exploratory competence: Cross-sectional, correlational, and experimental analyses. *Child Development, 51*, 1163–1178.

Bornstein, M. H. (1985). How infant and mother jointly contribute to developing cognitive competence in the child. *Proceedings of the National Academy of Sciences* (U.S.A.), *82*, 7470–7473.

    (1989). Sensitive periods in development: Structural characteristics and causal interpretations. *Psychological Bulletin, 105*, 179–197.

Bornstein, M. H., Miyake, K., Azuma, H., Tamis-LeMonda, C. S., & Toda, S. (1990). Responsiveness in Japanese mothers: Consequences and characteristics. *Annual Report of the Research and Clinical Center for Child Development* (pp. 15–26). Sapporo, Japan: University of Hokkaido.

Bornstein, M. H., & Tamis-LeMonda, C. S. (1989). Maternal responsiveness and cognitive development in children. In M. H. Bornstein (Ed.), *Maternal responsiveness: Characteristics and consequences* (pp. 49–61). San Francisco: Jossey-Bass.

    (1990). Activities and interactions of mothers and their firstborn infants in the first six months of life: Covariation, stability, continuity, correspondence, and prediction. *Child Development, 61*, 1206–1217.

Bruner, J. (1971). *The relevance of education.* New York: Norton.

Chevalier-Skolnikoff, S. (1982). A cognitive analysis of facial behavior in Old World monkeys, apes, and human beings. In C. T. Snowdon, C. H. Brown, & M. R. Petersen (Eds.), *Primate communication* (pp. 303–368). Cambridge: Cambridge University Press.

Clarke-Stewart, A. (1973). Interactions between mothers and their young children: Characteristics and consequences. *Monographs of the Society for Research in Child Development, 38* (6–7, Serial No. 153).

Coates, D. L., & Lewis, M. (1984). Early mother–infant interaction and infant cognitive status as predictors of school performance and cognitive behavior in six-year-olds. *Child Development, 55*, 1219–1230.

Comenius, J. A. (1628/1962). *Schola materni gremii.* German edition in J. Heubach (Ed.), *Informatorium der Mutterschule.* Heidelberg: Quelle & Unger, 1962. (Originally published 1628).

    (1657/1954). *Opera didactica omnia.* Amsterdam. German edition in A. Flitner

(Ed.), *Grosse Didaktik. Pädagogische Texte*, Vol. 1. Düsseldorf: Küpper, 1954. (Originally published 1657.)

Darwin, C. (1871). *The descent of man.* London: Murray.

DeCasper, A. J., & Fifer, W. P. (1980). Of human bonding: Newborns prefer their mothers' voice. *Science, 208*, 1174–1176.

Demany, L. (1982). Auditory stream segregation in infancy. *Infant Behavior and Development, 5*, 261–276.

Ehardt, C. L., & Blount, B. G. (1984). Mother–infant visual interaction in Japanese macaques. *Developmental Psychobiology, 17*, 391–405.

Eimas, P. D., Siqueland, E. R., Jusczyk, P., & Vigorito, J. (1971). Speech perception in infants. *Science, 171*, 303–306.

Fassbender C. (1989). *Auditory grouping and segregation processes in infancy.* Unpublished doctoral dissertation, Free University of Berlin.

Field, T., Woodson, R., Greenberg, R., & Cohen, D. (1983). Discrimination and imitation of facial expressions by term and preterm neonates. *Infant Behavior and Development, 6*, 485–490.

Fridlund, A. J., Ekman, P., & Oster, H. (1982). An evolutionary perspective on human facial displays. In A. Siegman & S. Feldstein (Eds.), *Nonverbal communication: A functional perspective* (pp. 143–224). Hillsdale, N.J.: Erlbaum.

Gardner, R. A., & Gardner, B. T. (1969). Teaching sign language to a chimpanzee. *Science, 165*, 664–672.

Harris, P. L. (1983). Infant cognition. In M. Haith & J. J. Campos (Eds.), *Infancy and developmental psychobiology* (pp. 689–782). Vol. 2 of P. H. Mussen (Gen. Ed.), *Handbook of child psychology.* New York: Wiley.

Hooff, J. A., van (1972). A comparative approach to the phylogeny of laughter and smiling. In R. A. Hinde (Ed.), *Non-verbal communication* (pp. 209–241). Cambridge: Cambridge University Press.

Kaye, K. (1982). *The mental and social life of babies: How parents create persons.* Chicago: University of Chicago Press.

Klinnert, M. (1984). The regulation of infant behavior by maternal facial expression. *Infant Behavior and Development, 7*, 447–465.

Kuhl, P. K., & Meltzoff, A. N. (1982). The bimodal perception of speech in infancy. *Science, 218*, 1138–1140.

Lasky, R. E., Syrdal-Lasky, A., & Klein, R. E. (1975). VOT discrimination by four- to six-and-a-half-month-old infants from Spanish environments. *Journal of Experimental Child Psychology, 20*, 215–225.

Lieberman P. (1984). *The biology and evolution of language.* Cambridge, Mass.: Harvard University Press.

Liedtke, M. (1976). *Evolution und Erziehung. Ein Beitrag zur integrativen pädagogischen Anthropologie* (2nd ed.). Göttingen: Vandenhoek & Ruprecht.

Lovejoy, C. O. (1981). The origin of man. *Science, 211*, 341–350.

Meltzoff, A. N., & Moore, M. K. (1983). Newborn infants imitate adult facial gestures. *Child Development, 54*, 702–709.

Newman, J. D., & Symmes, D. (1982). Inheritance and experience in the acquisition of primate acoustic behavior. In C. T. Snowdon, C. H. Brown, & M. R. Peterson (Eds.), *Primate communication* (pp. 259–278). Cambridge: Cambridge University Press.

Newson, J. (1979). Intentional behaviour in the young infant. In D. Schaffer & J. Dunn (Eds.), *The first year of life: Psychological and medical implications of early experience* (pp. 91–96). Chichester: Wiley.

Olson, S. L., Bates, J. E., & Bayles, K. (1984). Mother–infant interaction and the

228   Hanuš Papoušek and Marc H. Bornstein

development of individual differences in children's cognitive competence. *Developmental Psychology, 20,* 166–179.

Papoušek, H. (1967). Experimental studies of appetitional behavior in human newborns and infants. In H. W. Stevenson, E. H. Hess, & H. L. Rheingold (Eds.), *Early behavior: Comparative and developmental approaches* (pp. 249–277). New York: Wiley.

(1969). Individual variability in learned responses in human infants. In R. J. Robinson (Ed.), *Brain and early behavior* (pp. 251–266). London: Academic Press.

(1977). Entwicklung der Lernfähigkeit im Säuglingsalter. In G. Nissen (Ed.), *Intelligenz, Lernen und Lernstörungen* (pp. 75–93). Berlin: Springer.

Papoušek, H., & Bernstein, P. (1969). The functions of conditioning stimulation in human neonates and infants. In A. Ambrose (Ed.), *Stimulation in early infancy* (pp. 229–252). London: Academic Press.

Papoušek, H., & Papoušek, M. (1974). Mirror image and self-recognition in young human infants: I. A new method of experimental analysis. *Developmental Psychobiology, 7,* 149–157.

(1978). Interdisciplinary parallels in studies of early human behavior: From physical to cognitive needs, from attachment to dyadic education. *International Journal of Behavioral Development, 1,* 37–49.

(1979a). The infant's fundamental adaptive response system in social interaction. In E. B. Thoman (Ed.), *Origins of the infant's social responsiveness* (pp. 175–208). Hillsdale, N.J.: Erlbaum.

(1979b). Early ontogeny of human social interaction: Its biological roots and social dimensions. In M. von Cranach, K. Foppa, W. Lepenies, & D. Ploog (Eds.), *Human ethology: Claims and limits of a new discipline* (pp. 456–478). Cambridge: Cambridge University Press.

(1982). Integration into the social world: Survey of research. In P. M. Stratton (Ed.), *Psychobiology of the human newborn* (pp. 367–390). London: Wiley.

(1984). Learning and cognition in the everyday life of human infants. In J. S. Rosenblatt (Ed.), *Advances in the study of behavior* (Vol. 14, pp. 127–163). New York: Academic Press.

(1987a). *The structure and dynamics of early parental interventions: A potential contribution to evolution and ontogeny of speech.* Educational Resources Information Center. Urbana: Clearing House on Early Childhood Education. (ERIC Document No. 276 528).

(1987b). Intuitive parenting: A dialectic counterpart to the infant's integrative competence. In J. D. Osofsky (Ed.), *Handbook of infant development* (2nd ed., pp. 669–720). New York: Wiley.

(in press-a). Early integrative and communicative development: Pointers to humanity. In H. M. Emrich & M. Wiegand (Eds.), *Integrative biological psychiatry.* Berlin: Springer.

(in press-b). Early interactional signalling: The role of facial movements. In A. F. Kalverboer, B. Hopkins, & R. H. Geuze (Eds.), *A longitudinal approach to the study of motor development in early and later childhood.* Cambridge: Cambridge University Press.

Papoušek, H., Papoušek, M., & Koester, L. S. (1986). Sharing emotionality and sharing knowledge: A microanalytic approach to parent–infant communication. In C. E. Izard & P. Read (Eds.), *Measuring emotions in infants and children* (Vol. 2, pp. 93–123). Cambridge: Cambridge University Press.

Papoušek, H., Papoušek, M., Suomi, S., & Rahn, C. (1991). Preverbal communication and attachment: Comparative views. In J. L. Gewirtz & W. M. Kurtines (Eds.), *Intersections with attachment* (pp. 97–122). Hillsdale, N.J.: Erl-baum.

Papoušek, M., & Papoušek, H. (1981). Musical elements in the infant's vocalizations: Their significance for communication, cognition, and creativity. In L. P. Lipsitt (Ed.), Advances in infancy research (Vol. 1, pp. 163–224). Norwood, N.J.: Ablex.

(1989). Forms and functions of vocal matching in interactions between mothers and their precanonical infants. [Special issue]. *First Language, 9,* 137–158.

Papoušek, M., Papoušek, H., & Bornstein, M. H. (1985). The naturalistic vocal environment of young infants: On the significance of homogeneity and variability in parental speech. In T. Field & N. Fox (Eds.), *Social perception in infants* (pp. 269–297). Norwood, N.J.: Ablex.

Riksen-Walraven, J. M. (1978). Effects of caregiver behavior on habituation rate and self-efficacy in infants. *International Journal of Behavioral Development, 1,* 105–130.

Snowdon, C. T. (1982). Linguistic and psycholinguistic approaches to primate vocalization. In C. T. Snowdon, C. H. Brown, & M. R. Petersen (Eds.), *Primate communication* (pp. 212–238). Cambridge: Cambridge University Press.

Spelke, E. S. (1979). Perceiving bimodally specified events in infancy. *Developmental Psychology, 15,* 626–636.

Streeter, L. A. (1976). Language perception of 2-month-old infants shows effects of both innate mechanisms and experience. *Nature, 259,* 39–41.

Studdert-Kennedy, M. (1983). On learning to speak. *Human Neurobiology, 2,* 191–195.

Tamis-LeMonda, C. S., & Bornstein, M. H. (1989). Habituation and maternal encouragement of attention in infancy as predictors of toddler language, play, and representational competence. *Child Development, 60,* 738–751.

(1990). Language, play, and attention at one year. *Infant Behavior and Development, 13,* 85–98.

(1991). Individual variation, correspondence, stability, and change in mother and toddler play. *Infant Behavior and Development, 14,* 143–162.

Vauclair, J., & Bard, K. (1983). Development of manipulations with objects in ape and human infants. *Journal of Human Evolution, 12,* 631–645.

Vibbert, M., & Bornstein, M. H. (1989). Specific associations between domains of mother–child interaction and toddler referential language and pretense play. *Infant Behavior and Development, 12,* 163–184.

Werker, J. F., & Tees, R. C. (1984). Cross-language speech perception: Evidence for perceptual reorganization during the first year of life. *Infant Behavior and Development, 7,* 49–63.

12. Early ontogeny of vocal communication in parent–infant interactions

MECHTHILD PAPOUŠEK

A developmental–interactional approach to communication

Studies of the early stages of vocal communication between human parents and their infants call for specific methodological approaches that can capture the unique nature of this interacting system, namely, the wide difference between the integrative capacities and the communicative repertoires of the respective partners. According to Papoušek and Bornstein (chapter 11 of the present volume), the human infant is unique in both a precocious readiness to elicit and integrate experience in social interactions and in a crucial dependence on specifically adapted forms of stimulation. Conversely, the human parent is unique in a wide range of complementary behavioral adaptations, which include nonconscious forms of didactic support to the infant's integration of experience.

The initial imbalance is best exemplified in the discrepancy between the parent's mature speech – inaccessible to a newborn infant – and the infant's random vocal sounds – inconspicuous to an adult. Only specific compensatory adaptations in vocal repertoires and / or perceptual predispositions help to overcome critical gaps in communication.

This essay addresses the question of how both interacting partners achieve and profit from bidirectional vocal communication during early

The research described in this essay has been part of a long-term collaborative project, entitled "Intuitive Parenting of Infants in Comparative Perspectives," carried out by the Developmental Psychobiology Research Group at the Max Planck Institute for Psychiatry in Munich and the Laboratory of Comparative Ethology at the National Institute of Child Health and Human Development (NICHD) in Bethesda, Md. The research has been generously supported by the Deutsche Forschungsgemeinschaft and, during my sabbatical year of 1985–6, by the NICHD. The author owes special thanks to David Symmes, who provided substantial help with digital vocal analyses, to Shu-fen Chang-Hwang, C. Rahn; S. Suomi, J. Sykes, W. Thompson at the NICHD, and to G. Dirlich, C. Doermer, G. Kneitinger, and M. Radmacher at the Max Planck Institute for Psychiatry.

postnatal interactions, with particular respect to the infant's developing integrative and communicative capacities.

In this context, communication is viewed as a sequence of interactional processes, where both partners act as communicators and recipients and where each of them obtains and provides different types of information, with different vocal means and different functional gains. The following essential components of the process of communicating (identified by Smith, 1977) and their interrelations will be discussed: (1) the physical structure of the relevant vocal units; (2) the kind of information or messages provided by the communicator in vocal units; (3) the kind of information or meanings decoded by the recipient in concert with contextual sources of information; (4) the behavioral impact of vocal units on the recipient's responses and, in turn, the effect of recipient responses on the communicator.

In order to identify the relevant vocal units in early parent–infant interactions, it is necessary to consider intuitive and random behaviors, as well as specialized and intentional behaviors. The early ontogeny of close-range parent–infant vocal interchanges has long been excluded from systematic inquiry, owing to an overemphasis, in traditional ethological concepts, on infant crying (Ostwald, 1963) and, in psycholinguistic concepts, on intentional communication (Bates, 1987). From a systems perspective, all behaviors, whether specialized or random, whether intentional or intuitive, potentially provide information, but they become effective as signals only when they are perceived and responded to by a recipient. Whether communication functions or not depends much less on a communicator's intention to provide information than on the recipient's readiness and capacity to decode and integrate the transmitted information. Microanalytic techniques of behavioral analysis are necessary to detect unintentional, nonconscious forms of behavioral adaptations in both partners (Papoušek & Bornstein, chapter 11 in the present volume).

The kind of information that is encoded in vocal units can be indirectly assessed through analysis of the communicator's concurring behavioral-emotional states and nonvocal behaviors in relation to the interactional context. As pointed out by Marler (1984), scientific approaches to communication have been restricted in the past by a widespread erroneous equation of nonlinguistic vocal behaviors in human and nonhuman primates with emotion or affect, and by traditional artificial dichotomies between affect and integrative perceptual-cognitive processes (Malatesta, 1981). As evident in the differential alarm calls of vervet monkeys, for instance, vocal signals may be both "motivational" and "referential" (Marler, Evans, & Hauser, chapter 4 in the present volume; Seyfarth, Cheney, & Marler, 1980). In a similar vein, Bühler (1934) differentiated among three key functions of vocal signs: symptom, symbol, and appeal (Scherer, chapter 3 in the present volume). Smith (1977) concluded, from an extensive review of psychobiological research, that vocal signals convey a complex array of multifaceted messages, which may simultaneously refer to the communicator's internal states of arousal, affect, and / or integrative readiness; to his or her behavioral propensities and focus of interest; to external referents in the interactional context; and to identifying cues concerning individual identity, sex, age, and developmental stage. At the same time, the communicator's vocal signals may represent adaptive responses to preceding signals from the recipient.

The effective meanings and functions of vocal units can be most readily detected by analysis of the recipient's overt responses, which can be examined, for instance, with a combination of naturalistic interactional observations and playback studies. Whether recipient responses reside in preadapted behavioral propensities or not, they depend to a large degree on additional contextual sources of information, such as the communicator's simultaneous or sequential nonvocal behaviors and the interactional context (Seyfarth et al., 1980; Smith, 1977). Moreover, the recipient's perceptual predispositions or constraints, affective state and temperament, previous experience, expectations, attitudes, educational preoccupations, or cultural conventions each may codetermine which of the available messages is attended to and becomes significant for selecting an appropriate response.

The functional implications of vocal communication for the developing parent–infant relationship can be revealed in analyses of the immediate behavioral impact of vocal signals on both the recipient and the communicator. Long-term analyses can assess the contribution of communication to successful parenting, to the infant's development of integrative and communicative capacities, including speech, and to the quality of the parent–infant relationship.

This essay reviews a series of systematic empirical studies, each of which employs the developmental-interactional perspective just described but, at the same time, focuses on a seemingly narrow aspect of the process of communicating. The studies are confined to maternal face-to-face interactions with 2-month-old infants; to two classes of early vocal signals (the infant's voiced presyllabic vocalizations and the parent's prototypical speech melodies); and to a small number of acoustic parameters.

Two converging lines of collaborative empirical research are brought together: Each of them focuses on significant components of the process of communicating: namely, on physical structure, encoded messages, decoded meanings, adaptive functions, and determinants of one of the two classes of vocalizations. Acoustic analyses of salient units in the vocal repertoires of both partners were combined with behavioral microanalyses of naturalistic parent–infant interactions and with experimental verifications of the meanings and predicted behavioral impact of vocal units on the receiving partner. A comparative cross-cultural design (including ethnic groups with tone and stress languages) served to explore the relative contributions of cultural / linguistic and biological factors on vocal communication.

Infant vocal signaling

The vocal repertoire of the human newborn is dominated by the cry, a powerful innate signal that the newborn shares with the young of most mammalian species (Newman, 1985) and that functions adaptively in alarming, life-threatening situations (see Lester & Boukydis, chapter 8 in the present volume). The infant's cry elicits a preprogrammed set of adaptive psychophysiological responses and interventions from the social environment (Frodi, 1985). However, the communicative value of infant crying is far more limited than is generally acknowledged (Murray, 1979). It is true that infant crying promotes close contact with distant caretakers, but when used in close-range interactions prolonged crying is hard to tolerate and becomes disruptive because of its adverse physical characteristics (Ostwald, 1963). For close-range communication with young infants, parents must be able to decode and respond to much more subtle behavioral and contextual cues.

Beyond infant crying: Identification of relevant vocal units in the infant's presyllabic repertoire

Overshadowed by the cry, the infant's presyllabic vocalizations have long remained unrecognized as carriers of significant information. They have been traditionally described as void of meaning, as reflexive or random (Jakobson, 1941), as products of vocal play (Lewis, 1936) or exploration (Oller, 1980; Papoušek & Papoušek, 1981). Only gross categorizations of non-cry vocalizations into "distress / nondistress" or "positive / negative" sounds have commonly been used in studies of parent–infant interactions.

There is good reason, however, for paying increased attention to the infants non-cry, nonvegetative vocalizations (Papoušek & Papoušek, 1981). The early voiced sounds, or quasi-resonant nuclei, of the "phonation stage" (0–1 month; Oller, 1980) evolve from inconspicuous, involuntary by-products of respiration into precursors of vowels, or fully resonant nuclei, typical of the "gooing stage" (2–3 months), inasmuch as the elementary control of respiration, phonation, pitch, and resonance improves. They serve as vocal nuclei for the infant's procedural practising of basic phonatory and articulatory skills, in relation to both speech sounds (Oller, 1980) and musical elements (Papoušek & Papoušek, 1981). Moreover, because of their close dependence on phonation and on the rate and quality of respiration, the early voiced sounds are also optimal candidates for the transmission of fine-grain information on the infant's fluctuating behavioral-emotional states of arousal, comfort, and discomfort (ibid.). Thus they form the core of both an arbitrary sound–meaning system (as described by Oller and Eilers in chapter 9 of the present volume) and a nonarbitrary, expressive sound–meaning system (as described by Scherer in chapter 3).

The first line of research explored the structure, encoded messages, meanings, and determinants of voiced sounds that 2-month-old infants commonly produce during interactions with their mothers. One series of studies (Study 1, and Playback Study 1) was based on spontaneous interactions of 21 German mother–infant pairs (Papoušek, 1989; Papoušek, Papoušek, & Koester, 1986); another series (Study 2, and Playback Study 2) was based on interactions of 16 American and 16 Chinese mother–infant pairs (Papoušek, 1987, in press; Papoušek, Papoušek, & Symmes, 1991). Both series included a similar sequence of analyses: (1) assessment and acoustic analyses of the infant's interactional repertoire of voiced sounds; (2) videoanalysis of the infant's concurrent behavioral-emotional states; (3) examination of effects of state, individual, and culture on the physical structure of voiced sounds; and (4) experimental playback studies of recipient responses to the same samples of sounds in the absence of other behavioral or contextual cues.

Encoded information: Effects of behavioral-emotional states

The infants spent about 90% of recorded interaction times in states that fluctuated between alert inactivity with neutral affect and signs of readiness to attend; alert activity with signs of comfort and readiness to interact; and weariness or fussiness with signs of mild to moderate discomfort and a distinct need to reduce stimulatory input. States of maximum discomfort or cry were exceptional, because they typically disrupt face-to-face interactions. States of maximum comfort or joyful excitement were also rare, because of the infants' young age.

Infant states significantly affected the rate and perceptual qualities of their concurrently voiced sounds: Alert inactivity was associated with a lack of voicing or with a low rate of extremely brief, low-intensity fundamental voicing (termed *neutral sounds*). Alert activity was typically accompanied by relaxed single or repetitive vowel-like or cooing sounds (*comfort sounds*). Mild to moderate discomfort was indicated by similar sound types but with strained or fretful qualities (*discomfort sounds*). Maximum discomfort was associated with series of cries (*cry sounds*); joyful excitement with pleasure cries, laughter, elaborate cooing sounds, or squeals (*joy sounds*). Sonagrams of typical examples are displayed in Figure 12.1.

Acoustic correlates of state-related information

Acoustic measurements were obtained from hard-copy spectrograms and power spectra (performed at the point of peak amplitude and peak fundamental frequency). Although programs for digital vocal analysis have been successfully developed and adapted for the study of infant cry, available programs proved to be unreliable for the analysis of immature infant sounds because of the sounds' peculiar characteristics (low intensity, high pitch, pitch variability, divergent resonances, and high intra- and interindividual variability).

Acoustic comparisons of state-related classes of voiced units (neutral, comfort, discomfort, joy, and cry) showed consistent results in Study 1 (as previously reported, Papoušek et al., 1986) and Study 2 (as summarized in Table 12.1 from the combined samples of Chinese and American infants). Duration, peak fundamental frequency (*F*0), and *F*0 range were lowest in neutral sounds and increased with growing signs of both comfort or discomfort. Cry and joy sounds could not be differentiated on the basis of these parameters. Likewise, discomfort and comfort sounds did

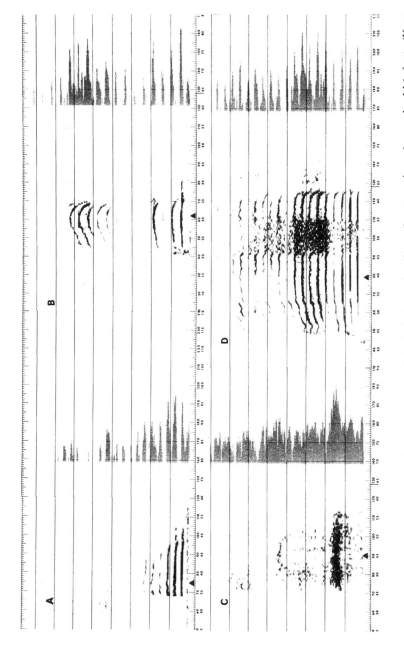

Figure 12.1. Spectrograms and power spectra of typical state-related vocalizations from 2-month-old infants (Kaye Elemetrics 7800, 45 Hz bandwidth, 0–8 kHz *F0* range). (A) Comfort sound; (B) discomfort sound; (C) pleasure cry; (D) cry.

Table 12.1. *Acoustic features of state-related vocal signals from 2-month-old infants*

	Joy $\bar{X}$	Comfort $\bar{X}$	Neutral $\bar{X}$	Discomfort $\bar{X}$	Cry $\bar{X}$	Comf/ disc.	Joy/ cry	Fried-man	r_s
Maternal state estimate (0–20)	3.9	6.9+++	9.2+++	13.2+++	17.4	+++	+++	***	.45***
Relative peak amplitude in frequency bands:									
1–2 kHz	0.85	0.69	0.72+	0.90++	1.28	+	++	***	.58**
2–4 kHz	0.88+	0.55	0.61+++	0.85++	1.23	+++	++	***	.52***
4–6 kHz	0.45+	0.26+	0.35+++	0.56++	0.84	+++	++	***	.54***
6–8 kHz	0.23	0.10	0.12+++	0.31+++	0.66	+++	++	***	.54***
Maximum fundamental frequency (Hz)	574.9+	363.9	325.5+++	464.6++	526.3	+++		***	.50***
Minimum fundamental frequency (Hz)	248.1	260.6	248.9+	299.0	302.1			*	.15
Harmonic with peak amplitude (Hz)	951.3	535.5	536.1+++	645.7+++	1,253.7	+		***	.35***
Fundamental frequency range (semitones)	14.6	5.8	4.7+	7.6+	9.6			*	.32***
Duration (ms)	1,023.0	467.0+++	269.0+++	539.0+++	1,398.0			***	.40***

+ $p<.05$; ++ $p<.01$; +++ $p<.001$ Wilcoxon Matched-Pairs Signed-Ranks Test.
* $p<.05$; ** $p<.01$; *** $p<.001$ Friedman Analysis of Variance.
Note: r_s, Spearman Rank Correlation between acoustic measures and Maternal States Estimates; number of infants, $N=32$ (16 American, 16 Chinese); number of vocal signals, $n=160$ (5 from each infant).

not differ in duration or in F0 range. But discomfort sounds significantly exceeded comfort sounds in peak F0 and in the relative amplitudes of spectral energy in all upper frequency bands. Similarly, cry sounds significantly exceeded joy sounds in the relative amplitudes of spectral energy in all upper frequency bands but had slightly lower peak frequencies. As will be discussed later in this essay, joy sounds did not differ from discomfort sounds in their spectral energy distribution.

The data provide first evidence that the physical structure of presyllabic interactional vocalizations reflects the infant's behavioral-emotional states. Thus, the infant's voiced sounds may be considered as "symptoms" of infant states (Bühler, 1934), or "motivational" signals (Marler, Evans & Hauser, chapter 4 in the present volume). The data suggest that certain acoustic parameters (vocal rate, duration, peak F0 and F0 range) are primarily influenced by the infant's arousal level, which is known to increase, from the state of alert inactivity, in two directions: to states of alert activity and joyful excitement, and to states of mild to severe discomfort (Scherer, 1985). The influence of positive or negative emotional factors (pleasure or displeasure, relaxation or strain, comfort or discomfort) is reflected in parameters of spectral energy. Similar differential effects of the two dimensions of arousal and hedonic tone have been found in emotional expressions of human adults (Scherer, 1985) and in parental speech (see the section in this chapter on parental vocal signaling).

Independent of infant state, individual voice characteristics significantly affected the acoustic features of infant sounds. Yet cultural origin and the infant's sex had no effects at the investigated age.

In summary, voiced sounds in the infant's presyllabic interactional repertoire carry differential information in relation to the infant's individual identity and to two dimensions of the infant's behavioral-emotional state: the dimension of general arousal, and the hedonic dimension of comfort versus discomfort.

Parental responsiveness to infant vocal signals

Students of early social interactions emphasize that parents treat infant vocalizations as a means of communication (Snow, 1977) and respond differentially to the infant's multimodal signals of comfort or discomfort (Keller & Schölmerich, 1987; Papoušek, Papoušek, & Bornstein, 1985). In many recent concepts of prelinguistic parent–infant interactions, parental responsiveness to infant crying or other signals is given crucial significance, for example, for the formation of secure parent–infant attachments (Frodi, 1985), for affective attunement (Field, 1985), and for the parent's intuitive didactic care (Papoušek & Papoušek, 1987). But systematic research on the parent's responsiveness has been limited to only a few standardized stimuli, in particular the infant's pain cry (Frodi, 1985; Lester & Boukydis, chapter 8 in the present volume). Moreover, not enough attention has been paid to separating and defining the relevant components of responsiveness, such as the parent's ability to decode information from infant signals, the parent's readiness to respond (response latency), and the quality of parental responses to infant signals.

Decoded information: Responses on the Infant State Barometer

Playback Study 1 (Papoušek, 1989) was conducted to investigate recipient responses to the common repertoire of interactional vocalizations. Fifty German infant sounds served as playback stimuli that had been identified and analyzed, both acoustically and in relation to infant state, in Study 1. Playback Study 1 focused on two questions: (1) whether single voiced units of 2-month-old infants convey information about the infant's behavioral-emotional state when played back in the absence of contextual and other behavioral cues; and (2) whether the ability to decode such information is determined by age, sex, parental status, and experience with infants.

A random sequence of 5 cry, 20 discomfort, 20 comfort, and 5 joy sounds was played back to six subject groups: mothers and fathers of same-age infants; multiparous and primiparous mothers of newborns; professionally experienced speech therapists; and 8-year-old children. An Infant State Barometer was designed, which allowed the subjects to respond intuitively rather than rationally and to estimate the infant's level of comfort or discomfort by moving a pointer along a bipolar visual analog scale. The two poles were marked, respectively, with a photograph of a smiling and a distressed infant face. Responses to the test sounds were analyzed as a function of sound category and subject group.

Categorical information. Recipient estimates of infant sounds significantly differed between comfort and discomfort sounds, and between discomfort and cry sounds, but not between joy sounds and other sound categories (Fig. 12.2). The most exact estimates were obtained from cries, followed by discomfort and comfort sounds. Joy sounds, however, con-

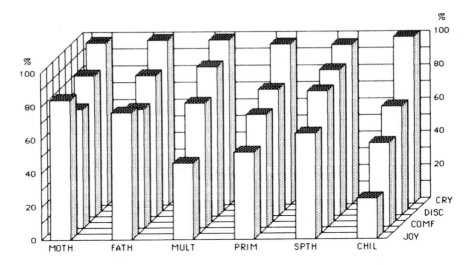

Figure 12.2. Determinants of correct decoding of state-related information: average percentages of correct differentiation of comfort/joy sounds versus discomfort/cry sounds. MOTH, FATH: mothers (*n* = 20) and fathers (*n* = 20) of 2-month-olds; MULT, PRIM: multiparous (*n* = 13) and primiparous (*n* = 12) mothers of newborns; SPTH: speech therapists (*n* = 20) with professional experience; CHIL: 8-year-old children (*n* = 9).

veyed ambiguous information. The estimates of "pleasure cries" and laughter showed a bimodal distribution, with one peak close to the comfort pole of the scale and the other peak close to the discomfort pole. Frequent misinterpretation of joy sounds as discomfort sounds may be explained by the joy sounds' spectral-energy characteristics. High-frequency energy increased similarly in both sound categories, as compared to comfort sounds (Table 12.1). Such an increase has been related to intrinsically unpleasant experience (Scherer, chapter 3 of the present volume). As pointed out by Wolff (1969), states of pleasurable excitement in young infants seem to be accompanied by unpleasantly high arousal levels, near the tolerance limits of the 2-month-old infant.

The results were replicated in Playback Study 2, where Chinese and American mothers each decoded 15 playback sounds from Chinese and American infants. Again, Chinese and American mothers had no difficulty inferring the infant's level of comfort or discomfort from the test sounds, with the exception of some of the joy sounds (Table 12.1, first row).

Graded information. During the test performance, subjects exhibited a strong tendency to relate each sound to the preceding one. They picked up subtle differences in degree of comfort or discomfort between the two sounds and modified their estimates relative to their estimate of the previous sound. The subjects' susceptibility to relational information has interesting implications for an understanding of naturalistic parent–infant interactions, where the parent typically receives and responds to dynamic variations in sequences of infant signals.

Infant state estimates significantly correlated with most acoustic parameters (Table 12.1, last column). The closer the estimates were to the pole of maximum discomfort, the higher were the relative spectral energy (in frequency bands above 1 kHz), the higher the peak $F0$ and the $F0$ range, and the longer the duration of sounds.

The data demonstrate that voiced sounds in the infant's presyllabic vocal repertoire effectively transmit both discrete information pertaining to the categorical distinction between comfort and discomfort and graded information pertaining to the relative intensity of affective arousal.

Recipient factors affecting responses to infant vocal signals

The recipient's ability to decode state-related information from isolated test sounds varied significantly as a function of age and experience but not in relation to parental status and sex (Playback Study 1, described in Papoušek, 1989) (Fig. 12.2). All groups read reliable, exact, and correct information from at least some sounds from each category. Overall, however, the four groups with parental or professional experience performed significantly better than the inexperienced groups of children and of primiparous mothers of newborns. Interestingly, children were even more reliable, exact, and correct in estimating cry sounds and some sounds of intense discomfort than the experienced groups, but they seemed to be at a loss with the majority of comfort and discomfort sounds and consistently misinterpreted joy sounds as discomfort sounds. Mothers and fathers who had immediate experience with same-age infants were the only recipients who correctly identified joy sounds as indicative of joyful excitement.

Playback Study 2 (Papoušek, in press) further showed that the mothers' state estimates were neither influenced by familiarity with infant voice, nor by cultural origin of test sounds, nor by their own cultural origin.

The results support the assumption that the ability to decode state-related information from infant sounds can be found universally in parents of varying status and sex and of different linguistic and cultural background. The performance is determined by an interaction of universal perceptual predispositions with experience. Experience has a negligible impact in responses to signals of severe discomfort but is crucial in responses to immature signals of joyful excitement.

Behavioral responses to infant vocal signals

Playback Study 2 examined (1) what other kinds of information, besides state-related information, are transmitted by infant sounds and (2) what kinds of spontaneous behavioral responses can be elicited in mothers by isolated sounds from 2-month-old infants (Papoušek, in press). Joy, comfort, neutral, discomfort, and cry sounds from 2-month-old Chinese and American infants were played back to the mothers at a later visit to the laboratory. Each mother was repeatedly tested with a random sequence of 15 sounds. Five sounds – one from each sound category – were from their own infant, 5 were standard sounds from an unfamiliar Chinese baby, and 5 were standard sounds from an unfamiliar American baby. In the first test run, mothers were encouraged to imitate the infant sounds. In the second run, mothers were asked to imagine that their baby was lying next door, alone in a crib, and vocalizing. The mother's task was to answer each sound so that babies could hear her. The final task was to identify which sounds had been produced by the mother's own infant.

Attribution of meaning. Most revealing were the mothers' spontaneous attributions of meaning, as evident in their spoken responses to the 15 test sounds. The 30 mothers responded with a total of 955 utterances, which were recorded and subjected to auditory and sonagraphic analysis. Response latencies, prosodic features, emotional responses, and linguistic content were analyzed. Content analysis revealed maternal references to the infant's concurrent activities, states, needs, or discrete emotions (Papoušek, in press). However, information on infant identity seemed to be insufficiently encoded in most of the single infant sounds. Identification of the mother's own infant's voice proved to be too difficult. Only 53% of maternal judgments were correct; 31% were false, and 16% were ambiguous.

Imitative and affective responses. The mother's deliberate attempts to match the test sounds indicated astonishing perceptual sensitivities and imitative capacities in relation to pitch, pitch contour, duration, loudness, dynamics, and affective tone (M. Papoušek, unpublished data). Similar capacities have been found in spontaneous vocal interchanges between mothers and their 2- to 5-month-olds (Papoušek & Papoušek, 1989). Reciprocal vocal matching is a regular component of naturalistic interactions and involves 34% to 56% of infant sounds.

In many mothers, the test sounds also elicited distinct emotional responses: empathy and concern as well as smiling and laughing (Papoušek, in press). Infant vocal sounds may induce affect in caretakers and contribute to affective attunement in early mother–infant relationships (Field, 1985).

Motherese responses and intuitive didactic caregiving tendencies. Strikingly, the playback of single infant sounds was sufficient to evoke motherese. As compared to adult-directed utterances from the same mothers, maternal responses to the test sounds were shortened, slowed down in tempo, raised in $F0$ and $F0$ range, included fewer syllables, and used simplified, repetitive melodic contours (Papoušek, in press).

In a recent study (Papoušek et al., 1991) the content of the mothers' spoken responses clearly indicated a number of typical intuitive didactic caregiving tendencies: *contingent rewarding,* or *greeting; encouraging a turn; encouraging imitation; evaluating infant state; reassuring of mother's presence; readiness to intervene; soothing,* or *discouraging* (see also the section in this essay on parental vocal signaling).

Test sounds from each of the five infant states elicited differential vocal responses from the mothers, in terms of both prosodic features and intuitive caregiving tendencies (Papoušek, in press):

Neutral infant sounds elicited the lowest rate of maternal responses and tendencies to encourage a turn or to reassure. Utterances were low in pitch and the shortest in duration.

Comfort sounds were answered with a high rate of utterances with short latencies, longer duration, and the slowest tempo. They evoked propensities to reward, to encourage another turn, or to greet, empathetic expressions of pleasure, and, in one third of the cases, spontaneous imitation. Mothers often attributed infant playing or talking, waking up, and happy feelings.

Joy sounds evoked a high rate of responses with short latencies, long duration, the highest rate of terminal rising contours, and the highest expansion of maximum frequencies. Utterances indicated propensities to reward, to encourage another turn, but also, in some cases, tendencies to evaluate the infant's state, to reassure, or to intervene. Mothers attributed infant playing, smiling, laughing, and happy feelings, and they spontaneously smiled or laughed themselves in many cases.

Responses to discomfort sounds were characterized by the longest latencies, the fastest tempo, and a high rate of staccato-like melodies with a final high-level contour. Mothers expressed readiness to intervene, or tendencies to evaluate the infant's state and to reassure of mother's presence. They referred to infant feelings of discomfort, anxiousness, or upsetness but rarely to particular physical needs.

Cry sounds elicited a high rate of responses with short latencies and, in many cases, spontaneous drowning of the test cry with overlapping, long, fast, high-pitch utterances, with a strong prevalence of final falling contours. Cries evoked most often readiness to intervene, to discourage infant crying, to evaluate, to reassure, or to soothe, and expressions of empathetic concern. Typical soothing responses with low pitch and slow tempo were surprisingly rare. They seem to require close-range contact with the infant. Discouraging tendencies were more frequent among the Chinese mothers, indicating cultural differences in tolerance of and educational attitudes toward infant crying.

The study also picked a few individual mothers with an apparent lack of differential responsiveness to state-related information and with unusual responses. They seemed to be preoccupied with their own affective state of anxiousness or showed aversive attitudes toward infant distress signals. Whereas most mothers attributed unhappy feelings to infant distress sounds, these mothers referred to anxiousness and anger. Thus, decoding capacities may also be hampered by the mother's own feelings, attitudes, or educational preoccupations.

Adaptive functions of infant vocal signaling

The reported studies clearly show that single voiced sounds from the infant's interactional repertoire are sufficient to induce typical intuitive parental behaviors. Infant sounds elicit motherese and imitative echoing and provide the mothers with significant cues which allow them to respond differentially with appropriate forms of intuitive didactic caregiving. If presented with isolated sounds, mothers most likely decode and respond to information on the infant's level of comfort or discomfort, behavioral state, and activities, and are less likely to respond to information on concrete needs and individual identity.

Recipient responsiveness seems to be based on perceptual and behavioral predispositions and – to a lesser degree – on the caregiver's experience and age. It is on this basis that the infant's interactional vocal sounds function as both symptoms of the infant's behavioral-emotional state and appeal to the caregiving environment, inasmuch as they elicit finely attuned, preadapted caregiving responses.

Parental vocal signaling

Beyond language: Identification of vocal signals in infant-directed speech

The second major line of research focused on the most prominent characteristic of parental speech to prelinguistic infants: melodic contours. Given the complexity, variety, and multimodal character of parent–infant vocal interchanges, this narrow focus could imply a critical reduction of information, disregarding cues from other relevant acoustic features of parental prosody, from linguistic codes, and from other modalities. However, substantial evidence has been accumulated that melodic contours are in fact, perceptually and acoustically, the salient units of parental speech to very young infants (Fernald & Simon, 1984; Papoušek et al., 1985; Stern, Spieker, Barnett, & MacKain, 1983).

Infant effects on structure and mode of parental vocal signaling

Melodic contours are offered as a small repertoire of simple, expanded, highly repetitive, discrete prototypes (Papoušek, Papoušek, & Haekel, 1987), and they are presented in a didactically adjusted mode, that is, with slow tempo, exaggerated contrasts, frequent repetitions, and contingency on preceding infant behaviors (Papoušek & Papoušek, 1984). Thus, the young infant's perceptual and integrative capacities and constraints seem to exert an immediate influence on the caretaker's vocal signaling. Both acoustic properties and didactic display of melodic contours enable the infant to attend to, process, and decode elementary units of speech from the beginning of life (Fernald, 1984; M. Papoušek & H. Papoušek, 1981, 1984; Papoušek, Papoušek, & Haekel, 1987; Trehub, 1990).

Interestingly, melodic contours are used without the parent's conscious awareness or control, as preadapted responses to vocal or other soliciting infant cues (see the section in the present chapter on responsiveness to infant signals). They are found universally in parents of both sexes, in nonparents, early in development, and in various cultures (Fernald, Taeschner, Dunn, Papoušek, Boysson-Bardies, & Fukui, 1989; Papoušek, 1987; Papoušek, Papoušek, & Haekel, 1987). Owing to these properties, melodic contours gain a special status of unconsciously delivered, cross-linguistic universals which belong to the core repertoire of intuitive parental care (Papoušek & Papoušek, 1987).

Encoded information: Relation to interactional caregiving contexts

Although it has become easier in recent years to trace and quantify melodic patterns, the messages and functions of melodic contours in prelinguistic parent–infant communication have hardly been explored. Melodic contours are most commonly viewed as purely "affective" signals (Fernald, chapter 13 in the present volume) although evidence in support of this assumption is limited and has not been convincing (Malatesta, 1981; Stern, Spieker, & MacKain, 1982). Other authors have pointed to the facilitatory role of intonation in processing linguistic information (Fernald & Mazzie, 1991). However, melodic contours in motherese to 2-month-olds seem to follow other rules than in adult-directed speech and to represent linguistically independent sources of information (Papoušek, & Haekel, 1987; Stern et al., 1982).

This assumption was examined in two studies, both of which followed a similar interactional-contextual approach. They analyzed (1) interrelations between maternal melodic contours and relevant interactional contexts of intuitive didactic care; (2) the kinds of information encoded in melodic contours; and (3) the extent to which contour–context relations are determined either by universal predapted programs or by linguistic and / or cultural variation. Study 1 examined German mother–infant pairs (Papoušek et al., 1985, 1986); Study 2 was a controlled, cross-cultural / cross-linguistic investigation of Mandarin Chinese and Caucasian American mother–infant pairs (Papoušek, 1987; Papoušek, Papoušek, & Symmes, 1991).

The latter two cultures were selected because of fundamental differences in both the cultural tradition and the role of melodic patterns in the phonological systems of tone and stress languages. In tone languages, specific $F0$ contours, or "tones," on the level of syllables carry lexical information (Eady, 1982). The crucial question was whether the lexical tone rules of Mandarin would constrain Chinese mothers in the use of expanded prototypical melodic contours when talking to young infants.

The mothers were observed, videotaped, and audiotaped during naturalistic interactions with their 2-month-old infants. Behavioral microanalyses were applied to analyze the infant's state and behaviors, maternal speech content, and the mothers' nonvocal intuitive caregiving behaviors (Papoušek & Papoušek, 1987). The microanalytic evaluations served to identify eight contexts of intuitive parental caregiving which proved to be highly repetitive and salient in close-distance mother–infant interchanges (Papoušek et al., 1991).

Maternal utterances were transcribed, translated, evaluated in terms of melodic contour types, and subjected to digital acoustic analyses of *F*0 contours. Statistical analyses determined the relative contribution of three factors to the total variance of melodic contours: caregiving context, individual style, and culture / language.

Context-related categorical information. Both studies showed significant functional links between the distribution of melodic contour types and the eight caregiving contexts. German, Chinese, and American mothers alike adjusted their choice of melodic contour types not only to preceding infant vocal signals but even more consistently in accordance with their intuitive didactic tendencies (Papoušek & Papoušek, 1984; Papoušek et al., 1991). The graphs in Figure 12.3 describe the highly corresponding profiles of contour preferences in relation to four caregiving contexts. Mothers from the three cultures preferred rising contours in turn-encouraging contexts, falling contours in the soothing context, and falling and bell-shaped contours in both rewarding and discouraging contexts.

Across all eight contexts, the profiles of contour preferences indicate a categorical contrast between the use of final rising contours in contexts in which mothers try to elicit attentional, visual, facial, vocal, or other behavioral turns, and the use of final falling contours in contexts in which mothers respond in approving, disapproving, distracting, or soothing ways to a preceding infant turn.

Linguists have traced back the syntactic and attitudinal meanings of adult-directed intonation to a similar basic dichotomy of meanings. A terminal rise is generally associated with open, receptive, nonassertive

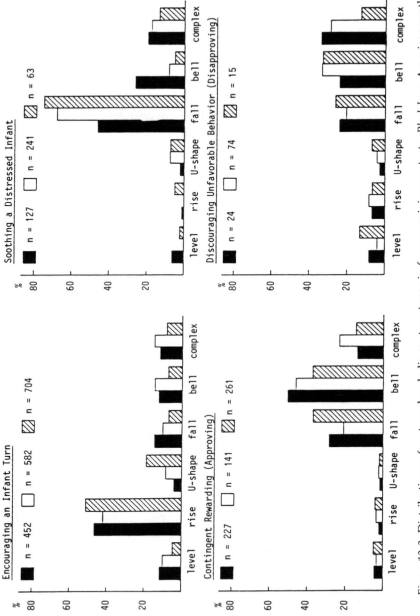

Figure 12.3. Distributions of maternal melodic contour types in four caregiving contexts. *Black bars*: American mothers (*n* = 10); *blank bars*: Mandarin Chinese mothers (*n* = 10); *striped bars*: German mothers (*n* = 21).

meanings, whereas falling intonation is associated with closed, conclusive, assertive, or reinforcing connotations (Cruttenden, 1981; Crystal, 1975).

When mothers communicate with their 2-month-olds, they reduce the complexity of adult-directed intonation patterns and replace the terminal rises or falls with global expanded rising (or U-shaped) and falling (or bell-shaped) melodies. Moreover, they use rising and falling patterns distinctively in turn-opening and turn-closing contexts and thus establish the most basic pattern of discourse, turn taking. As long as the infant is unable to sufficiently control his or her own turns, mothers provide a compensatory turn-taking frame, both by means of temporal pausing patterns (Kaye, 1982) and by melodic cues (M. Papoušek & H. Papoušek, 1991).

We found evidence of compensatory turn-taking frames on three levels of behavioral complexity. The most elementary opening / closing contrasts may be used to enhance or diminish the infant's affective arousal level and / or attentional processes. Once an optimal attentional level has been achieved for dyadic interchanges, mothers seem to use opening rises and closing falls to induce and reinforce the infant's active behavioral control of visual, facial, vocal, or other turns. The third level is evident in most of the early interactional games – conventional or idiosyncratic – which also provide turn-taking frames with an arousing / soothing dimension. Typical repetitive sequences include buildup of arousal and tension with a rising melody and a pause, contrasted with release of tension and calming down with a falling contour (Papoušek, Papoušek, & Harris, 1987).

Another contrast of context-related meanings of similar didactic significance was evident in the mother's approving or disapproving responses to preceding or ongoing infant behaviors. Discouraging contexts are rare in early infancy, but they occasionally appear in disruptive responses to infant fussiness or in attempts to distract and recapture the infant's attention. High-pitch, high-intensity discouraging responses are reminiscent of warning signals that human and nonhuman primates use in biologically threatening contexts (Jürgens, 1979). In both contexts – contingent rewarding and discouraging unfavorable behavior – falling and bell-shaped contours prevail (Fig. 12.3). The attention-getting, disruptive, and / or warning properties of discouraging falls or bells are encoded in brief, staccato-like, steep, high-pitch $F0$ contours, sometimes with negative emotional tone. In contrast, rewarding falls and bells are longer than falls and bells in other contexts and are displayed with intermediate $F0$ levels and wide $F0$ ranges.

Context-related graded information. Mothers not only preferred specific types of melodic contours in relation to the context, but they further modified or graded the acoustic shape of each type in close accordance with the interactional caregiving context (Papoušek et al., 1991). When rising contours were compared across different contexts, they had the highest $F0$ in the context of encouraging attention, where mothers tried to arouse a drowsy, inattentive infant. Rising contours were shorter and lower in average $F0$ when mothers encouraged a turn from an attentive infant. Rising contours were the longest in duration and the lowest in average and maximum $F0$, $F0$ range, and steepness when mothers evaluated the infant's state in response to infant cues of distress or weariness. An even more marked gradation across contexts was found in the shapes of falling contours between encouraging attention, on one side (highest $F0$, widest $F0$ range, steepest slope, shortest duration), and soothing on the other (lowest $F0$ and $F0$ ranges, flattest slope, longest duration). Figure 12.4 illustrates context effects on falling contours from two individual mothers.

The context-dependent gradations of maternal melodies add a crucial dimension to the rising–falling contrast. Encouraging rises with short, high-pitch, wide range, and steep contours on one end and soothing falls with long, low-pitch, low-range, and flat contours on the other represent opposite didactic tendencies along an arousing / soothing dimension which are expressed in both discrete and graded signal components.

Referential or symbolic information. The consistent association of distinctive melodic prototypes with repetitive contexts of intuitive parental care may endow melodic units with the function of contextual reference. Melodic contours represent salient integral components of interactional contexts which the infant may learn to process, to conceptualize, and to anticipate within the first months of life. Melodic contours do not carry referential information in a strictly linguistic sense. However, they certainly fulfil the assumptions of referential signaling as defined by Marler (1984). They refer to or symbolize concrete interactional events, guide the infant's attention and integrative processes to actions, persons and objects, and induce appropriate action tendencies in the infant (see the section in this essay on infant responsiveness).

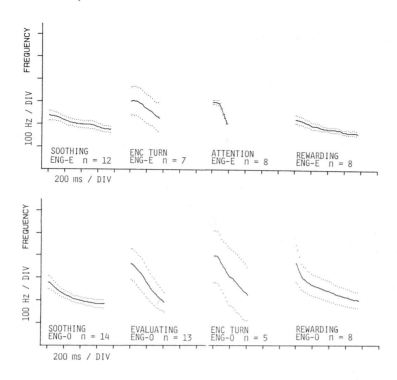

Figure 12.4. Contextual markers in maternal melodies: differentiation of falling melodies in relation to caregiving context. Patterns represent average contours and variabilities from 7-min interactions of two individual English-speaking mothers (ENG-E and ENG-O) with their 2-month-olds.

Affective information. Melodic contours in rewarding, discouraging, and soothing contexts seem to be particularly subject to emotional coloring in accordance with the type and level of the mother's emotional engagement. Evidence from a wide range of studies on vocal expression of emotions has shown that gradations in duration, and in the level, range, and slope of F0 contours, reflect different levels of psychophysiological arousal in the speaker (Scherer, 1985). The same kind of acoustic gradations characterize the infant's voiced sounds, from states of comfort, on one side, to states of maximum discomfort on the other (see the section in this essay on infant vocal signaling). Thus, although melodic contours alone are not sufficient to express the caretaker's emotional states, increasing levels of positive or negative emotional arousal may be reflected both in graded level, range, and slope of F0 (Fernald, chapter 13 of the present volume) and in expansions of falling contours into bell-shaped or sinusoidal contours (Crystal, 1975; Stern et al., 1982). Affect-related gradations may inform about the caretaker's overall interactive and affective engagement.

Melodic contours as symptom and / or appeal. The context-dependent acoustic gradations of maternal melodies, however, cannot be explained as symptoms of the mother's own affective arousal states alone. There is no doubt that infant distress signals and crying increase the mother's psychophysiological arousal (Boukydis & Burgess, 1982; Lester & Boukydis, chapter 8 of the present volume), but they simultaneously elicit the mother's soothing responses, characterized by prolonged, flattened, low-frequency melodies. Thus, when mothers respond to infant cues of tension or hyperarousal in contexts of evaluating state or soothing, they typically reduce the rate and intensity of stimulation and calm the infant. Their soothing melodies counterbalance the infant's hyperarousal. In contrast, when mothers respond to infant cues of passivity, inattentiveness, and hypoarousal in encouraging contexts, mothers employ various strategies to increase the infant's arousal level and readiness to respond. Mothers again counterbalance the infant's low level of arousal with melodies which are significantly shortened, steeper, and increased in level and range of $F0$.

Thus, the differential acoustic gradations of maternal melodic contours do not always mirror the infant's state of affective arousal, nor do they match the mother's own emotional state. Rather they reflect counterbalancing intuitive didactic tendencies in mothers who try to bring the infant back either into optimal states of active-alert waking or into sound sleep. Gradations along the arousing / soothing dimension play an eminent role in presyllabic parent–infant communication. Fine-grain moment-to-moment nuances are found abundantly in repetitive sequences of melodic units in maternal speech (Papoušek & Papoušek, 1987). Mothers use such variation in response to gradations in the infant's vocal cues to modulate the infant's fluctuating levels of arousal, attention, and readiness to interact.

The studies just described provide substantial evidence that both the types and acoustic gradations of melodic contours in maternal communication with 2-month-olds are closely tied to the mother's intuitive didactic care. Differential melodic contours signify and mediate the parent's intuitive didactic propensities in relation to arousing / soothing, turn opening / turn closing, or approving / disapproving dimensions of parental care. They are used to exert immediate influence on the infant's state; to induce infant turns; and to guide the infant in regulating arousal and attention, in getting control over visual, facial, and vocal behaviors, and in practising turn taking, imitation, play, and other communicative skills. Thus, "persuasive," "impressive," or "appeal" functions seem to prevail over primarily "expressive" or "symptom" functions in mother's melodic communication with 2-month-olds.

Information related to individual identification. Next to the effect of interactional context, individual speech style had a significant main effect of a similar order on the shapes of melodic prototypes. Figure 12.5 illustrates the striking individual differences among the average shapes of turn-encouraging rising contours from individual Chinese and American mothers. Individual variation in the mother's vocal tract, her style of vocal expressivity, and her emotional engagement may equally contribute to the observed differences in duration, level, range, and steepness of $F0$ contours. Such idiosyncratic variation within universal tendencies may provide the infant with salient cues for identification of and familiarization with individual caretakers.

Language- and culture-related information. American mothers differed from both Chinese and German mothers mainly in a higher extent of melodic expansion in infant-directed speech (Papoušek, 1987; Papoušek et al., 1991). Similar differences between American, European, and Asian mothers have been reported recently and related to differences in cultural conventions in the nonverbal display of attitudes or emotions (Fernald et al., 1989). Thus, melodic contours also include information on cultural rules of nonverbal expressivity.

The differences, however, were small in comparison with the striking cross-cultural similarities found in the observed contour–context relations. Mandarin-speaking mothers had no difficulty in providing their infants with the same kind of simplified prototypes in comparable contexts of intuitive caregiving as the American mothers. In fact, they tended to neglect linguistic information in favor of caregiving melodies and intuitively employed various "strategies" which allowed them to circumvent tonal constraints from the phonological system of their language. They were even ready to violate lexical tone rules in favor of context-bound caregiving melodies (H. Papoušek & M. Papoušek, 1991; Papoušek et al., 1991).

The reported studies provide convincing evidence that both the struc-

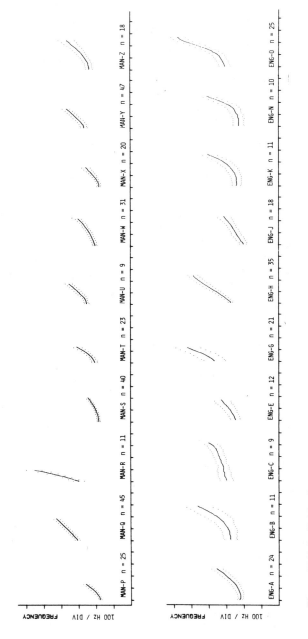

Figure 12..5. Individual markers: idiosyncratic differentiation of turn-encouraging average rising melodies from (*top*) 10 Chinese (MAN-P to MAN-Z) and (*bottom*) 10 American (ENG-A to ENG-O) mothers, as recorded during 7-min interactions with their 2-month-olds.

ture and messages of maternal melodies are used in intuitive caregiving contexts as cross-linguistic universals of parental communication with presyllabic infants.

Infant responsiveness to parental vocal signaling

The third playback study focused on the infant's decoding of the parent's melodic caregiving messages and addressed the crucial question of whether melodic contours differentially affect infant behaviors in a way which is predicted by their contextual meanings.

Early decoding of information

It has been well established that young infants are optimally prepared to discriminate and process melodic contours (Fernald, 1984; Trehub, 1990). Neonate infants identify and prefer their mother's voice, even when presented in a low-pass-filtered version (Fifer & Moon, 1988). Such evidence suggests that the human fetus is sensitive to at least some melodic and temporal information in speech. After birth, melodic contours in infant-directed speech effectively attract the infant's attention (Cooper & Aslin, 1989; Werker & McLeod, 1989) and account for the 4-month-old's selective listening preference for motherese over adult-directed talk (Fernald & Kuhl, 1987). Infant-directed speech is also more effective than adult-directed speech in eliciting positive affective responses in young infants, such as smiling, interest, and readiness to interact with the social environment (Werker & McLeod, 1989).

However, it has not yet been sufficiently explored whether infants are able to decode intuitive didactic caregiving information from contrastive pairs of infant-directed melodies. Sullivan & Horowitz (1983) compared infants' attentional responses to paired rising and falling melodies, but the results are difficult to interpret because of insufficiently controlled stimuli.

Differential behavioral responses to infant-directed vocal signals

In collaboration with Bornstein, Nuzzo, H. Papoušek, and Symmes (1990), we tested the effects of another contrastive pair – namely, approving and disapproving bell-shaped melodies – on infants' visual behavior in an infant-controlled auditory preference design. The stimulus pairs were produced by natural male and female voices and represented typical patterns of motherese without linguistic information. The reverse patterns were used as control against effects from global acoustic properties, duration, intensity, F0 range, and spectral energy. The two stimuli from each pair differed in duration, steepness of contours, and spectral energy but not in overall intensity, maximum F0, minimum F0, and F0 range (Fig. 12.6).

As expected, infants' visual attention to photographed faces of an adult stranger was significantly enhanced by the approving melodies but reduced by the disapproving melodies and not influenced by the reverse melodies. According to the data, infants differentially and adequately responded to a typical contrastive pair of intuitive caregiving melodies. Interestingly, the relevant information was not carried by global acoustic characteristics but by the dynamic shape of respective contours.

Fernald replicated the results with maternal speech samples from different cultures to 1-year-olds and showed that approving / disapproving melodies also elicit differential affective responses in 4-month-old infants (chapter 13 in the present volume).

The results confirm the assumption that melodic contours in parental communication with presyllabic infants have an immediate impact on the infant's behavior and function as communicative mediators of the parent's intuitive didactic care.

Conclusions: Adaptive functions of presyllabic vocal communication

It is of vital importance for any interacting system to make information available to the participants and enable each of them to utilize the available information. Yet it may be a unique feature of human parent–infant relationships that they largely rely on close-range, face-to-face communication. The reviewed research documents that, beyond the infant cry, bidirectional vocal communication functions effectively in early presyllabic mother–infant interactions, based on unintentional, nonconscious, and universal repertoires. Voiced units in the infant's precanonical repertoire and melodic units in maternal speech seem to be embedded in an asymmetrical didactic caregiving system which enables encoding and decoding of mutual information, in spite of initial critical gaps.

Infant voiced signals provide the mother with significant state-related cues which pertain to the infant's momentary integrative and interactional readiness. They elicit motherese, imitative echoing, and adequate

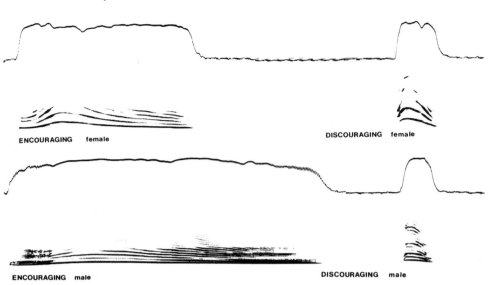

Figure 12.6. Rewarding and discouraging test stimuli spoken by natural female and male voices. Narrow-band (45 Hz) spectrograms, Kaye Elemetrics 7800, 0–8 kHz F0 range.

forms of intuitive didactic caregiving, on the basis of both universal predispositions and experience. Melodic contours in motherese mediate the mother's intuitive responsive care in relation to didactically significant dimensions of arousing / soothing, turn opening / turn closing, and approving / disapproving interventions. Thus they may support the infant's maturing regulation of arousal and attention, control over visual, facial, and vocal behaviors, and practise in turn taking, play, and imitation. The prototypical nature of contextually linked melodic units may facilitate the infant's perceptual decoding, familiarization with the mother, processing of contextual information, and joint attention and experience in relation to actions and objects.

Due to the mother's melodically mediated caregiving responses, the infant can learn in abundant episodes that his or her vocalizations have differential consequences and can affect the mother's behavior in predictable ways. Such experience alone may significantly reinforce the infant's early intentional display and refinement of differential vocal signaling. The infant's vocal signals, in turn, provide the mother with feedback information on the effectiveness of her intuitive caregiving interventions.

Thus, current evidence suggests that vocal communication offers immediate advantages to both interacting partners, particularly in relation to the infant's developing integrative and communicative capacities. An ultimate mutual advantage may be seen in the advancement of species-specific forms of thought and linguistic communication and in the promotion of specific forms of prosocial behaviors. Both – parental responsiveness to the infant's vocal sounds, and melodic prototypes in parental speech – may well represent cross-cultural universals in the early development of parent–infant communication. They seem to be at the core of biologically, rather than culturally, based programs for a species-specific support of the infant's developing prelinguistic communication and speech.

References

Bates, E., O'Connell, B., & Shore, C. (1987). Language and communication in infancy. In J. Osofsky (Ed.), *Handbook of infant development* (2nd ed.) (pp. 149–203). New York: Wiley.
Boukydis, C. F. Z., & Burgess, R. L. (1982). Adult physiological response to infant cries: Effects of temperament of infant, parental status, and gender. *Child Development, 53*, 1291–1298.
Bühler, K. (1934). *Sprachtheorie.* Jena: Fischer.
Cooper, R. P., & Aslin, R. N. (1989). The language environment of the young infant: Implications for early perceptual development. *Canadian Journal of Psychology, 43*, 247–265.
Cruttenden, A. (1981). Falls and rises: Meanings and universals. *Journal of Linguistics, 17*, 77–91.
Crystal, D. (1975). *The English tone of voice.* London: Arnold.
Eady, S. J. (1982). Differences in the F0 patterns of speech: Tone language versus stress language. *Language and Speech, 25*, 29–42.
Fernald, A. (1984). The perceptual and affective salience of mothers' speech to infants. In L. Feagans, C. Garvey, & R. Golinkoff (Eds.), *The origins and growth of communication* (pp. 5–29). Norwood, N.J.: Ablex.
Fernald A., & Kuhl, P. K. (1987). Acoustic determinants of infant preference for motherese speech. *Infant Behavior and Development, 10*, 279–293.
Fernald, A., & Mazzie, C. (1991). Prosody and focus in speech to infants and adults. *Developmental Psychology, 27*, 209–221.
Fernald, A., & Simon, T. (1984). Expanded intonation contours in mothers' speech to newborns. *Developmental Psychology, 20*, 104–113.
Fernald, A., Taeschner, T., Dunn, J., Papoušek, M., Boysson-Bardies, B., & Fukui, I. (1989). A cross-language study of prosodic modifications in mothers' and fathers' speech to preverbal infants. *Journal of Child Language, 16*, 977–1001.

Field, T. (1985). Attachment as psychobiological attunement: Being on the same wave length. In M. Reite & T. Field (Eds.), *The psychobiology of attachment and separation* (pp. 415–454). Orlando, Fla.: Academic Press.

Fifer, W. P., & Moon, C. (1989). Early voice discrimination. In C. von Euler, H. Forssberg, & H. Lagerkrantz (Eds.), *The neurobiology of early infant behavior* (pp. 277–286). Basingstoke: Macmillan.

Frodi, A. (1985). Variations in parental and nonparental response to early infant communication. In M. Reite & T. Field (Eds.), *The psychobiology of attachment and separation* (pp. 351–367). Orlando, Fla.: Academic Press.

Jakobson, R. (1941). *Kindersprache, Aphasie und allgemeine Lautgesetze.* Uppsala: Almquist & Wiksell.

Jürgens, U. (1979). Vocalization as an emotional indicator: A neuroethological study in the squirrel monkey. *Behaviour, 69,* 88–117.

Kaye, K. (1982). *The mental and social life of babies: How parents create persons.* Chicago: University of Chicago Press.

Keller, H., & Schölmerich, A. (1987). Infant vocalizations and parental reactions during the first four months of life. *Developmental Psychology, 23,* 62–67.

Lewis, M. M. (1936). *Infant speech: A study of the beginning of language.* New York: Harcourt, Brace.

Malatesta, C. Z. (1981). Infant emotion and the vocal affect lexicon. *Motivation and Emotion, 5,* 1–23.

Marler, P. (1984). Animal communication: Affect or cognition? In K. R. Scherer & P. Ekman (Eds.), *Approaches to emotion* (pp. 345–365). Hillsdale, N.J.: Erlbaum.

Murray, A. D. (1979). Infant crying as an elicitor of parental behavior: An examination of two models. *Psychological Bulletin, 86,* 191–215.

Newman, J. D. (1985). The infant cry of primates: An evolutionary perspective. In B. M. Lester & C. F. Z. Boukydis (Eds.), *Infant crying: Theoretical and research perspectives* (pp. 307–323). New York: Plenum.

Oller, D. K. (1980). The emergence of the sounds of speech in infancy. In G. Yeni-Komshian, J. Kavanagh, & C. Ferguson (Eds.), *Child phonology: Vol. 1. Production* (pp. 93–112). New York: Academic Press.

Ostwald, P. F. (1963). *Soundmaking: The acoustic communication of emotion.* Springfield, Ill.: Thomas.

Papoušek, H., & Papoušek, M. (1984). Learning and cognition in the everyday life of human infants. In J. Rosenblatt (Ed.), *Advances in the study of behavior* (Vol. 14, pp. 127–163). New York: Academic Press.

(1987). Intuitive parenting: A dialectic counterpart to the infant's integrative competence. In J. D. Osofsky (Ed.), *Handbook of infant development* (2nd ed., pp. 669–720). New York: Wiley.

(1991). Innate and cultural guidance of infants' integrative competencies: China, the United States, and Germany. In M. H. Bornstein (Ed.), *Cultural approaches to parenting* (pp. 23–44). Hillsdale, N.J.: Erlbaum.

Papoušek, H., Papoušek, M., & Koester, L. S. (1986). Sharing emotionality and sharing knowledge: A microanalytic approach to parent–infant communication. In C. E. Izard & P. Read (Eds.), *Measuring emotions in infants and children* (Vol. 2, pp. 93–123). Cambridge: Cambridge University Press.

Papoušek, M. (1987). Models and messages in the melodies of maternal speech in tonal and nontonal languages. Paper presented to the Sixth Biennial Meeting of the Society for Research in Child Development, Baltimore. April.

(1989). Determinants of responsiveness to infant vocal expression of emotional state. *Infant Behavior and Development, 12,* 505–522.

(in press). Responsiveness to infant cry and non-cry vocalizations. In B. M. Lester, J. D. Newman, & F. A. Pedersen (Eds.), *Social and biological aspects of infant crying*. New York: Plenum.

Papoušek, M., Bornstein, M. H., Nuzzo, C., Papoušek, H., & Symmes, D. (1990). Infant responses to prototypical melodic contours in parental speech. *Infant Behavior and Development, 13*, 539–545.

Papoušek, M., & Papoušek, H. (1981). Musical elements in the infant's vocalizations: Their significance for communication, cognition, and creativity. In L. P. Lipsitt (Ed.), *Advances in Infancy Research* (Vol. 1, pp. 163–224). Norwood, N.J.: Ablex.

(1984). Categorical vocal cues in preverbal parent–infant communication. Paper presented to the International Congress of Infant Studies, New York. April.

(1989). Forms and functions of vocal matching in interactions between mothers and their precanonical infants. [Special issue]. *First Language, 9*, 137–158.

(1991). Preverbal vocal communication from zero to one: Preparing the ground for language acquisition. In M. E. Lamb & H. Keller (Eds.), *Infant development: Perspectives from German-speaking countries* (pp. 299–328). Hillsdale, N.J.: Erlbaum.

Papoušek, M., Papoušek, H., & Bornstein, M. H. (1985). The naturalistic vocal environment of young infants: On the significance of homogeneity and variability in parental speech. In T. Field & N. Fox (Eds.), *Social perception in infants* (pp. 269–297). Norwood, N.J.: Ablex.

Papoušek, M., Papoušek, H., & Haekel, M. (1987). Didactic adjustments in fathers' and mothers' speech to their three-month-old infants. *Journal of Psycholinguistic Research, 16*, 491–516.

Papoušek, M., Papoušek, H., & Harris, B. J. (1987). The emergence of play in parent–infant interactions. In D. Görlitz & J. F. Wohlwill (Eds.), *Curiosity, imagination, and play: On the development of spontaneous cognitive and motivational processes* (pp. 214–246). Hillsdale, N.J.: Erlbaum.

Papoušek, M., Papoušek, H., & Symmes, D. (1991). The meanings of melodies in motherese in tone and stress languages. *Infant Behavior and Development, 14*, 414–440.

Scherer, K. R. (1985). Vocal affect signaling: A comparative approach. In J. S. Rosenblatt, C. Beer, M. C. Busnel, & P. J. B. Slater (Eds.), *Advances in the Study of Behavior* (Vol. 15, pp. 189–244). New York: Academic Press.

Seyfarth, R. M., Cheney, D. L., Marler, P. (1980). Monkey responses to three different alarm calls: Evidence for predator classification and semantic communication. *Science, 210*, 801–803.

Smith, W. J. (1977). *The behavior of communicating*. Cambridge, Mass.: Harvard University Press.

Snow, C. E. (1977). The development of conversation between mothers and babies. *Journal of Child Language, 4*, 1–22.

Stern, D. N., Spieker, S., Barnett, R. K., & MacKain, K. (1983). The prosody of maternal speech: Infant age- and context-related changes. *Journal of Child Language, 10*, 1–15.

Stern, D. N., Spieker, S., & MacKain, K. (1982). Intonation contours as signals in maternal speech to prelinguistic infants. *Developmental Psychology, 18*, 727–735.

Sullivan, J. W., & Horowitz, F. D. (1983). The effects of intonation on infant attention: The role of the rising intonation contour. *Journal of Child Language, 10*, 521–534.

Trehub, S. E. (1990). The perception of musical patterns by human infants: The provision of similar patterns by their parents. In W. C. Stebbins & M. Berkley (Eds.), *Comparative perception: Vol. 1. Discrimination* (pp. 429–459). New York: Wiley Interscience.

Werker, J. F., & McLeod, P. J. (1989). Infant preference for both male and female infant-directed talk: A developmental study of attentional and affective responsiveness. *Canadian Journal of Psychology, 43,* 230–246.

Wolff, P. H. (1969). The natural history of crying and other vocalizations in early infancy. In B. Foss (Ed.), *Determinants of Infant Behavior* (Vol. 4, pp. 81–109). London: Methuen.

13. Meaningful melodies in mothers' speech to infants

ANNE FERNALD

In "A Biographical sketch of an Infant" (1877), Darwin reported that his son "understood intonation and gestures" before he was a year old, whereas his linguistic competence was still very limited. The idea that intonation and gesture can be "understood" has been more congenial to ethologists studying animal communication than to researchers interested in human communication. Ethologists agree that some higher nonhuman primate species use pitch, intensity, rhythm, and other "gradient" dimensions of sound in order to convey meaningful information about intentions and motivational states (e.g., Green, 1975). They also agree that this ability greatly enhances communicative potential among conspecifics, in comparison with species whose signal repertoire is limited to "discrete" categories of vocalization (e.g., Bastian, 1965; Marler, 1976). In research on human communication, however, language is regarded as the medium of meaning, with intonation and gesture relegated to peripheral status. The evolutionary advance in the chimpanzee's use of pitch and intensity to reveal motivations and intentions is majestically upstaged by the evolution of language. If Darwin's paternal observations were correct, however, human infants also rely on intonation and gesture in the prelinguistic period, before they are able to use the semantic power of language to comprehend meaning.

In this essay, I propose that infants first make sense out of human speech through the intonation patterns of the mother's voice. After reviewing empirical evidence on the acoustic characteristics of maternal speech to infants in different cultures, I present a model of developmental changes in the functional significance of prosody in infant-directed vocalizations over the first year of life. A hypothesis central to this model is that infants indeed "understand intonation" before understanding language, as Darwin suggested. This claim is discussed in relation to ethological conceptions of the meaningfulness of vocal signals in animal communication.

Prosodic characteristics of maternal speech to infants

That adults tend to speak to infants in an odd and characteristic fashion is a commonplace observation. It was Charles Ferguson, in 1964, who first offered a coherent description of the linguistic features of child-directed speech, including simplified syntax as well as phonological and lexical modifications. In the six languages described by Ferguson, which included English, Spanish, Arabic, Comanche, Gilyak, and Marathi, the use of elevated pitch and exaggerated intonation in adult speech to children was among the most prominent characteristics observed across cultures. Such exaggerated prosody in mothers' speech has also been reported anecdotally in languages as diverse as Sinhalese (Meegaskumbura, 1980), Japanese (Chew, 1969), and Latvian (Ruke-Dravina, 1976).

These reports by linguists and anthropologists of a distinctive prosodic register used in speech to children have now been substantiated by acoustic analyses of the global prosodic features of parental speech in several languages, including English (e.g., Garnica, 1977; Stern, Spieker, Barnett, & MacKain, 1983), German (Fernald & Simon, 1984; Papoušek, Papoušek, & Haekel, 1987), and Mandarin Chinese (Grieser & Kuhl, 1988; Papoušek & Papoušek, 1991). In a recent cross-language analysis of parental prosody in French, Italian, Japanese, German, and British and American English, we found that fathers as well as mothers in these languages modified their intonation when addressing a preverbal infant, in comparison with typical adult-directed speech (Fernald, Taeschner, Dunn, Papoušek, Boysson-Bardies, & Fukui, 1989). The prosodic modifications most consistently observed in this literature on speech to infants include higher mean fundamental frequency ($F0$), higher $F0$ minima and $F0$ maxima, greater $F0$ variability, shorter utterances, and longer pauses. The expansion of $F0$ range is also common in infant-directed speech, although more consistently in mothers' than in fathers' speech (ibid.).

While instrumental studies of parental speech have revealed prosodic modifications essentially comparable across cultures, there is also evidence suggesting interesting cross-cultural variability. In both the Mandarin Chinese (Papoušek & Papoušek, 1991) and Japanese samples (Fernald et al., 1989), mothers seem to show less expansion of $F0$ range than in the American and European samples, although the differences are small and the findings inconsistent (see Grieser & Kuhl, 1988). Of the cultures studied so far, American middle-class parents show the most extreme prosodic modifications in speech to infants, differing significantly from other language groups in the extent of intonational exaggeration (Fernald et al., 1989). These results may reflect cultural differences in "display rules" governing the public expression of emotion. In Asian cultures, the exaggeration of facial or vocal expression is less acceptable than in middle-class American culture, where emotional expressiveness is not only tolerated but expected (Ekman, 1972). In any case, the cross-cultural variations in the prosody of speech to children reported to date are relatively minor, and the few reports of cultures in which no special infant-directed register is used (e.g., Ratner & Pye, 1984) are difficult to interpret (Fernald et al., 1989). The common pattern of results emerging from cross-language research on parental speech is one of remarkable consistency across cultures in the use of exaggerated intonation in speech to infants.

While the majority of descriptive studies of infant-directed intonation have focused on global properties, such as the mean fundamental frequency per utterance across a representative speech sample, a few studies have investigated the fine structure of prosodic contours in specific interactional contexts. The question of interest in this research has been the relation of prosodic form to communicative function in such common maternal activities as comforting or praising the infant, eliciting the infant's attention, or prohibiting the infant from doing something. When soothing a distressed infant, for example, mothers are more likely to use falling than rising $F0$ contours (Fernald, Kermanschachi, & Lees, 1984; Papoušek, Papoušek, & Bornstein, 1985). Rising $F0$ contours are used more frequently to engage attention and elicit a response from the infant (Ferrier, 1985; Ryan, 1978), while bell-shaped $F0$ contours are used to maintain the infant's attention (Stern, Spieker, & MacKain 1982). These results show that maternal prosody is responsive to the infant's affective state and that mothers use intonation differentially to regulate infant attention and arousal (see also M. Papoušek, chapter 12 in the present volume).

In addition to these general regulatory goals, several other common communicative intentions appear to be associated with fairly stereotyped prosodic patterns in maternal speech. A recent study of infant-directed speech in French, German, Italian, and English documented the characteristics of prosodic melodies typically used to convey particular communicative intentions (Fernald, 1987; Fernald et al., 1989). During the recording sessions for the cross-language study just described, we used standardized scenarios to elicit four typical kinds of interaction between mother and infant: (1) *attention bid:* Mother calls infant's attention to a new toy; (2) *approval:* Mother praises infant for retrieving an object; (3) *prohibition:* Mother tries to stop infant from touching a forbidden object; (4) *comfort:* Mother soothes infant. Across language groups, we found characteristic prosodic patterns associated with each of the four interactional contexts (Figs. 13.1–13.4). Attention bids (Fig. 13.1) and approval vocalizations (Fig. 13.2) were high in mean $F0$ and wide in $F0$ range, although they differed in amplitude envelope characteristics. While approvals were consistently characterized by a rise–fall $F0$ contour, attention bids were more variable in contour shape. Prohibition (Fig. 13.3) and comfort (Fig. 13.4) vocalizations were both relatively low in mean $F0$ and narrow in $F0$ range, although these two categories also differed in amplitude envelope and temporal features. Prohibitions, typically short and intense, had a sharp rise-time that gave a "staccato" quality to the rising or falling $F0$ contour. Comforts, in contrast, were longer, less intense, and "legato" in quality, typically with falling $F0$ contours (see also M. Papoušek, chapter 12 in the present volume).

These recent cross-language studies of early mother–infant communication reveal that the global prosodic features of mothers' speech, as well as the association of prosodic forms with particular communicative functions, share striking similarities across cultures. Because research in this area has focused almost exclusively on urban populations that are both educated and child centered, it is too early to assert that the use of exaggerated prosody in infant-directed speech is truly universal. However, it is clear that across a wide variety of languages and cultures parents speak to their preverbal infants using prosodic melodies quite unlike those used in normal adult conversation.

The functional significance of prosody in mothers' speech to infants

While cultures can differ impressively in caretaking practices and attitudes toward infants, maternal behaviors such as nursing and rocking infants are not only universal but also similar in form across cultures. This narrow range of variability in certain human parenting behaviors presumably reflects functional constraints related to their undeniable biological utility. Speech to children may not be as stereotyped as feeding

ATTENTION

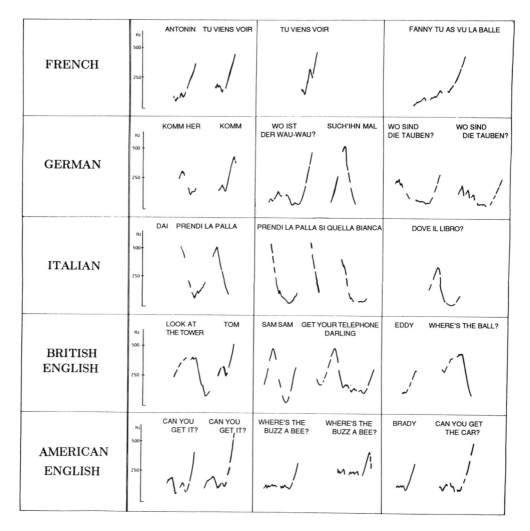

Figure 13.1 Cross-language comparison of attention bid vocalizations in mothers' speech to 12-month-old infants. (Examples of *F0* contours from 3 subjects in each language.)

APPROVAL

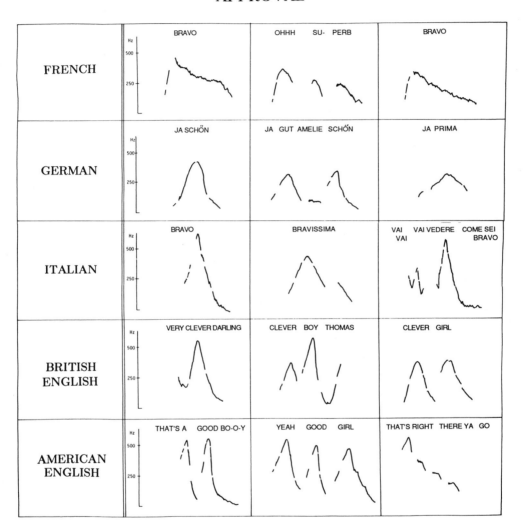

Figure 13.2. Cross-language comparison of approval vocalizations in mothers' speech to 12-month-old infants. (Examples of *F*0 contours from 3 subjects in each language.)

PROHIBITION

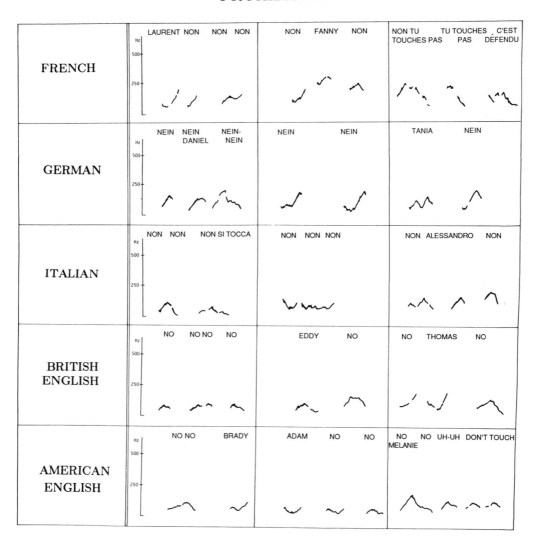

Figure 13.3. Cross-language comparison of prohibition vocalizations in mothers' speech to 12-month-old infants. (Examples of *F*0 contours from 3 subjects in each language.)

COMFORT

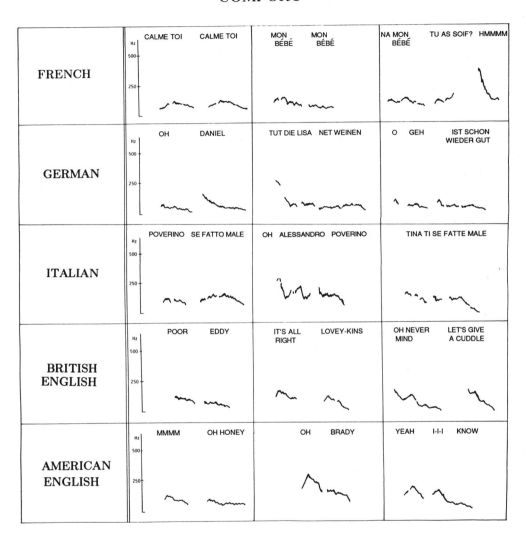

Figure 13.4. Cross-language comparison of comfort vocalizations in mothers' speech to 12-month-old infants. (Examples of *F*0 contours from 3 subjects in each language.)

and soothing behaviors, yet the relatively narrow range of variation in prosodic form suggests that the widespread use of exaggerated vocal melodies in adult speech to infants across diverse cultures may also be attributed to their biological utility (Fernald, 1991). In the model presented here, I argue that the prosodic patterns of maternal speech serve psychobiological functions central to the development of communication in the first year of life.

The idea that the special characteristics of language input to young infants have developmental consequences is, of course, not new. However, research in this area has focused most commonly on linguistic features of child-directed speech, in relation to linguistic-outcome measures of child language production (e.g., Newport, Gleitman, & Gleitman, 1977; Furrow, Nelson, & Benedict, 1979), an emphasis which reflects the assumption that the primary function of mothers' speech is to teach language. The fact that mothers use exaggerated intonation even with newborns (Fernald & Simon, 1984), long before language learning is a central issue, suggests that this prosodic dimension of early language input serves other purposes as well in the first months of life. While language learning is an important developmental goal which may eventually be facilitated by prosodic as well as linguistic features of mothers' speech to infants, other more primitive prosodic functions are effective earlier in the prelinguistic period.

The model in Figure 13.5 represents the changing role of maternal prosody in communication with the infant over the first year of life. While the initial influence of intonation is primarily perceptual and emotional, the characteristic melodies of mothers' speech increasingly take on affective meaning and convey to the preverbal infant important information about communicative intentions. It is only later in the first year that maternal prosody begins to play a more specifically linguistic role, facilitating speech segmentation and possibly enhancing comprehension. Even then, the melodies of mothers' speech retain their attentional salience and affective power, influential in social interaction and used increasingly in the service of learning language.

As indicated in Figure 13.5, the earliest functions of exaggerated prosodic contours spoken to infants derive from their enhanced perceptual prominence and their effectiveness in modulating attention and infant state (Fernald, 1984). Even newborns are responsive to such prosodic parameters as frequency (Wormith, Pankhurst, & Moffitt, 1975), intensity (Steinschneider, Lipton, & Richmond, 1966), rise-time (Kearsley, 1973), and rhythm (Demany, McKenzie, & Vurpillot, 1977). More im-

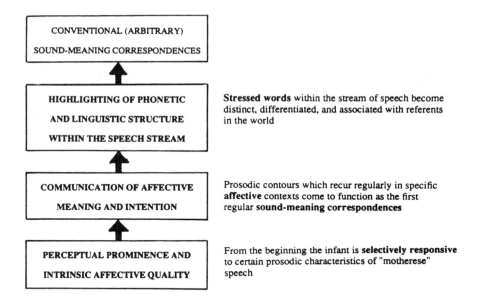

Figure 13.5. A model of developmental changes in the functions of prosody in mothers' speech to infants over the first year of life.

portantly, the prosodic contours of mothers' speech – simple in form, expanded in F0 range, and highly repetitive – seem to provide a form of acoustic stimulation particularly appropriate to the auditory sensitivities and limited cognitive-processing abilities of the young infant. For example, discrimination of speech sounds embedded in multisyllabic sequences is facilitated in infant-directed speech (Karzon, 1985). In comparison with adult-directed prosody, the prominent melodies of mothers' speech presumably also fare better in competition with background sounds, providing a more optimal figure–ground relation for the infant still unskilled at localizing sound sources and recognizing auditory patterns (Fernald, 1984).

The power of infant-directed speech to elicit and maintain attention has been shown in several recent experiments investigating the listening preferences of infants from 1–4 months of age (Cooper & Aslin, 1989; Fernald, 1985; Werker & McLeod, 1989). In each of these studies, infants responded selectively by choosing to listen longer or more frequently to infant-directed speech than to adult-directed speech. In follow-up experiments designed to assess the influence of various prosodic features on the preference for infant-directed speech, we used synthetic stimuli with no linguistic content, derived from natural samples of speech addressed to infants and adults (Fernald & Kuhl, 1987). These stimuli consisted of frequency-modulated sine waves which isolated either fundamental frequency, intensity, or duration, corresponding to the prosodic parameters of pitch, loudness, and temporal pattern. We found that 4-month-old infants showed a listening preference only for the $F0$ contours of infant-directed speech with amplitude held constant, suggesting that pitch modulation is the prosodic feature most critical in eliciting the infant preference.

In addition to perceptual salience, the melodies of mothers' speech have emotional qualities accessible even to the neonate. As Lewis observed, in *Infant Speech* (1936 / 1951), the mother's voice "is not a neutral stimulus" for the newborn; "it possesses an affective character for the child – in other words it evokes a response" (p. 52). One of the most notable of these responses is the infant's smile, which can be elicited very early by infant-directed speech. Wolff (1987) found that infants smiled consistently to the voice when presented alone, but not to the face alone, in the first month after birth, and that a high-pitched voice was considerably more effective than a low-pitched voice in eliciting infant smiling. Werker and McLeod (1989) have shown that infants are affectively more responsive and show more readiness for social engagement when listening to infant-directed speech than when listening to adult-directed speech. These recent findings substantiate Lewis's observation that "from the outset, heard adult speech comes to the child steeped in affective quality" (1936 / 1951, p. 42).

At the next level of the model depicted in Figure 13.5, the infant continues to respond affectively to the vocal melodies of mothers' speech, although in an increasingly differentiated fashion. The explanation offered by Lewis for this development is that the "intrinsic affective quality" of speech to the infant is continually associated with other behaviors and situations, such as soothing melodies used in conjunction with rocking, and arousing melodies accompanied by smiles and other engaging forms of visual stimulation (ibid.). Although the infant is not yet processing linguistic content in the mother's vocalizations, the melodies of her speech begin to give the infant access to her feelings and intentions. When pleased with the infant, she might say, "Good!" or "That's right!", with a wide-range rise–fall $F0$ contour, to reward or encourage the child. The melody itself is pleasing to the infant, and its effectiveness is further reinforced by the social contexts in which it repeatedly occurs.

When the mother's intention is to warn or to scold the infant, she is unlikely to use this melody of approval. Instead she might say, "No!" or "Don't touch that!", with a short, sharp prosodic contour, lower in pitch and louder, to interrupt the infant's activity. In this way, the characteristic prosodic contours of infant-directed speech, used continually to express particular communicative intentions, come to function as the first regular correspondences between sound and meaning for the preverbal infant.

The fact that maternal vocalizations similar in communicative intent are also similar in acoustic form, as shown in Figures 13.1–13.4, provides indirect evidence for the claim that prosodic contours could offer reliable cues to the mother's communicative intent. However, such findings reveal nothing about whether these different melodies are perceived as distinctive, nor whether infant-directed prosodic contours are any more informative than adult-directed prosodic contours. A recent study with adult subjects provided a first step toward answering these questions (Fernald, 1989a). Here we used content-filtered speech to investigate the power of intonation to reveal the communicative intent of the speaker. Natural samples of infant-directed American English speech were recorded from five mothers of preverbal infants in the four interactional contexts described earlier – approval, prohibition, attention bid, and comfort – and also while the mother was playing a hiding game with the infant. Analogous samples of adult-directed speech were also recorded, using standardized role-playing scenarios. For example, for the attention-bid vocalization, the wife was instructed to call her husband, who was seated in a chair reading a newspaper, to come to the window to see something interesting. In adult-directed speech, *telephone greeting* was substituted for the infant-directed *game* category, both highly stereotyped vocal patterns. Fifty infant-directed and adult-directed vocalizations were electronically filtered and presented to 80 subjects, all either experienced parents or students inexperienced with infants. Subjects were asked to judge the communicative intent of the speaker, given a five-alternative forced choice. Regardless of the extent of their previous experience with infants, listeners were able to use intonation to identify the speaker's intent with significantly greater accuracy in infant-directed speech than in adult-directed speech, as is reflected in the graph in Figure 13.6. These findings suggest that the prosodic patterns of infant-directed speech are more informative than those of adult–adult speech and may provide the infant with reliable cues to the communicative intent of the speaker.

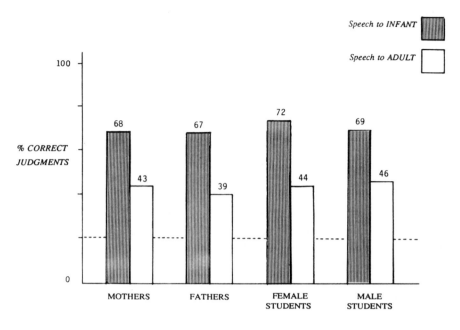

Figure 13.6. Mean percentage of correct judgments of speaker's communicative intent in infant-directed and adult-directed vocalizations across four groups of subjects. (Chance performance is indicated by dotted line.)

The real question of interest here is whether the melodies of mother's speech are meaningful to infants. Indirect evidence on prosodic regularities associated with particular communicative intentions, and on the ability of adults to use intonation to recognize communicative intent, can indicate only that the prosodic contours of infant-directed speech are potentially meaningful, in the sense that these melodies vary systematically and prominently with the context of interaction. In order to demonstrate that infants are in fact able to decode the prosodic information in mothers' speech, it is obviously necessary to test infants directly. In a recent series of experiments, we have investigated infant responsiveness to the melodies of mothers' speech (Fernald, 1989b). The hypothesis tested was that young infants would respond selectively and appropriately to approval and to prohibition vocalizations, two characteristic sound–meaning pairs in infant-directed speech, even when spoken in languages with which the infants were completely unfamiliar.

During testing, 4-month-old infants from monolingual American English families sat on the mother's lap in a three-sided booth. On the left and right sides were identical pictures of a woman's face with a neutral emotional expression, and loudspeakers connected to two tape recorders in an adjacent, sound-isolated control room. In the center, a concealed video camera relayed an image of the infant's face to a videorecorder in the control room. From the loudspeaker on one side of the booth, subjects heard infant-directed approval vocalizations in either a familiar or an unfamiliar language, while from the opposite loudspeaker they heard infant-directed prohibitions in the same language. Eight approval and eight prohibition trials were given in random order. Each sound presentation continued as long as the infant remained oriented to the appropriate side, for a maximum of 20 sec per trial.

Infants listened to approval and prohibition vocalizations in four unfamiliar languages: German, Italian, Greek, or Japanese. Two different experiments were run in Japanese, so that we could use one set of stimulus tapes recorded by a Japanese mother in the laboratory, where semantic content was controlled, and a second set of stimulus tapes consisting of excerpts from the spontaneous infant-directed speech of three Japanese mothers, recorded during home visits. In addition to the unfamiliar languages, we included two native-language controls, one using nonsense syllables spoken with American English intonation, and one using natural American English speech. Twenty infants participated as subjects in each of these seven experiments. The dependent measure of primary interest was the infants' affective responsiveness while listening to infant-directed approval and prohibition vocalizations. Affective responsiveness was measured on a 5-point scale, ranging from frown (1) to full smile (5), coded off-line by a judge blind to the experimental condition of the subject.

Infants listening to German, Italian, Greek, English, or English nonsense syllables responded with significantly more positive affect to infant-directed approvals than to prohibitions, and with more negative affect to prohibitions than to approvals. One of the salient prosodic characteristics of ordinary prohibitions to infants, increased loudness, had been deliberately eliminated in advance as a cue in these experiments; both approvals and prohibitions were presented at the same intensity level, in order not to startle the infants. Even without this powerful cue, infants responded with appropriate affect to vocalizations in languages which they were hearing for the first time, as well as in a familiar language. This selective affective responsiveness was not shown for all languages, however. In both Japanese conditions, infants listened with neutral affect to approvals as well as to prohibitions.

Why should American infants respond affectively to positive and negative maternal vocalizations in three unfamiliar European languages and in English but not in Japanese? As mentioned earlier, the pitch range used by Japanese mothers in infant-directed speech is narrower than that used by European mothers (Fernald et al., 1989). This attenuation of $F0$ range was also characteristic of both sets of Japanese stimuli used in these experiments. In fact, when we asked adult English speakers to rate the affect and the intensity of infant-directed vocalizations from the English-, European-, and Japanese-language tapes, they judged Japanese to be less intense. There was also confusion, in the responses to some Japanese vocalizations, as to whether the affect was positive or negative, consistent with other findings that Japanese facial and vocal expressions of emotion are difficult to decode (Magno-Caldognello & Kori, 1983; Shimoda, Argyle, & Riccibitti, 1978).

The results of these infant listening experiments support the idea that preverbal infants are affectively responsive to the prosodic patterns of mothers' speech, even in unfamiliar languages. However, the finding that 4-month-old infants familiar with English respond affectively to approvals and prohibitions in European languages but not in Japanese may indicate that cultural differences in mother–infant interaction are already influential at this early age. On the one hand, it could be that the prosodic forms used to express approval and prohibition in Japanese speech to infants are different from those found in European languages. While we do not yet have adequate data to address this issue, our observations so far suggest that the $F0$ contours of Japanese mothers' speech are not substantially different in form from those of European mothers. Approval vocalizations are typically rise–fall $F0$ contours similar to those shown in Figure 13.2, although narrower in $F0$ range. Similarly, Japanese prohibitions share the $F0$ characteristics shown in Figure 13.3, although they are often much less intense. A second possibility is that 4-month-old infants have already been influenced by experience in their own culture and respond with positive affect only to those approval vocalizations similar in prosodic range to those with which they are familiar. Since German, Italian, and Greek are all languages spoken in cultures which encourage vocal expressiveness, infant-directed approvals in those languages are similar to those in English in their use of wide $F0$ range and are thus "familiar" to the American infant. Research in progress on the prosodic characteristics of Japanese mothers' speech and on the responsiveness of Japanese infants to approval and prohibition vocalizations in Japanese and other languages will enable us to further explore these intriguing questions.

At the third level of the model depicted in Figure 13.5, the prosodic patterns of infant-directed speech begin to serve linguistic functions, as the child gradually develops the ability to use language to extract meaning from the mother's vocalizations. In the earlier preverbal period, before speech becomes meaningful through linguistic structure, the infant perceives intonation contours holistically, not yet attending closely to segmental units within the melody. Toward the end of the first year, words begin to emerge from the melody, and the mother's prosody helps to draw the infant's attention to linguistic units within the stream of speech. When showing picture books to infants just learning to speak, mothers very consistently introduce new labels for unfamiliar objects at the peaks of their intonation contours (Fernald & Mazzie, 1991). This prosodic strategy may help the infant to identify word boundaries and acquire new lexical items. Gleitman and Wanner (1982) have proposed that infants are biologically predisposed to pay special attention to stressed words. By exaggerating prosodic contours and using emphatic stress to introduce new linguistic information, mothers may quite intuitively accommodate this infant bias, helping the child in the formidable task of parsing spoken language.

As infants acquire language, they begin to recognize the many arbitrary and conventional associations of sound and meaning in their language. What the English child learns is *dog* the Japanese child recognizes as *inu* and the French child as *chien*. It is this accomplishment that is usually celebrated as the beginning of "language comprehension." According to the model depicted in Figure 13.5, however, comprehension begins much earlier. Speech first becomes meaningful to the infant through prosody rather than through words, and through associations of sound and meaning that are not arbitrary.

The meaning of "meaning" in the prosody of speech to infants

Our conception of "meaning" in human speech is dominated by the power of language to refer. Through mastery of the conventional association between a sound and a class of referents, the English-speaking child learns that the word *dog* refers to the family pet as well as to similar animals. When the mother says "dog," the child demonstrates comprehension by searching for a dog. Through language, the mother can put her thoughts, feelings, and intentions into words and make them accessible to the child who has learned what these words mean. This ability to decode conventional sound–meaning combinations in order to gain access to other minds is a stunning breakthrough, both in the evolution of primate communication and in the development of the individual human infant. But it does not mark the first appearance of "meaningful" vocal communication.

As I have argued in the preceding section, the preverbal infant gains early access to the mother's feelings and intentions through the prosody of her speech. Prior to the time when the mother's speech sounds have impact through their symbolic power to refer beyond themselves, the prosody of her voice can influence the infant directly. When her intention is to soothe, she rocks the infant and speaks with a low, sustained pitch (see Fig. 13.4), using sounds like "shhhh" as well. Just as rocking has a direct calming effect on the infant (e.g., Byrne & Horowitz, 1981), the acoustic features of the sounds the mother uses also function to calm the infant. Low frequencies, sustained tones, and white-noise signals have all been shown to be effective as unconditioned stimuli in reducing infant distress (Bench, 1969; Birns, Blank, Bridger, & Escalona, 1965; Watterson & Riccillo, 1983). When the mother's goal is to arouse the infant, she uses $F0$ contours higher in frequency, often with rising pitch (see Fig. 13.1), thus exploiting acoustic features known to function effectively in alerting signals (Patterson, 1982). In both soothing and arousing the infant, the mother accomplishes her intentions, in part, through her use of sound. However, the communicative force of her vocalizations derives not from their arbitrary, assigned meanings in a symbolic code but from the more immediate power of music to alert, to alarm, to soothe, and to delight.

The sense of the term *meaning* suggested here, obviously different from the referential meaning of the linguists, is closer to ethologists' understanding of meaning in vocal communication among nonhuman primates. Unlike speech sounds, the associations between sounds and meanings in primate signal systems are regarded as nonarbitrary, in two respects. First, the acoustic features of primate calls often reflect adaptations to the functions these calls accomplish. For example, the frequency spectrum of long-distance vocalizations among African monkeys is optimally efficient for transmission through the forest canopy (Waser & Waser, 1977). In human mother–infant interaction as well, we have seen how the acoustic characteristics of infant-directed vocalizations contribute to their functional efficiency. Second, primate calls are unlearned and often are strongly influenced by the emotional state of the animal. While some alarm calls do appear to have specific external referents (Seyfarth, Cheney, & Marler, 1980), information about the motivational state of the calling animal remains central to the meaning of most primate calls (Marler, 1984). In this respect too, the melodies of human mothers' speech to infants are analogous, in that they are similar across cultures and rich in information about the mother's feelings.

In comparison with language, the semantic potential of vocal communication among higher nonhuman primates seems primitive. Yet in comparison with the inflexible and limited vocal repertoires of lower primates, chimpanzee vocalizations allow enormous subtlety in social communication. Chimpanzees are able to use gradations in pitch and intensity, in conjunction with facial expressions and posture, to convey vital information about their needs, desires, and future behavior (Marler, 1976). The predisposition to be moved by as well as to interpret the emotions of others, and the ability to discern the intentions and motivations of others through expressions of the voice and face, are remarkable evolutionary advances in communicative potential found among the higher primates. These nonverbal interactive skills are at the heart of human communication as well. While the use of language gives humans access to other minds that is immeasurably more powerful and intricate than that of other primates, human symbolic communication builds on our primate legacy, a foundation of affective communication established in the preverbal period (Fernald, 1991).

Conclusion

By the time infants develop the prerequisite cognitive skills for interpreting speech sounds as symbols, they have had a long experience responding to the mother's vocalizations as meaningful in other ways. The characteristic melodies of mothers' speech are used to elicit and maintain the infant's attention, to modulate arousal, to communicate emotions, and to facilitate speech segmentation, with a developmental progression from the more general attentional and affective functions in the early months to linguistic functions toward the end of the first year. The attentional and affective functions of infant-directed speech are primary, engaging the infant in social interaction and enabling the baby to experience emotional communion with others months before communication through symbols is possible. Through this early experience of sharing feelings and intentions by means of prosody, speech first becomes meaningful to the infant. According to Halliday (1975), babies are "learning how to mean" when they express their desires and intentions through intonation and gesture before they express them through language. These words echo Darwin's much earlier insight (1877), that infants are learning how to understand meaning through intonation and gesture as well.

References

Bastian, J. (1965). Primate signaling systems and human languages. In I. Devore (Ed.), *Primate behavior: Field studies of monkeys and apes* (pp. 585–606). New York: Holt, Rinehart & Winston.

Bench, J. (1969). Some effects of audio-frequency stimulation on the crying baby. *Journal of Auditory Research, 9,* 122–128.

Birns, B., Blank, M., Bridger, W. H., & Escalona, S. K. (1965). Behavioral inhibition in neonates produced by auditory stimuli. *Child Development, 36,* 639–645.

Byrne, J. M., & Horowitz, F. D. (1981). Rocking as a soothing intervention: The influence of direction and type of movement. *Infant Behavior and Development, 4,* 207–218.

Chew, J. J., Jr. (1969). The structure of Japanese baby talk. *Association of Teachers of Japanese, 6,* 4–17.

Cooper, R. P., & Aslin, R. N. (1989). The language environment of the young infant: Implications for early perceptual development. *Canadian Journal of Psychology, 43,* 247–265.

Darwin, C. (1877). A biographical sketch of an infant. *Mind 2,* 286–294.

Demany, L., McKenzie, B., & Vurpillot, E. (1977). Rhythm perception in early infancy. *Nature, 266,* 718–719.

Ekman, P. (1972). Universals and cultural differences in facial expressions of emotion. In J. Cole (Ed.), *Nebraska Symposium on Motivation 1971* (pp. 207–283). Lincoln: University of Nebraska Press.

Ferguson, C. A. (1964). Baby talk in six languages. *American Anthropologist, 66,* 103–114.

Fernald, A. (1984). The perceptual and affective salience of mothers' speech to infants. In L. Feagans, C. Garvey, and R. Golinkoff (Eds.), *The origins and growth of communication* (pp. 5–29). Norwood, N.J.: Ablex.

(1985). Four-month-old infants prefer to listen to motherese. *Infant Behavior and Development, 8,* 181–195.

(1987). *Form and function in the prosody of mothers' speech to infants.* Paper presented to the Society for Research in Child Development, Baltimore. April.

(1989a). Intonation and communicative intent in mothers' speech to infants: Is the melody the message? *Child Development, 60,* 1497–1510.

(1989b). *Emotion and meaning in mothers' speech to infants.* Paper presented to the Society for Research in Child Development, Kansas City. April.

(1991). Human maternal vocalizations to infants as biologically relevant signals. An evolutionary perspective. In J. H. Barkow, L. Cosmides, & J. Tooby (Eds.), *The adapted mind: Evolutionary psychology and the generation of culture.* Oxford: Oxford University Press.

Fernald, A., Kermanschachi, N., & Lees, D. (1984). *The rhythms and sounds of* soothing: Maternal vestibular, tactile, and auditory stimulation and infant state. Paper presented to the International Conference on Infant Studies, New York. April.

Fernald, A., & Kuhl, P. K. (1987). Acoustic determinants of infant preference for motherese speech. *Infant Behavior and Development, 10,* 279–293.

Fernald, A., & Mazzie, C. (1991). Prosody and focus in speech to infants and adults. *Developmental Psychology, 27,* 209–221.

Fernald, A., & Simon, T. (1984). Expanded intonation contours in mothers' speech to newborns. *Developmental Psychology, 20,* 104–113.

Fernald, A., Taeschner, T., Dunn, J., Papoušek, M., Boysson-Bardies, B., & Fukui, I. (1989). A cross-language study of prosodic modifications in mothers' and fathers' speech to preverbal infants. *Journal of Child Language, 16,* 477–501.

Ferrier, L. J. (1985). Intonation in discourse: Talk between 12-month-olds and their mothers. In K. Nelson (Ed.), *Children's language* (Vol. 5, pp. 35–60). Hillsdale, N.J.: Erlbaum.

Furrow, D., Nelson, K., & Benedict, H. (1979). Mothers' speech to children and syntactic development: Some simple relationships. *Journal of Child Language, 6,* 423–442.

Garnica, O. (1977). Some prosodic and paralinguistic features of speech to young children. In C. E. Snow and C. A. Ferguson (Eds.), *Talking to children: Language input and acquisition* (pp. 63–88). Cambridge: Cambridge University Press.

Gleitman, L. R., & Wanner, E. (1982). Language acquisition: The state of the state of the art. In E. Wanner and L. R. Gleitman (Eds.), *Language acquisition: The state of the art* (pp. 3–48). Cambridge: Cambridge University Press.

Green, S. (1975). Variation of vocal pattern with social situation in the Japanese monkey (*Macaca fuscata*): A field study. In L. A. Rosenblum (Ed.), *Primate behavior: Developments in field and laboratory research* (Vol. 4, pp. 1–102). New York: Academic Press.

Grieser, D. L., & Kuhl, P. K. (1988). Maternal speech to infants in a tonal language: Support for universal prosodic features in motherese. *Developmental Psychology, 24,* 14–20.

Halliday, M. A. K. (1975). *Learning how to mean: Explorations in the development of language.* London: Arnold.

Karzon, R. G. (1985). Discrimination of polysyllabic sequences by one- to four-month-old infants. *Journal of Experimental Child Psychology, 39,* 326–342.

Kearsley, R. B. (1973). The newborn's response to auditory stimulation: A demonstration of orienting and defensive behavior. *Child Development, 44,* 582–590.

Lewis, M. M. (1936 / 1951). *Infant speech: A study of the beginnings of language.* London: Routledge & Kegan Paul. (Original work published 1936).

Magno-Caldognetto, E., & Kori, S. (1983). Intercultural judgment of emotions expressed through voice: The Italians and the Japanese. Paper presented to the 10th International Congress of Phonetic Sciences, Utrecht, Netherlands.

Marler, P. (1976). Social organization, communication and graded signals: The chimpanzee and the gorilla. In P. P. G. Bateson and R. A. Hinde (Eds.), *Growing points in ethology.* Cambridge: Cambridge University Press.

    (1984). Animal communication: Affect or cognition? In K. R. Scherer and P. Ekman (Eds.), *Approaches to emotion* (pp. 345–365). Hillsdale, N.J.: Erlbaum.

Meegaskumbura, P. B. (1980). Tondol: Sinhala baby talk. *Word, 31,* 287–309.

Newport, E. L., Gleitman, H., & Gleitman, L. R. (1977). Mother I'd rather do it myself: Some effects and non-effects of maternal speech style. In C. E. Snow and C. A. Ferguson (Eds.), *Talking to children: Language input and acquisition* (pp. 109–149). Cambridge: Cambridge University Press.

Papoušek, H., & Papoušek, M. (1991). Innate and cultural guidance of infants' integrative competencies: China, the United States, and Germany. In M. H. Bornstein (Ed.), *Cultural approaches to parenting* (pp. 23–44). Hillsdale, N.J.: Erlbaum.

Papoušek, M., Papoušek, H., & Bornstein, M. H. (1985). The naturalistic vocal environment of young infants: On the significance of homogeneity and variability in parental speech. In T. Field & N. Fox (Eds.), *Social perception in infants* (pp. 269–297). Norwood, N.J.: Ablex.

Papoušek, M., Papoušek, H., & Haekel, M. (1987). Didactic adjustments in fathers' and mothers' speech to their three-month-old infants. *Journal of Psycholinguistic Research, 6,* 49–56.

Patterson, R. D. (1982). *Guidelines for auditory warning systems.* London: Civil Aviation Authority.

Ratner, N. B., & Pye, C. (1984). Higher pitch in BT is not universal: Acoustic evidence from Quiche Mayan. *Journal of Child Language, 2,* 515–522.

Ruke-Dravina, V. (1976). Gibt es Universalien in der Ammensprache? *Salzburger Beiträge zur Linguistik, 2,* 3–16.

Ryan, M. (1978). Contour in context. In R. Campbell & P. Smith (Eds.), *Recent advances in the psychology of language* (pp. 237–251). New York: Plenum.

Seyfarth, R. M., Cheney, D. L., & Marler, P. (1980). Vervet monkey alarm calls. Semantic communication in a free-ranging primate. *Animal Behaviour, 28,* 1070–1094.

Shimoda, K., Argyle, M., & Riccibitti, P. (1978). The intercultural recognition of emotional expressions by three national racial groups: English, Italian, and Japanese. *European Journal of Social Psychology, 8,* 169–179.

Steinschneider, A., Lipton, E. L., & Richmond, J. B. (1966). Auditory sensitivity in the infant: Effect of intensity on cardiac and motor responsivity. *Child Development, 37,* 233–252.

Stern, D. N., Spieker, S., Barnett, R. K., & MacKain, K. (1983). The prosody of maternal speech: Infant age and context related changes. *Journal of Child Language, 10,* 1–15.

Stern, D. N., Spieker, S., & MacKain, K. (1982). Intonation contours as signals in maternal speech to prelinguistic infants. *Developmental Psychology, 18,* 727–735.

Waser, P. M., & Waser, M. S. (1977). Experimental studies of primate vocalizations: Specializations for long-distance propagation. *Zeitschrift für Tierpsychologie, 43,* 239–263.

Watterson, T., & Riccillo, S. C. (1983). Vocal suppression as a neonatal response to auditory stimuli. *Journal of Auditory Research, 23,* 205–214.

Werker, J. F., & McLeod, P. J. (1989). Infant preference for both male and female infant-directed-talk: A developmental study of attentional and affective responsiveness. *Canadian Journal of Psychology, 43,* 230–246.

Wolff, P. H. (1987). *The development of behavioral states and the expression of emotions in early infancy.* Chicago: University of Chicago Press.

Wormith, S. J., Pankhurst, D., & Moffitt, A. R. (1975). Frequency discrimination by young infants. *Child Development, 46,* 272–275.

Author index

Italic page numbers indicate page of bibliographic entry.

Subject index

acoustic analysis (*see also* vocal signal)
  and digital signal-processing, 150–1
  and spectrography, 149
acoustic correlates of motivation, 45–
  7, 51–4
affect (*see also* emotion; state)
  vocal expression of, 43, 44, 46, 49,
    51, 54–5, 57
    as appeal, 54–7; in human pre-
      verbal communication, 217
    in human infant, 235, 238
    as symbol, 48–54
    as symptom, 44–8, 238
affiliative chuck, 133
aggressive encounter, 90–1
agonistic encounter, 88, 90
alarm call, *see* call
allomothering, 135–6
alphabetic level of vocal sound, 175–6
alphabetic units in language, 178
ambiguity in signal, *see* signal
American sign language, 36
amplitude modulation, 21
anencephalic infant, 31, 148
animal studies (*see also* human stud-
    ies; primate studies)
  black-capped chickadee, 72, 189
  California ground squirrel, 72, 75
  cat, 31
  chicken, food call, 77
  chinchilla, 20
  dog, 20
  frog, 8
  lung fish, 7
  prairie dog (black-tailed and Gunni-
    son's), 72
appeal
  nonlinguistic form of, in humans,
    54–7, 217

  in vocal expression of affect, 54–7
appraisal patterns, 49–51
approval in infant-directed speech,
    248–9, 265, 267, 274–6
arousal, *see* state
attention bid in infant-directed
    speech, 265, 266
attention in human infant
  effect of infant-directed speech on,
    249, 270–1
  effect of maternal didactics on, 219
  predisposition to, related to
    stressed words, 277
attribute concept of vocalization, 92,
    98
auditory agnosia, 24
auditory perception
  and agnosia in humans, 24
  categorical, in monkey, 19–23, 106–
    10, 117
  and central perceiving system, 17–
    23
  comparison monkey vs. humans,
    19–23, 111–12, 113, 115
  and difference limen, 111
  and experimental lesions, 23–4
  and frequency discrimination, 111
  general sensitivity of, 115
  motor theory of, 56
  as precursor of linguistic percep-
    tion, 20–1
  as precursor of phonetic percep-
    tion, 20–1
  and predisposition for stressed
    word, 277
  and right-ear advantage, 23, 25, 107
  of vocal signal, 103, 111, 113
  and voice onset time, 19
autism, early infantile, 198–200